SOFTWARE MANUAL
FOR THE
ELEMENTARY FUNCTIONS

WILLIAM J. CODY, JR.
Argonne National Laboratory

and

WILLIAM WAITE
**Department of Electrical Engineering
University of Colorado**

Prentice-Hall, Inc., Englewood Cliffs, New Jersey 07632

Library of Congress Cataloging in Publication Data

Cody, William James
  Software manual for the elementary functions.

  (Prentice-Hall series in computational mathematics)
  Bibliography: p.
  1. Functions--Data processing. I. Waite, William
McCastline, joint author. II. Title. III. Series.
QA331.C635 1980   519.5   80-14411
ISBN 0-13-822064-6

Prentice-Hall Series in Computational Mathematics
Cleve Moler, Advisor

© 1980 by Prentice-Hall, Inc., Englewood Cliffs, N.J. 07632

Printed in the United States of America

10 9 8 7 6 5 4 3 2 1

Prentice-Hall International, Inc., *London*
Prentice-Hall of Australia Pty. Limited, *Sydney*
Prentice-Hall of Canada, Ltd., *Toronto*
Prentice-Hall of India Private Limited, *New Delhi*
Prentice-Hall of Japan, Inc., *Tokyo*
Prentice-Hall of Southeast Asia Pte. Ltd., *Singapore*
Whitehall Books Limited, *Wellington, New Zealand*

To our two Joannes

CONTENTS

PREFACE

This manual is intended to provide guidance towards the preparation and testing of elementary function subroutines for non-vector oriented digital computers. We believe it will be useful to systems programmers, teachers, students of numerical analysis, hobbyists and anyone else concerned or curious about how the elementary functions might be computed. The functions covered are the usual assortment of algebraic, trigonometric, and transcendental functions of real argument, including those required by algebraic languages such as Fortran and Basic. Where programs are included, they are written in Fortran.

Fortran also influences the terminology and notation used: We frequently use the symbol * to mean multiplication, use ** to represent exponentiation, and talk about the SQRT program, for example. But the ideas, algorithms, and programs presented are more widely applicable. Many of the algorithms and accompanying test programs have been implemented in Basic and PL/I by the authors and their students, and some have even been implemented on programmable hand calculators. Nevertheless, the authors make no warranty of any kind with regard to the material in this manual. It is the reader's responsibility to verify that the material is both correct and appropriate for his intended usage.

A magnetic tape containing the Fortran source code for all of the test programs, the random number generators and the environmental inquiry program in this manual are available from either of two sources:

> National Energy Software Center
> Argonne National Laboratory
> 9700 South Cass Avenue
> Argonne, Illinois 60439
>   (Phone: 312-972-7250)

International Mathematical and Statistical
    Libraries, Inc.
Sixth Floor, GNB Building
7500 Bellaire Boulevard
Houston, Texas 77036
    (Phone: 713-772-1927)

Information regarding distribution charges and tape formats can be obtained directly from either source.

Almost the entire text of this manual has been prepared on a computer. While this process has simplified the writing and proofing of our work, it has also introduced limitations on the use of mathematical symbols and notation. Subscripts, for example, had to be inserted by hand and therefore were avoided wherever possible. We apologize for any resulting awkwardness in our presentation.

We owe much to W. Kahan and the late Hirondo Kuki who were especially influential over the years in molding some of the ideas presented here. We are grateful to Argonne National Laboratory for its support of this project and to our colleagues there who contributed so much. We especially thank B. Garbow who patiently read and commented on several versions of the manuscript, R. Clark and W. Tippie who provided special graphics programs for typesetting and flow charting, S. Pieper who developed important enhancements to the text editing program which facilitated the photo typesetting, and G. Pieper who prepared our computer text files for typesetting and otherwise assisted editorially. Finally, we thank the many colleagues and students around the world who tried various versions of our algorithms and provided useful criticism.

1. INTRODUCTION

The proliferation of mini- and micro-computers has involved ever larger numbers of people in the creation of basic software. Subprograms for the elementary functions are an essential part of such software in a wide variety of applications. These subprograms are often the basic building blocks of an application and as such must be efficient and accurate. The algorithms chosen for them must exploit the hardware of the particular target computer to achieve these goals.

Many pitfalls await a systems programmer who attempts to implement basic function routines using information gleaned from a calculus text. The treatment by Hart and his co-authors [1968] provides some guidance, but its theoretical orientation makes it difficult for the non-mathematician to use, and it ignores many algorithmic details dictated by considerations of computer architecture. This manual is designed as a "cookbook," containing specific "recipes" for the preparation of software for the elementary functions and information on testing procedures. Some material presented here is new, particularly the coefficients used in some of the algorithms and the testing material. Many of the techniques suggested for implementing the algorithms are old enough to be considered folklore by some numerical analysts, but they are gathered together in one place for the first time.

Our intent is to make this work useful to as wide an audience as possible, but especially to systems programmers not familiar with numerical analysis or numerical programming. To this end we have made comments in the implementation notes which our numerically oriented colleagues may find trite, but which our experience indicates the non-numerically oriented will find useful. The technical discussions have also been kept simple, with references suggested for those desiring more detailed discussion.

Chapter 2 of this work discusses the general principles behind the choice of algorithms and the assumptions made about the computer hardware and software environments in which these algorithms are to be implemented. Chapter 3 discusses techniques for testing the accuracy of elementary function subprograms in general, and for testing in the environments described in Chapter 2 in particular. Chapters 4 through 13 contain the recommended algorithms. The discussion for each function includes general comments about the algorithm, a flow chart, detailed implementation notes for several different machine environments, a discussion of performance testing, and a Fortran program to provide minimal testing. Finally, there is a glossary of important concepts and terms, as well as appendices containing certain Fortran subroutines required by the test programs.

Each algorithm has been implemented as a parameterized body of Janus (Haddon and Waite [1978]) text. By setting specific parameters and processing this text with the general-purpose macro processor STAGE2 (Waite [1973]), a Janus program tailored to a particular machine is obtained. We have tested the Janus implementations on a number of machines with various parameter settings to validate the algorithms. While the results are not always as good as the best individual efforts achieved by programming in assembly language and choosing algorithms that exploit specific hardware features of a particular computer, they do demonstrate that these algorithms often come acceptably close.

2. PRELIMINARIES

For expository purposes we will often classify computers according to pertinent arithmetic characteristics. Efficient implementation of our algorithms will then require a detailed knowledge of the particular arithmetic system being used, where the term arithmetic system refers to the combination of the hardware or software for the arithmetic operations and the scheme for representing numbers in the machine. Because there is a great variation in arithmetic systems, we can discuss them only in general terms here, but the important details of a specific arithmetic system can usually be determined from the manual describing the instruction set for the particular machine.

We assume every computer can perform the four basic arithmetic operations for integers because this capability is essential for indexing and addressing. Integer arithmetic is exact with two exceptions. First, there is a largest integer which can be accommodated in the representation scheme, placing a practical bound on the magnitude of integers that can be stored in the machine. If we assume that at most n-digit integers can be stored, then the product of two such integers is too large to be stored as an integer. On many machines the full double-length integer product is developed in the arithmetic registers, with the least significant n digits of the product stored as the result and an *overflow* error indicated if the product exceeds n digits. Overflow is also possible in addition and subtraction provided the integers involved are large enough. Unless overflow occurs, however, the result of adding, subtracting or multiplying two integers is exact and again an integer.

The second exception to exact integer arithmetic is division. The exact result of integer division is an integer plus a proper fraction as a remainder. Similar to multiplication, many machines develop both the integer and the fraction (appropriately rounded or truncated) in the arithmetic registers, but the fraction is ignored in storing the result.

The possibilities for scientific computation using only integer arithmetic are limited, primarily because scientific computation is dominated by non-integer quantities. It is possible but awkward to use integer arithmetic on such numbers. For example, if the computer uses decimal integers but data must be represented to hundredths, then scaling by one hundred gives integer quantities that can be combined by addition and subtraction without error. However, the product of two such numbers contains four places after the decimal point and must be rescaled before being used further. Similarly, unless the dividend is rescaled before division, the quotient will not be an integer.

Integer arithmetic with an implied scale factor is generically called fixed-point arithmetic, although we will reserve that term in a moment to denote a specific scaling. Two extremes of scaling are possible: no scaling, which implies pure integer arithmetic with the "decimal point" at the extreme right of the digits, and "total" scaling with the "decimal point" at the extreme left of the digits. This latter case, in which the stored number represents a proper fraction, a quantity less than one in magnitude, is what we will call *fixed-point* arithmetic (Ralston [1976]). The main differences that distinguish fixed-point arithmetic from integer arithmetic are as follows:

a) every stored number is either zero or a proper fraction;

b) in multiplication, the most significant n digits of the double-length product are retained, not the least significant. Thus overflow is impossible, but *underflow* (a result too small, hence indistinguishable from zero) is possible;

c) the fractional part of the quotient is retained instead of the integer part, and overflow is signaled if the integer part is non-zero. Thus overflow occurs in division unless the divisor is greater in magnitude than the dividend.

Many computers extend the instruction set for integer arithmetic to accommodate fixed-point arithmetic by adding fractional multiply and divide instructions. This procedure is not difficult when double-length integer products and quotients are already available. The add and subtract operations are identical to the integer operations.

Scientific computation is facilitated by representing numbers in a pseudo-scientific notation and using fixed-point arithmetic. Thus a number x is represented as

$$x = \pm f \cdot B^{**}e, \ 0 \leq f < 1,$$

where f is the fractional part of the number, B is the base for the scaling, and e is the exponent. Such a number is stored in two parts, the fraction and an integer representing the exponent. The base B, which is 10 in normal scientific notation, is usually compatible with the internal number system for the computer. Thus B will ordinarily be 10 on a decimal computer but will be 2, 4, 8, or 16 on a machine that works primarily in binary. In any case, the value of B is understood and not explicitly stored.

Multiplication and division in this system are simple, involving fixed-point multiplication or division of the fractional parts of the numbers, addition or subtraction of the exponents, and appropriate prescaling to avoid overflow in division. Addition and subtraction become complicated, however, requiring appropriate prescaling of the operands to align them and to avoid overflow.

It is only natural that this scheme should be implemented as a separate arithmetic system, called a *floating-point* system, and supported by the instruction set on many computers. The additional instructions may appear as hardware instructions, or they may invoke software subprograms. In either case, the floating-point representation usually differs slightly from the representation just presented. In particular, we can think of a number x as being represented in *normalized* form by

$$x = \pm f \cdot B^{**}e, \ 1/B \leq f < 1,$$

unless $x = 0$, in which case $f = 0$ and the value of e varies with the implementation. Normalization refers to the lower bound on f, which is now called e *significand*. B is the *radix* of the representation, and e is the exponent. In order to make our algorithms independent of the actual representation of x, we state them in terms of the components f, B, and e. For example, we define functions below which access the f and e components of a floating-point number. These functions hide details of the representation; their values depend only upon the values of x and B and upon the relationship stated above.

The arithmetic performed on floating-point numbers varies from one machine to another in two characteristics that will affect the performance of our algorithms. These are the method of fitting overlength intermediate results back to working precision, and the availability of guard digits. In an n-digit floating-point arithmetic system, more than n digits are frequently required to represent the true result of an arithmetic operation, but only the n most significant digits can be retained in the machine. In the *chop* mode of rounding, any extra digits in the true result are ignored, while in a *round* mode the retained significand is rounded up or down, depending in various ways upon the magnitude of the digits to be discarded.

Often at an intermediate stage of an arithmetic operation the significand of the result requires a *renormalization shift* of one or more digit positions to the left to compensate for loss of leading digits. If the arithmetic operations generate only the first n digits of the intermediate result, counting possible leading zeros, then there are no extra digits to shift into the low-order positions during renormalization, and we say there are no *guard digits*. However, if extra digits are generated and participate in renormalization shifts, thus protecting the low-order positions, we say there are guard digits. Some arithmetic operations on a machine may have guard digits, while others on the same machine may not. Lack of guard digits for addition/subtraction may cause inaccuracies when subtracting numbers slightly less than an integer power of the radix from numbers slightly larger than that power of the radix, while lack of guard digits for multiplication may mean that $1.0 \cdot x \neq x$.

We can now distinguish several broad classes of machines. We will always assume the existence of some form of floating-point arithmetic. We will also assume that the radix B is either 10 or a small integral power of 2, i.e., B is 2, 4, 8, 10 or 16. Thus we will classify machines as binary ($B = 2$), decimal ($B = 10$), non-decimal ($B \neq 10$), etc. We can also distinguish between fixed-point and floating-point machines by classifying a machine as fixed-point whenever its floating-point operations are extremely slow in comparison to its fixed-point operations. Typically, the floating-point instructions are implemented by software in this case. To be useful, we further assume that a fixed-point machine is a non-decimal machine and that the number of bits in a fixed-point (fractional) number is at least as great as the number of bits in the floating-point significand. In certain explicitly noted cases we will assume that there are more bits in the fixed-point representation than in the floating-point significand (e.g., see the implementation notes for SQRT).

On non-decimal floating-point machines we will assume that, say, b bits are available for the representation of the significand. If $B = 2$, normalization requires that $1/2 \leq f < 1$ unless $f = 0$, and the left-most bit of f is 1. Thus all b bits are potentially significant. If $B = 4$, however, it is possible that $1/4 \leq f < 1/2$ so that the left-most bit of f is 0, in which case only b-1 of the available bits are potentially significant. Similarly, if $B = 16$, there may be as many as three leading zero bits and thus only b-3 potentially significant bits in f. This phenomenon of loss of potentially significant bits in the representation of f for $B = 4$, 8 or 16, which is due entirely to the accidental magnitude of x, is termed *wobbling precision*. As an example of its impact, in hexadecimal arithmetic ($B = 16$) the significand of the constant 2/pi contains no leading zero bits while that for the constant pi/2 contains three leading zero bits. Thus division by 2/pi is potentially one decimal place more accurate than multiplication by pi/2 in this system.

A more subtle form of wobbling precision is present in all floating-point arithmetic systems. Consider two machine numbers $X = (1+eps) \cdot B^{**}(n)$ and $Y = (1-eps) \cdot B^{**}(n)$, where eps is a small positive quantity. The exponent in the floating-point representation of X is one greater than the exponent in the representation of Y, even though X and Y are almost equal. If u represents one unit in the last digit of the significand of X and v represents one unit in the last digit of the significand of Y, then for all practical purposes

$(u/X) = B \cdot (v/Y)$,

and u is a larger fraction of X than v is of Y. This has implications when we discuss relative error in the next chapter.

The algorithms presented in Chapters 4 through 13 are each accompanied by implementation notes for specific broad classes of machines. These notes describe details of the implementation consistent with the characteristics of the target arithmetic systems. The notes for fixed-point machines, for example, incorporate proper scaling (even of the given coefficients) to avoid fixed-point overflow and to maintain maximum precision in the computed result. Similarly, computations are organized to minimize the effects of wobbling precision on machines where that can be important. We have tried to indicate why some of the suggestions are made, but we have not tried to provide background for every suggestion because to do so would turn our "cookbook" of "recipes" into a ponderous text on practical numerical analysis.

In most of the algorithms the number of coefficients and the number of significant digits in each coefficient vary with the length of the significand. Usually several sets of coefficients are given, each set intended to be used with a range of machine precisions. The algorithms for floating-point machines allow for at least 60-bit significands on non-decimal machines and 18 decimal places on decimal machines; the algorithms for fixed-point machines generally assume a maximum of 48 significant bits, or about 14 decimal places, in a fixed-point number. Coefficients must be found elsewhere for machines with greater precision, although the general algorithmic outline is still valid. One source of coefficients is the book by Hart et al. [1968], which contains approximations good to about 25 decimal places (roughly 80 bits) of significance. Taylor series and continued fraction expansions can be found in Abramowitz and Stegun [1964] and Lyusternik et al. [1965].

Coefficients and other numerical values used in the algorithms can only be as accurate as their representation in the computer. The problems associated with representation in a decimal computer are well understood. For example, the constant .3 can be represented without error, i.e., *exactly,* in a decimal machine, but its reciprocal cannot because it is non-terminating. Relatively few decimal fractions can be represented exactly in binary because binary arithmetic is incommensurate with decimal. Ordinarily this will not cause any problem provided the program to convert decimal data to binary limits conversion error to the final bit or two. However, there are a few constants in our algorithms for which exact machine representation is essential. These constants will always be specified so that exact representation is possible (even being given in octal when the binary representation is important), and they will be clearly labeled. We assume that such constants will be converted to their machine representation before being implanted in the function subroutines, thereby avoiding any possible error in automatic conversion.

We define a number of functions, or pseudo-operations, which will simplify the presentation of our algorithms. While the realization of these functions as either macro instructions for the assembler or as stand-alone subprograms may facilitate the implementation of our algorithms, such realizations are not essential. For some machines the functions may be too difficult to implement in the full generality required of macros, in which case they should be regarded as merely expository devices for describing the algorithms. Any instruction sequence achieving the desired result can be used in place of a particular function.   It is the end result which is important,   not how it is achieved.

ADX(X,N):   augments the integer exponent in the floating-point representation of X by N,   thus scaling X by the N-th power of the radix.   For example,

$$ADX(1.0,2) = 4.0$$

on binary machines because $4.0 = 1.0 \cdot 2^2$.   This operation is equivalent to SETXP($X,N+$INTXP(X)) and is valid only when X is nonzero and the result neither overflows nor underflows.

AINT(X):   equivalent to FLOAT(INT(X)).   This is a standard Fortran intrinsic function.

AINTRND(X):   equivalent to FLOAT(INTRND(X)).

FIX(X):   returns   the   fixed-point fraction closest   to   the floating-point number X.   This operation is only valid when $|X| < 1.0$.

FLOAT(N):   returns the floating-point representation of the integer N. This is a standard Fortran intrinsic function.

INT(X):   truncates the floating-point number X to an integer and converts the result to integer format.   For example,

$$INT(-3.14) = -3   .$$

This is a standard Fortran intrinsic function.

INTRND(X):   returns the integer representation of the integer closest to the floating-point number X.   (If X is equidistant from two integers, either may be chosen.) For example,

$$INTRND(-1.57) = -2   .$$

INTXP(X):   returns the integer representation of the exponent in the normalized representation of the floating-point number X.   For example,

$$INTXP(3.0) = 2$$

on binary machines because $3.0 = (0.75) \cdot 2^2$. This operation is valid only when X is nonzero.

REFLOAT(f): returns the floating-point representation of the fixed-point fraction f.

SETXP(X,N): returns the floating-point representation of a number whose significand is the significand of the floating-point number X, and whose exponent is the integer N. For example,

    SETXP(1.0,3) = 4.0

on binary machines because $1.0 = (0.5) \cdot 2^1$ and $4.0 = (0.5) \cdot 2^3$. This operation is only valid when X is nonzero and the result neither overflows nor underflows.

Our algorithms avoid improper arguments for these functions; the functions themselves need not verify that their arguments are valid if their only usage is in our algorithms. (For further discussion of some of these functions, see Cody [1977] and Sterbenz [1973].)

Finally, there is a simple notation convention which we will follow. Small letters will usually designate mathematical quantities, and capital letters will designate machine quantities. Thus, sqrt(x) will represent the mathematical square root of the variable x, while SQRT(X) will represent the result from the square root subroutine with the floating-point machine variable X as an argument. Similarly, sqrt(X) will mean the mathematical square root of the number represented by the machine variable X. Deviations from this convention will occur, such as the use of f to denote the floating-point significand of a number, but in such cases the distinction between mathematical and machine quantities should either be clear from context or unimportant.

3. PERFORMANCE TESTING

Each of our function discussions includes a Fortran program to demonstrate the capabilities and limitations of any program that evaluates the function. Output from these demonstration programs includes evidence that no major programming blunders have been made, statistical estimates of the overall accuracy of the program, and verification that all error conditions have been properly trapped. Detailed descriptions of specific tests are included in the discussions of the individual functions; the basic concepts of performance testing are presented here.

Consider accuracy testing first. There are two types of error associated with any numerical computer program. The first is the error attributable to errors in the data. Let $y = f(x)$ be a differentiable function. Then

$$dy/y = x\ f'(x)/f(x)\ dx/x$$

is an analytic relation between the relative error dx/x (called the *inherited error*) in the function argument and the corresponding relative error dy/y (called the *transmitted error*) in the function value. Because the transmitted error depends solely upon the analytic properties of the function and the inherited error, it is beyond the control of the function subprogram. All other errors, such as those due to inexact representation of constants in the program, truncation of series expansions, cancellation of significant digits in forming a sum, and rounding errors, are grouped together and called *generated error.*

Ideally, accuracy tests should measure only the error directly attributable to the program, i.e., the generated error. This can be accomplished by a direct comparison of computed results with "correct" results obtained for the same arguments by a different algorithm (to eliminate systematic programming errors) in higher precision arithmetic (Cody [1969]). Properly done, such tests give very reliable accuracy statistics, but the effort required is often orders of magnitude greater than that to prepare the program being tested. The design of such tests requires a detailed knowledge of the computer arithmetic system. In addition, when higher precision arithmetic is not available in the hardware, as is often the case in the environments that concern us, it must be provided as special software. Tests requiring such knowledge and effort are not appropriate for our present purposes.

Instead, the accuracy tests we use involve measuring the error in mathematical identities such as sqrt(x^2) = $|x|$. But the error that is measured in this case is not limited to generated error from the function program, because identities involve operations beyond the evaluation of the function. Identities that unduly magnify or distort the function error must be avoided whenever possible. For example, the SQRT function maps the interval (.25,1) into the interval (.5,1). Because there are exactly twice as many floating-point numbers in the first interval as the second on binary computers, the SQRT function must map an average of two different arguments into each result. Squaring the result can return at most one of the possible original arguments. Thus the calculation (SQRT(X))**2 statistically can be expected to return X for only about half of the arguments, even though the SQRT function may perform flawlessly. On the other hand, the operation of multiplying a number by itself maps each argument from the interval (.5,1) into a unique result in the interval (.25,1). Because this mapping is usually accurate to within a rounding error, the calculation SQRT(X**2) may be expected to return X in most of those cases where SQRT(X) is accurate. Thus the computation

SQRT(X**2) - X

is more useful for measuring the generated error in the SQRT routine than the computation

(SQRT(X))**2 - X.

Only rarely does an identity contaminate the generated error as little as this one does. In most cases the difference between the measured error and the generated error can be roughly estimated. Where possible, the estimates for the identities we use are included in the notes for testing the individual functions.

Care must also be taken to select identities that are independent of the subroutine being tested. For example, if the cosine of an angle is calculated by first calculating the sine and then using the identity $\sin^2(x)+\cos^2(x)=1$, then this identity becomes useless for determining the accuracy of either the sine or the cosine because the computed function values automatically satisfy the identity regardless of their accuracy.

Once the identity has been selected, it is necessary to choose the test intervals. These should be chosen so that each test has a specific purpose. Most function subroutines first reduce the given argument to a related argument in a small primary interval and obtain other parameters related to the argument reduction. They then evaluate an appropriate function approximation for the reduced argument and reconstruct the desired function value from these components. A test that exercises the routine over the primary interval tests the accuracy of the main approximation independent of the argument reduction. Other intervals should be chosen to determine the additional error incurred in argument reduction and the effect of increasing argument size.

Statistics of interest for each interval include the maximum magnitude of the relative error, MRE, which approximates the worst-case behavior of the function in the interval, and the root mean square relative error, RMS, which indicates the overall quality. These are defined by

$$MRE = \max\ |RE|$$

and

$$RMS = \ \text{sqrt}[(1/N)\ \text{sum}(RE)^2],$$

where the max and sum are to be taken over all arguments. For each argument $RE = [F(x) - f(x)]/f(x)$, where $F(x)$ is the calculated function value, $f(x)$ is the "correct" value, and $f(x) \neq 0$. Our test programs print MRE, the argument that led to MRE, and RMS for each interval.

On machines with radix B the measures can be converted to the number of correct base-B digits by dividing the log of the statistic by $\log(B)$. For example, on binary machines if

$$MRE = 4.759E-07,$$

then

$$\ln(MRE)/\ln(2) = -21.00,$$

and MRE represents a nominal error of 1 unit in the 21st significant bit. This result must be interpreted carefully, however. Recall the discussion in Chapter 2 of the relative value of the last digit position in the significands of two approximately equal numbers with differing exponents. Suppose that $F(x) = 1+eps$ and $F(y) = 1-eps$ for a small positive eps, and that each has an error of one unit in the last digit of the significand. Then the RE for $F(x)$ reports about one less, correct base-B digit than does the RE for $F(y)$.

A random number generator should be used to select arguments from each interval. Our test programs now use the uniform random number generator RAN provided in Appendix A. This generator is designed to return only about 29 random bits and is not suitable for machines with longer significands without some additional synthesis of low-order bits. Randomness in the low-order bits is not as crucial as randomness in the high-order bits for our purposes, but it is essential that the low-order bits not all be 0. One possibility for longer significands is to combine pairs of random numbers by appropriately scaling the second and adding it to the first. Of course, any other generator could be used in place of RAN. If one is not already available, the Fortran-coded generators RAND (Schrage [1979]) and URAND (Forsythe, Malcolm and Moler [1977]) are very portable. RAND is new, but URAND has been used extensively and has a good reputation. One disadvantage to URAND is that it uses double-precision floating-point arithmetic in several places. In addition, it uses DATAN and DSQRT programs to determine values of pi/4 and sqrt(3). These subroutines could be circumvented on a particular machine by using numerical values of the constants instead.

Random numbers drawn from a uniform distribution do not realistically duplicate the distribution of numbers encountered in actual computation, which follow a logarithmic distribution (Knuth [1969]). For small intervals the difference is not important. For large intervals, however, the difference can be dramatic. About 90% of the numbers from a uniform distribution over the interval $(1,10^{10})$ will exceed 10^9, while only 10% will be that large from a logarithmic distribution. The latter will also provide about 10% of its numbers in the subinterval $(1,10)$, whereas the uniform distribution will essentially provide none. When logarithmically distributed numbers are desired, they can be obtained from a uniform distribution; for example,

$$x = a \cdot \exp[y \cdot \ln(b/a)]$$

is logarithmically distributed over (a,b) if y is uniformly distributed over $(0,1)$. Our test program for SQRT uses the logarithmic generator RANDL provided in Appendix A. This in turn uses the above relation with RAN and the exponential routine EXP. Even though RAN provides only 29 random bits, the numbers obtained from RANDL may be considered to be random to the precision of the exponential routine with one exception. The exception, which does not arise in our use, is that these numbers should not be used in tests requiring the logarithm of a random number when the floating-point precision is greater than 29 bits.

In addition to random argument accuracy tests just described, test programs ought to check specific arguments which might cause or detect trouble. These may include the largest and smallest (in magnitude) arguments acceptable to a routine, arguments spanning the endpoints of the primary interval of computation, and selected pairs of arguments x and $-x$ for functions with even or odd symmetry. The purpose of these tests is to verify that a subroutine does work properly at the advertised extremes of its domain, that it provides smooth transition across boundaries separating different computational paths within the routine, and that basic analytic properties of the function are preserved. Monotonicity is extremely difficult to achieve and to detect in a subroutine, and tests for it are probably not worth including in general performance testing. Many of the other special tests are included in our test programs.

Each of our test programs uses information about the floating-point arithmetic system. The radix and precision of the system are required by all of the programs, and some of them require additional information about the largest and smallest positive floating-point numbers, whether the arithmetic rounds or chops, etc. The programs now call upon the environmental inquiry subprogram MACHAR presented in Appendix B, which dynamically determines these and other environmental parameters by exercising the floating-point arithmetic. The program is successful on most current computers but fails whenever the active arithmetic registers retain floating-point quantities to more precision than stored numbers and use that extra precision in subsequent computations. MACHAR must be modified to force the storage and retrieval of important intermediate results on such machines. (The test programs may also fail in such cases, and the notes indicate some, but perhaps not all, places where they too must be modified.) MACHAR need not be used at all if the necessary environmental information can be supplied as static data, with accompanying modifications to the test programs to accommodate this, of course.

The function notes include typical results obtained by the test programs when applied to our algorithms and to selected existing system library programs on a variety of computers with differing characteristics. Most of our algorithms were implemented in Janus for these tests, but some were implemented in assembly language or Fortran. The library programs were drawn from libraries accompanying Fortran compilers provided by the machine manufacturers or from installation-developed libraries such as the one at Argonne National Laboratory. Because system libraries frequently change (and, we hope, improve), such libraries are identified by version where possible.

The error figures tabulated for our algorithms are indicative of the errors to be expected when the algorithms are implemented on other machines. Minor deviations from these typical values will occur in specific implementations, but any major increase is probably due to a programming error. Such errors can usually be found quickly by stepping through an execution of the function applied to the argument which led to MRE. Test results for some library programs, particularly those on the IBM 370, are included because the programs are superb. Such results allow a comparison of test results for our algorithms with those for programs that have been individually designed by master craftsmen for maximum performance on a specific machine. Test results for other library programs are included because they indicate what happens when certain critical steps in our algorithms are omitted. Such results have been selected only to illustrate the diagnostic capabilities of our test programs; they are not intended as an indication of the current status of any library nor as a condemnation of any function program.

4. SQRT

a. General Discussion

The square root exists and is computable for every non-negative floating-point number X. Assume $X > 0$, and let $X = f \cdot B**e$, $1/B \leq f < 1$, $2 \leq B \leq 16$. Then

$$\text{sqrt}(X) = \text{sqrt}(f) \cdot B**(e/2)$$

if e is even, and

$$\text{sqrt}(X) = [\text{sqrt}(f)/\text{sqrt}(B)] \cdot B**[(e+1)/2]$$

if e is odd. The computation of sqrt(X) then consists of three steps: the reduction of the given argument X to the related parameters f and e, the computation of sqrt(f), and the reconstruction of sqrt(X) from these results.

The computation of sqrt(f) begins with an appropriate low-accuracy initial approximation y_0. Successively more accurate approximations are then generated using Newton iteration in the form of Heron's formula:

$$y_i = (y_{i-1} + f/y_{i-1})/2, \quad i = 1,2,\ldots,j.$$

If the relative error in the n-th iterate is d, then the relative error in the $(n+1)$-th iterate is approximately $d^2/2$. Thus each iteration doubles the number of correct significant digits in the square root.

b. Flow Chart for SQRT(X)

(Assume $X = \pm f \times B^{**}e$, $1/B \le f < 1$)

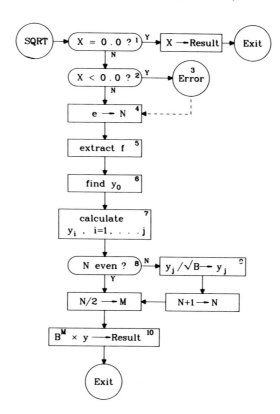

Note: Small integers indicate an implementation note.

c. Implementation Notes, Non-Decimal Fixed-Point Machines

1) Consider fixed-point instructions for efficiency.

2) Consider fixed-point instructions for efficiency.

3) If execution is to continue rather than terminate, then a default function value should be provided in addition to an error message. Usually this default value is the computed square root of $|X|$; i.e., computation continues with $|X|$.

4) In terms of our operations (see Chapter 2),

   $$N = INTXP(X) \quad .$$

5) Convert to fixed point here. We assume that $B = 2^{**}k$ with $k = 1$, 2, 3 or 4 and that the fixed-point representation of a number contains at least as many bits as the floating-point significand (plus two extra if the Newton iteration with $f/4$ described in Note 7 is used). In terms of our operations (see Chapter 2),

   $$f = FIX(SETXP(X,0))$$

   returns a fixed-point f such that $1/B \leq f < 1$.

   This is the final value of f for binary machines, but it must be scaled by c on non-binary machines so that $1/2 \leq c \cdot f < 1$, where $c = 2^{**}r$ and r is the number (possibly 0) of leading zero bits in the first base-B digit of f. There will be a corresponding rescaling after the Newton iteration (see Note 7). The scaling here can be accomplished in two ways. If bit manipulation instructions are available, extract the first $k+1$ bits of f (assuming the first bit is a sign bit), use them as an index to retrieve r from an appropriate integer array, and then shift f left r bits. Otherwise, set $r=0$, test f, and repeatedly shift f left one bit at a time, replacing r by $r+1$ each time, until $1/2 \leq f$. In either case save r for later use.

6) Use the following approximation (Lyusternik et al. [1965]):

   $$y_0 = a + b \cdot f,$$

where

$$a = .42578 \text{ (decimal) or } .33177\text{--}7 \text{ (octal)}$$

and

$$b = .57422 \text{ (decimal) or } .44600\text{--}0 \text{ (octal)}.$$

See Note 7 for accuracy estimates and an alternate start.

7) The following table gives the accuracy in bits of successive Newton iterates starting from the above estimate of y_0.

	Iteration #		
0	1	2	3
6.50	14.00	28.99	58.99

This table thus specifies the number j of Newton iterations necessary to determine sqrt(f) to a given accuracy. For example, $j = 2$ is sufficient when there are 24 bits in the floating-point significand for X. There may be more than 24 bits in f in this case, but only the first 24 bits of sqrt(f) will be used in the floating-point result.

All Newton iterations may take the form

$$y_i = y_{i-1}/2 + (f/2)/y_{i-1} \quad ,$$

where division by 2 may be accomplished with a shift operation and $f/2$ may be precomputed. It is important that the order of operations be strictly observed if overflow is to be avoided.

If $j>1$ and there are sufficient extra bits in the fixed-point representation to protect the accuracy of $f/4$, an alternate computation of y_2 may require fewer storage accesses and hence be quicker. Let

$$y_0 = a + b*f,$$

where now

$$a = .212885 \text{ (decimal) or } .15477\text{--}7 \text{ (octal)}$$

and

$\qquad$ b = .28711   (decimal) or .22300--0 (octal).

Then

$$z = (y_0/2) + ((f/4)/y_0)/2$$
and
$$y_2 = z + (f/4)/z,$$

where the quantity $f/4$ should be precomputed and all divisions by powers of 2 should be done with shift operations. The indicated order of operations is important to avoid overflow. In particular, summing the components of z before dividing by 2 may lead to overflow in the sum.

For non-binary machines, $k > 1$, the final Newton iterate y_j must now be multiplied by $c' = sqrt(1/c) = sqrt[2^{**}(-r)]$, where c' and r are defined in Note 5. Omit this rescaling if $r = 0$. Otherwise, use r as an index to retrieve the value of c' from an array of length k. Although $r \le k-1$, the extra array value will be needed later (see Note 9). It is important that c' be specified as accurately as possible. We suggest direct use of the fixed-point machine representation (see Chapter 2). The octal values of c' are

r	c'
1	.55202 36314 77473 63110
2	.40000 00000 00000 00000
3	.26501 17146 37635 71444
4	.20000 00000 00000 00000

8) When machine instructions for testing specific bits in an integer are available, the parity of N can be determined from its integer representation. On machines with either sign-magnitude or 2's complement representation, the low-order bit is 0 for even numbers and 1 for odd numbers. On machines with 1's complement representation, the sign and low-order bits agree for even numbers and disagree for odd numbers.

9) In fixed point, $y_j/sqrt(B)$ must be implemented as

$\qquad$ y_j • sqrt(1/B).

The array c' described in Note 7 for non-binary machines already contains sqrt($1/B$) as the k-th element. This array does not exist for binary machines, but the value for c' specified in Note 7 for $r = 1$ should be used here.

10) Let $Y = $ REFLOAT(y_j) and use ADX(Y,M) to augment the exponent of Y (see Chapter 2). The operation SETXP(Y,M) is not safe; $Y = 0.5-eps$ is possible at this point, but it has a floating-point representation that includes a non-zero exponent, and the SETXP operation would produce an incorrect result.

d. Implementation Notes, Binary Floating-Point Machines

1) Consider fixed-point instructions for efficiency.

2) Consider fixed-point instructions for efficiency.

3) If execution is to continue rather than terminate, then a default function value should be provided in addition to an error message. Usually this default value is the computed square root of $|X|$; i.e., computation continues with $|X|$.

4) In terms of our operations (see Chapter 2),

$$N = INTXP(X) \quad .$$

5) In terms of our operations (see Chapter 2),

$$f = SETXP(X,0) \quad .$$

6) Use the following approximation (Hart et al. [1968]):

$$y_0 = .41731 + .59016 * f.$$

See Note 7 for accuracy estimates.

7) The following table gives the accuracy in bits of successive Newton iterates starting from the above estimate of y_0.

	Iteration #		
0	1	2	3
7.04	15.08	31.16	63.32

Using this table and knowing the number of bits in the representation of f, we can determine the correct value for j. For example, if there are 24 bits in f, then $j=2$ is sufficient to determine sqrt(f) to within roundoff error.

All Newton iterations may take the form

$$y_i = .5 * (y_{i-1} + f/y_{i-1}),$$

where the multiplication by .5 may be accomplished with an $ADX(y_i, -1)$ operation (see Chapter 2).

If $j > 1$, the value of y_2 can be formed as

$$z = (y_0 + f/y_0)$$

$$y_2 = .25 * z + f/z,$$

where the multiplication by .25 may be an $ADX(z, -2)$ operation. This saves one multiply or ADX over the unmodified use of Heron's formula twice.

8) When machine instructions for testing specific bits in an integer are available, the parity of N can be determined from its integer representation. On machines with either sign-magnitude or 2's complement representation, the low-order bit is 0 for even numbers and 1 for odd numbers. On machines with 1's complement representation, the sign and low-order bits agree for even numbers and disagree for odd numbers.

9) Because multiplication is usually faster than division, we suggest that $y_j/\text{sqrt}(B)$ be implemented as

$$y_j * \text{sqrt}(.5),$$

where
$$\text{sqrt}(.5) = .70710\ 67811\ 86547\ 52440\ \dots\ (\text{decimal})$$
$$= .55202\ 36314\ 77473\ 63110\quad (\text{octal}).$$

It is important that this constant be specified as accurately as possible. We suggest direct use of the machine representation (see Chapter 2).

10) Use $ADX(y_j, M)$ to augment the exponent of y_j (see Chapter 2). The operation $SETXP(y_j, M)$ is not safe; $y_j = 1.0$ is possible at this point, but it has a floating-point representation that includes a non-zero exponent, and the SETXP operation would produce an incorrect result.

e. Implementation Notes, Non-Binary Floating-Point Machines

1) Consider fixed-point instructions for efficiency.

2) Consider fixed-point instructions for efficiency.

3) If execution is to continue rather than terminate, then a default function value should be provided in addition to an error message. Usually this default value is the computed square root of $|X|$; i.e., computation continues with $|X|$.

4) In terms of our operations (see Chapter 2),

$$N = \text{INTXP}(X) \quad .$$

5) In terms of our operations (see Chapter 2),

$$f = \text{SETXP}(X,0) \quad .$$

6) We assume the worst case for non-binary machines; i.e., $B = 16$, and $1/16 \leq f < 1$. Then two reasonable choices for y_0 exist (Fike [1968]):

$$R1: \quad y_0 = .223607 + .894427 \cdot f$$

and

$$R2: \quad y_0 = .580661 + f/2 - .086462/(f + .175241).$$

The selection between $R1$ and $R2$ should be based on efficiency. Starting with $R1$ and doing one Newton iteration generally require fewer overall operations to achieve slightly more accuracy than $R2$, but $R2$ trades a relatively expensive floating-point multiplication for a floating-point add. See Note 7 for accuracy estimates.

7) The following table gives the accuracy in bits and decimal places of successive Newton iterates starting from $R1$ and $R2$ (Fike [1968]):

	Iteration #			
	1	2	3	4
R1 (bits)	7.33	15.66	32.32	65.65
(decimals)	2.21	4.71	9.73	19.76
R2 (bits)	15.27	31.54	64.08	129.16
(decimals)	4.60	9.49	19.29	38.88

Using this table and knowing the number of bits or decimal places in the representation of f, we can determine the correct value for j. For example, if there are 24 bits in f, and y_0 is determined using $R1$, then $j=3$ is sufficient to determine sqrt(f) to within roundoff error.

On non-binary machines the first $j-1$ Newton iterations may take the form

$$y_i = .5 * (y_{i-1} + f/y_{i-1}),$$

but the final iteration should be of the form

$$y_i = y_{i-1} + .5 * (f/y_{i-1} - y_{i-1}).$$

If $j>1$, the value of y_2 can be formed as

$$z = (y_0 + f/y_0)$$

$$y_2 = .25 * z + f/z,$$

which saves one multiply over the unmodified use of Heron's formula twice.

8) When instructions are available on non-decimal machines for testing specific bits in an integer, the parity of N can be determined from its integer representation. On machines with either sign-magnitude or 2's complement representation, the low-order bit is 0 for even numbers and 1 for odd numbers. On machines with 1's complement representation, the sign and low-order bits agree for even numbers and disagree for odd numbers.

9) Because multiplication is often faster than division, we suggest that $y_i/\text{sqrt}(B)$ be implemented as

$$y_i \cdot \text{sqrt}(1/B),$$

where $\text{sqrt}(1/B)$ is the stored constant. It is important that this constant be specified as accurately as possible. We suggest direct use of the machine representation (see Chapter 2). Appropriate constants are given below:

B	sqrt(1/B)
4	.2 (base 4)
8	.26501 17146 37635 71444 (octal)
10	.31622 77660 16837 93320 (decimal)
16	.4 (hexadecimal)

10) Use $\text{ADX}(y_i,M)$ to augment the exponent of y_i (see Chapter 2). The operation $\text{SETXP}(y_i,M)$ is not safe; $y_i = 1.0$ is possible at this point, but it has a floating-point representation that includes a non-zero exponent, and the SETXP operation would produce an incorrect result.

f. Testing

The tests are divided into four major parts. First is a random argument test to determine the accuracy of the basic Newton iteration, i.e., the accuracy of the square root when the argument lies in the primary range and no argument reduction is necessary. Second is a similar test using random arguments outside the primary range, and with odd exponent, to test the argument reduction and subsequent multiplication by sqrt(1/B). Third is a series of short tests with special arguments, including arguments close to the largest and smallest in magnitude representable in the machine. Finally there is a test with zero as an argument to verify that an error return is not triggered, and a test with a negative argument to verify that an error return is triggered.

The random argument tests measure the relative difference between the two sides of the identity

$$sqrt(x^2) = x.$$

See Chapter 3 for a discussion of the choice of this identity. Thus we measure

$$E = [sqrt(x^2) - x] / x$$

for x drawn randomly (logarithmically distributed) from an interval (r,s) with $r > 0$.

For the first test r = sqrt(1/B), where B is the radix of the floating-point number representation (see Glossary), and s = 1. This particular choice of interval will contaminate the error on some machines, particularly those with B = 16. To see this, assume that B = 16 and that there are b bits (not base-16 digits) available for the representation of the significand of a floating-point number. As described in Chapter 2, such numbers suffer from "wobbling precision." Table 4.1 compares the number of possible significant bits in the representation of X, $X*X$ and SQRT($X*X$) for X drawn from subintervals of (r,s) = (1/4,1). Because $X*X$ cannot generally be represented exactly, there is a rounding error in the argument for the SQRT routine. We can assume that this inherited error (see Glossary) is limited to one unit

TABLE 4.1

Wobbling Precision in Hexadecimal

Interval	Possible Significant Bits in		
	X	X·X	SQRT(X·X)
(1/4, sqrt(2)/4)	b-1	b-3	b-2
(sqrt(2)/4, 1/2)	b-1	b-2	b-1
(1/2, sqrt(2)/2)	b	b-1	b
(sqrt(2)/2, 1)	b	b	b
(1 , sqrt(2))	b-3	b-3	b-3
(sqrt(2) , 2)	b-3	b-2	b-3
(2 ,2·sqrt(2))	b-2	b-1	b-2
(2·sqrt(2), 4)	b-2	b	b-2

TABLE 4.2

Typical Results for SQRT Tests

Test	Machine	B	Library or Program	Reported Loss of Base-B Digits in	
				MRE	RMS
1	CDC 6400	2	Ours	0.50	0.26
	IBM/370	16	Ours	0.75	0.41
	CDC 7600	2	FTN 4.6	0.50	0.00
	IBM/370	16	FTX 2.2	0.75	0.24
2	CDC 6400	2	Ours	2.00	1.31
	IBM/370	16	Ours	1.00	0.81
	CDC 7600	2	FTN 4.6	0.99	0.00
	IBM/370	16	FTX 2.2	0.00	0.00

in the last bit position. From the formula in Chapter 3, the corresponding transmitted error (see Glossary) is then a half unit in the last bit position. This means that the value returned by SQRT can have only one more bit of precision than the argument. Thus, the precision of function values for arguments drawn from the first interval is not so great as the precision of the original arguments, and the testing process is contaminated. The contamination is unavoidable if we are to test in the primary range using this identity. Nevertheless, we expect the test to report accuracies only slightly less than machine precision for good implementations of SQRT. The results given in Table 4.2 all show a loss of less than one base-B digit for the MRE (see Chapter 3), and a loss of less than half a digit for the RMS.

For the second test we choose $r = 1$ and $s = \text{sqrt}(B)$. Then $X \cdot X$ is drawn from the interval $(1,B)$, and the previous contamination due to wobbling precision is eliminated. Table 4.1 illustrates the situation for $B = 16$. Test results for this interval must be interpreted carefully, however. In Chapter 3 we discussed how a last-digit error in a number of the form 1+eps is B times more significant than a last-digit error in a number of the form 1-eps. That is precisely the situation we have here; all of the calculated square roots are less than 1 for the first interval, and all of them are greater than 1 for this second interval. Thus a last digit error in this test is B times more significant than a last digit error in the first test, and this test should report larger errors than the first. The MRE might report a loss of one base-B digit on non-binary machines and perhaps two bits on binary machines. The RMS should report the loss of a large fraction of a digit on non-binary machines, and perhaps a little more than one bit on binary machines. The results given in Table 4.2 illustrate this. The library program tested on the IBM machine is superb; the identity was always satisfied exactly. The library routine on the CDC machine is also superb; the identity was satisfied exactly for all except a handful of arguments, and the MRE reported a loss of only one bit. Our algorithm fared a little worse in each case. The MRE for both the IBM and CDC versions was limited to the last bit of the result, however. It occurred for $x = 1.0006$ on the IBM machine, and for $x = 1.0060$ on the CDC machine.

```
C       PROGRAM TO TEST SQRT
C
C       DATA REQUIRED
C
C          NONE
C
C       SUBPROGRAMS REQUIRED FROM THIS PACKAGE
C
C          MACHAR - AN ENVIRONMENTAL INQUIRY PROGRAM PROVIDING
C                   INFORMATION ON THE FLOATING-POINT ARITHMETIC
C                   SYSTEM.  NOTE THAT THE CALL TO MACHAR CAN
C                   BE DELETED PROVIDED THE FOLLOWING SIX
C                   PARAMETERS ARE ASSIGNED THE VALUES INDICATED
C
C                      IBETA  - THE RADIX OF THE FLOATING-POINT SYSTEM
C                      IT     - THE NUMBER OF BASE-IBETA DIGITS IN THE
C                               SIGNIFICAND OF A FLOATING-POINT NUMBER
C                      EPS    - THE SMALLEST POSITIVE FLOATING-POINT
C                               NUMBER SUCH THAT 1.0+EPS .NE. 1.0
C                      EPSNEG - THE SMALLEST POSITIVE FLOATING-POINT
C                               NUMBER SUCH THAT 1.0-EPSNEG .NE. 1.0
C                      XMIN   - THE SMALLEST NON-VANISHING FLOATING-POINT
C                               POWER OF THE RADIX
C                      XMAX   - THE LARGEST FINITE FLOATING-POINT NO.
C
C          RANDL(X) - A FUNCTION SUBPROGRAM RETURNING LOGARITHMICALLY
C                     DISTRIBUTED RANDOM REAL NUMBERS.  IN PARTICULAR,
C                         A * RANDL(ALOG(B/A))
C                     IS LOGARITHMICALLY DISTRIBUTED OVER (A,B)
C
C          RAN(K) - A FUNCTION SUBPROGRAM RETURNING RANDOM REAL
C                   NUMBERS UNIFORMLY DISTRIBUTED OVER (0,1)
C
C
C       STANDARD FORTRAN SUBPROGRAMS REQUIRED
C
C          ABS, ALOG, AMAX1, FLOAT, SQRT
C
C
C       LATEST REVISION - AUGUST 2, 1979
C
C       AUTHOR - W. J. CODY
C                ARGONNE NATIONAL LABORATORY
```

```
C
C
      INTEGER I,IBETA,IEXP,IOUT,IRND,IT,J,K1,K2,K3,MACHEP,
     1          MAXEXP,MINEXP,N,NEGEP,NGRD
      REAL A,AIT,ALBETA,B,BETA,C,EPS,EPSNEG,ONE,RANDL,R6,R7,
     1     SQBETA,W,X,XMAX,XMIN,XN,X1,Y,Z,ZERO
C
      IOUT = 6
      CALL MACHAR(IBETA,IT,IRND,NGRD,MACHEP,NEGEP,IEXP,MINEXP,
     1            MAXEXP,EPS,EPSNEG,XMIN,XMAX)
      BETA = FLOAT(IBETA)
      SQBETA = SQRT(BETA)
      ALBETA = ALOG(BETA)
      AIT = FLOAT(IT)
      ONE = 1.0E0
      ZERO = 0.0E0
      A = ONE / SQBETA
      B = ONE
      N = 2000
      XN = FLOAT(N)
C-----------------------------------------------------------------
C     RANDOM ARGUMENT ACCURACY TESTS
C-----------------------------------------------------------------
      DO 300 J = 1, 2
        C = ALOG(B/A)
        K1 = 0
        K3 = 0
        X1 = ZERO
        R6 = ZERO
        R7 = ZERO
C
        DO 200 I = 1, N
          X = A * RANDL(C)
          Y = X * X
          Z = SQRT(Y)
          W = (Z - X) / X
          IF (W .GT. ZERO) K1 = K1 + 1
          IF (W .LT. ZERO) K3 = K3 + 1
          W = ABS(W)
          IF (W .LE. R6) GO TO 120
          R6 = W
          X1 = X
  120     R7 = R7 + W * W
```

```
    200     CONTINUE
C
        K2 = N - K1 - K3
        R7 = SQRT(R7/XN)
        WRITE (IOUT,1000)
        WRITE (IOUT,1010) N,A,B
        WRITE (IOUT,1011) K1,K2,K3
        WRITE (6,1020) IT,IBETA
        W = -999.0E0
        IF (R6 .NE. ZERO) W = ALOG(ABS(R6))/ALBETA
        WRITE (IOUT,1021) R6,IBETA,W,X1
        W = AMAX1(AIT+W,ZERO)
        WRITE (IOUT,1022) IBETA,W
        W = -999.0E0
        IF (R7 .NE. ZERO) W = ALOG(ABS(R7))/ALBETA
        WRITE (IOUT,1023) R7,IBETA,W
        W = AMAX1(AIT+W,ZERO)
        WRITE (IOUT,1022) IBETA,W
        A = ONE
        B = SQBETA
    300 CONTINUE
C----------------------------------------------------------------
C     SPECIAL TESTS
C----------------------------------------------------------------
      WRITE (IOUT,1040)
      X = XMIN
      Y = SQRT(X)
      WRITE (IOUT,1041) X,Y
      X = ONE - EPSNEG
      Y = SQRT(X)
      WRITE (IOUT,1042) EPSNEG,Y
      X = ONE
      Y = SQRT(X)
      WRITE (IOUT,1043) X,Y
      X = ONE + EPS
      Y = SQRT(X)
      WRITE (IOUT,1044) EPS,Y
      X = XMAX
      Y = SQRT(X)
      WRITE (IOUT,1045) X,Y
C----------------------------------------------------------------
C     TEST OF ERROR RETURNS
C----------------------------------------------------------------
```

```
      WRITE (IOUT,1050)
      X = ZERO
      WRITE (IOUT,1051) X
      Y = SQRT(X)
      WRITE (IOUT,1055) Y
      X = -ONE
      WRITE (IOUT,1052) X
      Y = SQRT(X)
      WRITE (IOUT,1055) Y
      WRITE (IOUT,1100)
      STOP
 1000 FORMAT(22H1TEST OF SQRT(X*X) - X //)
 1010 FORMAT(I7,47H RANDOM ARGUMENTS WERE TESTED FROM THE INTERVAL /
     1 6X,1H(,E15.4,1H,,E15.4,1H)//)
 1011 FORMAT(19H SQRT(X) WAS LARGER,I6,7H TIMES, /
     1      12X,7H AGREED,I6,11H TIMES, AND /
     2       8X,11HWAS SMALLER,I6,7H TIMES.//)
 1020 FORMAT(10H THERE ARE,I4,5H BASE,I4,
     1      46H SIGNIFICANT DIGITS IN A FLOATING-POINT NUMBER  //)
 1021 FORMAT(30H THE MAXIMUM RELATIVE ERROR OF,E15.4,3H = ,I4,3H **,
     1 F7.2/4X,16HOCCURRED FOR X =,E17.6)
 1022 FORMAT(27H THE ESTIMATED LOSS OF BASE,I4,
     1  22H SIGNIFICANT DIGITS IS,F7.2//)
 1023 FORMAT(40H THE ROOT MEAN SQUARE RELATIVE ERROR WAS,E15.4,
     1     3H = ,I4,3H **,F7.2)
 1040 FORMAT(26H1TEST OF SPECIAL ARGUMENTS//)
 1041 FORMAT(19H SQRT(XMIN) = SQRT(,E15.7,4H) = ,E15.7//)
 1042 FORMAT(25H SQRT(1-EPSNEG) = SQRT(1-,E15.7,4H) = ,E15.7//)
 1043 FORMAT(18H SQRT(1.0) = SQRT(,E15.7,4H) = ,E15.7//)
 1044 FORMAT(22H SQRT(1+EPS) = SQRT(1+,E15.7,4H) = ,E15.7//)
 1045 FORMAT(19H SQRT(XMAX) = SQRT(,E15.7,4H) = ,E15.7//)
 1050 FORMAT(22H1TEST OF ERROR RETURNS//)
 1051 FORMAT(38H SQRT WILL BE CALLED WITH THE ARGUMENT,E15.4/
     1       41H THIS SHOULD NOT TRIGGER AN ERROR MESSAGE//)
 1052 FORMAT(38H0SQRT WILL BE CALLED WITH THE ARGUMENT,E15.4/
     1       37H THIS SHOULD TRIGGER AN ERROR MESSAGE//)
 1055 FORMAT(24H SQRT RETURNED THE VALUE,E15.4///)
 1100 FORMAT(25H THIS CONCLUDES THE TESTS )
C     ---------- LAST CARD OF SQRT TEST PROGRAM ----------
      END
```

5. ALOG/ALOG10

a. General Discussion

Let $X = f \cdot B \cdot \cdot m$, $1/B \leq f < 1$, where B is the radix of the
floating-point number system (see Glossary). Assume for the moment that
$B = 2 \cdot \cdot k$, i.e., that the machine is non-decimal. Determine g and n so
that $f = g \cdot 2 \cdot \cdot (-n)$, $1/\text{sqrt}(2) \leq g < \text{sqrt}(2)$. Then

$$\ln(X) = (k \cdot m - n) \ln(2) + \ln(g)$$

and

$$\log(X) = \log(e) \cdot \ln(X) = \ln(X) / \ln(10),$$

where ln denotes the natural (base e)   logarithm and log denotes the
common (base 10)   logarithm.   The computation of a logarithm thus
involves three distinct steps: the reduction of a given argument to a
related argument in a small, logarithmically symmetric interval about 1;
the computation of the logarithm for this reduced argument;   and the
reconstruction of the desired logarithm from its components.   Only the
third step need vary with the type of logarithm wanted.

The roles of $\ln(X)$ and $\log(X)$ must be interchanged to preserve
accuracy in the above algorithm when $B = 10$.   In particular, g and n
must be chosen so that $f = g \cdot 10 \cdot \cdot (-n)$, $1/\text{sqrt}(10) \leq g < \text{sqrt}(10)$.   Then

$$\log(X) = m - n + \log(g)$$

and $\ln(X)$, when needed, is determined from the second relation above.

The logarithm of the reduced argument can be determined in many ways.   In our algorithm we return to the assumption that $B \neq 10$ (modifications for the case $B = 10$ should be obvious) and define

$$s = (g-1)/(g+1).$$

Then

$$\ln(g) = \ln((1+s)/(1-s))$$

is evaluated using a minimax rational approximation generated especially for this work.   This approximation is expressed in terms of the auxiliary variable $z = 2s$ (but we work directly with s when $B = 10$).

In general the computation of $\ln(X)$ is well-behaved numerically. The term $(k \cdot m - n) \cdot \ln(2)$ dominates for most values of X, and small rounding errors in $\ln(g)$ do not alter the value of $\ln(X)$.   However, when $k \cdot m - n$ vanishes, i.e., when $X = g$, the accuracy of $\ln(g)$ becomes vital. Because

$$\ln(g) = 2s + s \sum_{i=1}^{\infty} a_i s^{2i}, \quad g > 0,$$

this in turn requires accuracy of z.   In the flow chart and implementation notes that follow, z can be determined directly from f without explicit evaluation of either g or s.   The computation varies with the class of machine to maximize the accuracy of z.

b. Flow Chart for ALOG(X)/ALOG10(X)

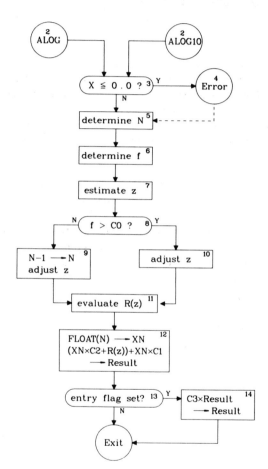

(Assume $X = \pm f \times B^{**}e$, $1/B \leq f < 1$) [1]

Note: Small integers indicate an implementation note.

c. Implementation Notes, Non-Decimal Fixed-Point Machines

1) In this case $B = 2**k$; $k = 1$, 2, 3, or 4; and $1/B \leq f < 1$.

2) These may be alternate entry points to one subroutine, in which case ALOG10 should set a flag and ALOG should clear that flag (see Note 13).

   When multiple entries are not supported, ALOG and ALOG10 must be separate subroutines. In that case ALOG can be a self-contained subroutine which is called by ALOG10, or there can be a separate computational subroutine starting with the error test (see Note 3) which is called by both ALOG and ALOG10. In either case, multiplication by $C3$ (see Notes 13 and 14) occurs after return to ALOG10.

3) On machines that do not support multiple entry points, this is a natural point at which to begin a new subroutine.

4) If execution is to continue rather than terminate, then a default function value should be provided in addition to the error message. If $X = 0$, this function value is usually the negative of the largest floating-point number. Otherwise, it is the computed log of the absolute value of X; that is, the computation continues with $|X|$.

5) The radix B is assumed to be $2**k$. In this and the next step, we must determine N and a scaled value of f such that

   $$X = f * 2 ** N, \quad .5 \leq f < 1.$$

   As an initial estimate (see Chapter 2)

   $$N = INTXP(X) \quad .$$

6) As an initial estimate of f (see Chapter 2)

   $$f = SETXP(X,0) \quad .$$

If $k \neq 1$, our estimates of N and possibly of f need modification. First let

    N = k • N;

then test f, and repeatedly shift f left one bit at a time, replacing N by $N-1$ each time, until $.5 \leq f < 1$. If bit manipulation instructions are available, it may be more efficient to extract the first k bits of f and use them to determine the number of places to shift f and the corresponding adjustment on N.

7) This and the next few steps are critical if accuracy is to be retained for arguments close to 1 and at the same time the number of floating-point operations is to be minimized. The rational function to be evaluated is $R(z) = z + z \cdot r(z^2)$, where $r(z^2)$ is defined below (see Note 11), $z = 2s$, and $s = (g-1)/(g+1)$. Because z can be quite small, there may be little significance in its fixed-point representation. To retain precision in the rational function, it is best to perform the final multiplication and addition by z in floating point. However, evaluation of z itself in floating point involves an expensive floating-point divide. Therefore we compromise, trading the floating-point divide for a loss in precision for arguments very close to 1 as long as this loss can be kept acceptably small. Toward this end, we reformulate the computation to use a scaled value of $g-1$ in floating point in the last few critical steps and to carry out the rest of the computation in properly scaled fixed point. Thus, if $z = znum/zden$,

    ln(g) = 4•znum•[.25/zden+(.25/zden)•r(z²)]

where all but the final multiplication by 4•*znum* is carried out in fixed point. Begin as follows (where fixed-point division by 2 is a shift operation):

    f - .5 --> y   in floating point

    FIX(y) --> znum

    znum/2 + .5 -->zden   in fixed point.

8) This test is best made in fixed point by comparing *znum* against

$$CO = sqrt(.5) - .5$$
$$= .20710\ 67811\ 86547\ 52440.$$

9) No adjustment of z is necessary.

10) Recall that y is a floating-point quantity and that *znum* and *zden* are fixed-point quantities. Then

$$y - .5 \rightarrow y$$

$$znum - .5 \rightarrow znum$$

$$zden + .25 \rightarrow zden.$$

11) We use scaled fixed point to evaluate a rational approximation $r(z^2)$ derived especially for this work. Let b be the number of bits in the significand of a floating-point number. Then

for $b \leq 24$

$$\begin{aligned}
C &= 0.0 \\
a0 &= 0.06908\ 84357 \\
b0 &= 0.82908\ 97767 \\
b1 &= -0.125
\end{aligned}$$

for $25 \leq b \leq 32$

$$\begin{aligned}
C &= 0.01360\ 09546\ 862 \\
a0 &= 0.04862\ 85276\ 587 \\
b0 &= 0.69735\ 92187\ 803 \\
b1 &= -0.125
\end{aligned}$$

for $33 \leq b \leq 48$

$$\begin{aligned}
C &= 0.00444\ 45515\ 10980\ 33 \\
a0 &= 0.05523\ 07791\ 33055\ 91 \\
a1 &= -0.00889\ 05729\ 08757\ 20 \\
b0 &= 0.70010\ 94180\ 58381\ 82 \\
b1 &= -0.22363\ 05368\ 10708\ 18 \\
b2 &= 0.01562\ 5
\end{aligned}$$

Recalling that *znum* and *zden* are fixed-point quantities, form
$z = znum/zden$ and $w = z^2$. Then evaluate

   $r(z^2) = w * (C + A(w)/B(w))$

in fixed point, where C can be ignored when it is zero, and where
$A(w)$ and $B(w)$ are polynomials in w with coefficients $a0$, $a1$, ...,
aN, and $b0$, $b1$, ..., bM, respectively. Use nested multiplication.
For example, for $33 \leq b \leq 48$,

   $B(w) = (b2 * w + b1) * w + b0.$

Next, form $v = .25/zden$, and evaluate $q(z) = v + v*r(z^2)$ in fixed
point. Now let $Q(z) = \text{REFLOAT}[q(z)]$ and form $R(z) = (4*y)*Q(z)$ in
floating point. Note that an ADX operation (see Chapter 2) may be
quicker than floating-point multiplication of y by 4 when $B \leq 4$.
Use ADX(y,2) on binary machines, and ADX(y,1) when $B = 4$.

12) See Chapter 2 for the definition of FLOAT. Because floating-point
multiplies are expensive, this step should be bypassed when $N = 0$.
Otherwise, use

      C1 = 355/512 = .543 (octal)
      C2 = -2.12194 44005 46905 827679 E-4

where $C2$ is rounded at the appropriate point.

13) Ignore this step if ALOG10 is a separate subroutine.

14) Use the following constant rounded to machine precision:

      C3 = log(e)
         = 0.33626 75425 11562 41615 (octal)
         = 0.43429 44819 03251 82765 (decimal).

Direct use of the machine representation (see Chapter 2) will
preserve accuracy.

d. Implementation Notes, Non-Decimal Floating-Point Machines

1) In this case $B = 2**k$; $k = 1, 2, 3,$ or 4; and $1/B \leq f < 1$.

2) These may be alternate entry points to one subroutine, in which case ALOG10 should set a flag and ALOG should clear that flag (see Note 13).

   When multiple entries are not supported, ALOG and ALOG10 must be separate subroutines. In that case ALOG can be a self-contained subroutine which is called by ALOG10, or there can be a separate computational subroutine starting with the error test (see Note 3) which is called by both ALOG and ALOG10. In either case, multiplication by $C3$ (see Notes 13 and 14) occurs after return to ALOG10.

3) On machines that do not support multiple entry points, this is a natural point at which to begin a new subroutine.

4) If execution is to continue rather than terminate, then a default function value should be provided in addition to the error message. If $X = 0$, this function value is usually the negative of the largest floating-point number. Otherwise, it is the computed log of the absolute value of X; that is, the computation continues with $|X|$.

5) The radix B is assumed to be $2**k$. In this and the next step, we must determine N and a scaled value of f such that

$$X = f \cdot 2 ** N, \quad .5 \leq f < 1.$$

   As an initial estimate (see Chapter 2)

$$N = INTXP(X) \quad .$$

6) As an initial estimate of f (see Chapter 2)

$$f = SETXP(X,0) \quad .$$

If $k \neq 1$, our estimates of N and possibly of f need modification. First let

$$N = k \cdot N;$$

then test f, and repeatedly replace f by $f+f$ and N by $N-1$ until $.5 \leq f < 1$.

If bit manipulation instructions are available, it may be more efficient to use them to adjust f and N. One possibility is to extract the first base-B digit of the significand of f and use it as an index to retrieve an integer j and the corresponding constant $2^{**}j$ from appropriate arrays. Then replace N by $N-j$, and f by $f \cdot (2^{**}j)$.

7) Omit this step. The next few steps are critical if accuracy is to be retained for arguments close to 1. The rational function to be evaluated is $R(z) = z + z \cdot r(z^2)$, where $r(z^2)$ is defined below (see Note 11), $z = 2s$ and $s = (g-1)/(g+1)$. Because of possible wobbling precision (see Glossary) when $k \neq 1$ and rounding problems, we reformulate the computation of s to use a scaled value of $g-1$.

8) CO = sqrt(.5) = .70710 67811 86547 52440.

9) At this point make an initial determination of $znum$ and $zden$ rather than an adjustment of z.

   $f - .5 \longrightarrow znum$

   $znum \cdot .5 + .5 \longrightarrow zden.$

10) At this point make an initial determination of $znum$ and $zden$ rather than an adjustment of z. Do not combine constants in $znum$.

   $(f-.5) - .5 \longrightarrow znum$

   $f \cdot .5 + .5 \longrightarrow zden.$

11) We use a rational approximation $r(z^2)$ derived especially for this work. Let b be the number of bits in the significand of a floating-point number. Then

for b ≤ 24

a0 = -0.55270 74855 E+0
b0 = -0.66327 18214 E+1
b1 = 0.10000 00000 E+1

for 25 ≤ b ≤ 32

a0 = -0.46490 62303 464 E+0
a1 = 0.13600 95468 621 E-1
b0 = -0.55788 73750 242 E+1
b1 = 0.10000 00000 000 E+1

for 33 ≤ b ≤ 48

a0 = 0.37339 16896 31608 66 E+1
a1 = -0.63260 86623 38596 65 E+0
a2 = 0.44445 51510 98033 23 E-2
b0 = 0.44807 00275 57364 36 E+2
b1 = -0.14312 35435 58853 24 E+2
b2 = 0.10000 00000 00000 00 E+1

for 49 ≤ b ≤ 60

a0 = -0.64124 94342 37455 81147 E+2
a1 = 0.16383 94356 30215 34222 E+2
a2 = -0.78956 11288 74912 57267 E+0
b0 = -0.76949 93210 84948 79777 E+3
b1 = 0.31203 22209 19245 32844 E+3
b2 = -0.35667 97773 90346 46171 E+2
b3 = 0.10000 00000 00000 00000 E+1

Form z = $znum/zden$ and w = z^2. Then evaluate

$r(z^2)$ = w * $A(w)/B(w)$,

where $A(w)$ and $B(w)$ are polynomials in w with coefficients $a0$, $a1$, ..., aN, and $b0$, $b1$, ..., bM, respectively. Use nested multiplication. For example, for 49 ≤ b ≤ 60,

$B(w)$ = ((w + b2) * w + b1) * w + b0.

Note that explicit multiplication by $b3 = 1.0$ is best avoided. Finally, evaluate $R(z) = z + z \cdot r(z^2)$. Note that $z \cdot [1+r(z^2)]$ is mathematically equivalent but not so accurate.

12) See Chapter 2 for the definition of FLOAT. Use the following values:

$C1 = 355/512 = .543$ (octal)
$C2 = -2.12194\ 44005\ 46905\ 827679$ E-4

where $C2$ is rounded at the appropriate point.

13) Ignore this step if ALOG10 is a separate subroutine.

14) Use the following constant rounded to machine precision

$C3 = \log(e)$
$= 0.33626\ 75425\ 11562\ 41615$ (octal)
$= 0.43429\ 44819\ 03251\ 82765$ (decimal).

Direct use of the machine representation (see Chapter 2) will preserve accuracy.

e. Implementation Notes, Decimal Floating-Point Machines

1) In this case $B = 10$ and $.1 \le f < 1$.

2) These may be alternate entry points to one subroutine, in which case ALOG should set a flag, and ALOG10 should clear that flag (see Note 13).

   When multiple entries are not supported, ALOG and ALOG10 must be separate subroutines. In that case ALOG10 can be a self-contained subroutine which is called by ALOG, or there can be a separate computational subroutine starting with the error test (see Note 3) which is called by both ALOG and ALOG10. In either case, multiplication by $C3$ (see Notes 13 and 14) occurs after return to ALOG.

3) On machines that do not support multiple entry points, this is a natural point at which to begin a new subroutine.

4) If execution is to continue rather than terminate, then a default function value should be provided in addition to the error message. If $X = 0$, this function value is usually the negative of the largest floating-point number. Otherwise, it is the computed log of the absolute value of X; that is, the computation continues with $|X|$.

5) In terms of our operations (see Chapter 2),

   $$N = \text{INTXP}(X) \quad .$$

6) In terms of our operations (see Chapter 2),

   $$f = \text{SETXP}(X,0) \quad .$$

7) Omit this step.

8) $C0 = \text{sqrt}(.1) = .31622\ 77660\ 16837\ 93320$.

9) Rather than adjust z, we rescale f here. Thus, this step becomes

   $$10.0 \cdot f \longrightarrow f$$

10) Omit this step.

11) In this case we modify the flow chart to use the variable
$s = (f-1)/(f+1)$ instead of z. To preserve accuracy near $f = 1$,
calculate s as follows:

    s = ((f-0.5)-0.5) / (f + 1.0).

We use a rational approximation $r(s^2)$ derived especially for this
work. Let d be the number of digits in the significand of a
floating-point number. Then

                    for d ≤ 7

        a0 = 0.10756 13712 E+1
        a1 = -0.60368 24627 E+0
        b0 = 0.37150 53570 E+1
        b1 = -0.43144 78001 E+1
        b2 = 0.10000 00000 E+1

                    for 8 ≤ d ≤ 10

        a0 = -0.29156 81437 901 E+1
        a1 = 0.31630 34915 570 E+1
        a2 = -0.67358 16014 777 E+0
        b0 = -0.10070 40695 423 E+2
        b1 = 0.16966 98140 210 E+2
        b2 = -0.81908 00454 670 E+1
        b3 = 0.10000 00000 000 E+1

                    for 11 ≤ d ≤ 15

        a0 = 0.85167 31987 23885 403 E+1
        a1 = -0.13682 37024 15026 896 E+2
        a2 = 0.62503 65112 79083 731 E+1
        a3 = -0.71433 38215 32264 273 E+0
        b0 = 0.29415 75017 23226 173 E+2
        b1 = -0.64906 68274 09428 483 E+2
        b2 = 0.47925 25604 38733 968 E+2
        b3 = -0.13210 47835 01562 817 E+2
        b4 = 0.10000 00000 00000 000 E+1

for $16 \leq d \leq 18$

```
a0 = -0.26044 70024 05557 63612 E+2
a1 =  0.55408 59120 41205 93097 E+2
a2 = -0.39273 74102 03156 25018 E+2
a3 =  0.10333 85715 14793 86456 E+2
a4 = -0.74101 07841 61919 23924 E+0
b0 = -0.89955 20778 81033 11704 E+2
b1 =  0.24534 76188 68489 34790 E+3
b2 = -0.24430 30353 41829 54205 E+3
b3 =  0.10710 97891 15668 00857 E+3
b4 = -0.19373 23458 32854 78594 E+2
b5 =  0.10000 00000 00000 00000 E+1
```

Form $w = s^2$. Then evaluate

$r(s^2) = w * A(w)/B(w),$

where $A(w)$ and $B(w)$ are polynomials in w with coefficients $a0$, $a1$, ..., aN, and $b0$, $b1$, ..., bM, respectively. Use nested multiplication. For example, for $8 \leq d \leq 10$,

$B(w) = ((w + b2) * w + b1) * w + b0.$

Note that explicit multiplication by $b3 = 1.0$ is best avoided. Finally, evaluate $R(s) = s*[C+r(s^2)]$, where

$C = 2 * \log(e) = 0.86858\ 89638\ 06503\ 65530.$

12) See Chapter 2 for the definition of FLOAT. For the base-10 log the second part of this step simplifies to $XN + R(s)$.

13) Ignore this step if ALOG is a separate subroutine.

14) Use the following constant rounded to machine precision:

$C3 = \ln(10) = 2.30258\ 50929\ 94045\ 68402.$

f. Testing

The tests are divided into five major parts. First is a random argument test of $\ln(x)$ for x very close to 1, checking the accuracy of the computation of s. Second are tests of both $\ln(x)$ and $\log(x)$ for x in the primary range, checking the accuracy of the evaluation of $\ln(g)$ or $\log(g)$, as appropriate, and the conversion between natural and common logarithms. Third is a test of $\ln(x)$ for x reasonably large, checking the accuracy of the computations involving the exponents m and n. Fourth is a series of short tests with special arguments, and a cursory check of the property

$$\ln(x) = -\ln(1/x).$$

Finally, the error returns are checked for $x \leq 0$.

The evaluation of the logarithm is relatively insensitive to small errors in the argument except for arguments close to 1, as we noted in the general discussion above. To see this analytically, let

$$y = \ln(w).$$

Then

$$dy = dw/w,$$

and we see that the absolute error in $\ln(w)$ is roughly equal to the relative error in the argument w. This assures us that small errors in the argument have little effect on the accuracy of the function value except when $\ln(x)$ is small in magnitude, i.e., except for arguments close to 1.

The first test compares $\ln(x)$ for x close to 1 against the truncated Taylor series

$$TS(x) = - \sum_{i=1}^{4} (1-x)^i / i,$$

with the truncation error approximately bounded in magnitude by $(1-x)^5/5$. Let $X = f \cdot B^{**}m$, $1/B \leq f < 1$, where B is the radix of the floating-point number system (see Glossary), and assume there are t base-B digits in the representation of f. Then, if X is restricted so

that $|X-1| \leq B**(-t/2)$, TS(X) can be used to compute ln(X) to within
rounding error on the machine, provided care is taken in evaluating $1-X$
and in combining the various terms of TS.   Because the test procedure
involves   the   direct   comparison of two evaluations of ln(X),   the
possibility of systematic error exists were the subroutine being tested
to implement this same Taylor series, but there is no problem for
implementations of the algorithm advocated here.   We expect the test
program to report accuracies approaching machine precision in this first
test.   The results tabulated in Table 5.1 generally show a loss of one
base-B digit or less for the MRE (see Chapter 3), and a loss of a small
fraction of a digit for the RMS.   The larger errors for our program on
the GP L3055 are probably due to the final multiplication by ln(10).   We
do not know the reason for the larger than expected MRE for the FTN 4.7
routine on the CDC 7600.   Arguments close to 1.0 are handled carefully,
because the errors would be much larger if they were not.   In any case
the errors are not large enough to be of concern.

Although tests for ln(x) and log(x) over the primary range of
arguments should differ slightly for decimal and non-decimal machines,
we wish to use the same procedures for both classes of machines.   We
therefore assume that ln(x) is the primary computation and log(x) a
secondary one on non-decimal machines and that the roles are reversed on
decimal machines.   Then in places where the test procedures should
differ slightly, our procedures favor non-decimal machines for ln(x) and
decimal machines for log(x).

The second test checks ln(x) for x in the primary range with the
identity

$$\ln(x) = \ln(17x/16) - \ln(17/16).$$

Thus we measure

$$E = \{\ln(x) - [\ln(17x/16) - \ln(17/16)]\} / \ln(x)$$

for $1/\text{sqrt}(2) \leq x \leq 15/16$.   The restricted range assures that both x and
$17x/16$ have the same exponents m and n in the algorithm described
earlier and that neither argument gets too close to 1.   There are two
possible sources of error contamination in using this identity.   The
first is the roundoff error introduced in computing $17x/16$ from the
assumed exact argument x.   This roundoff error is eliminated on
non-decimal machines by perturbing the machine argument X to a nearby

TABLE 5.1

Typical Results for ALOG/ALOG10

Test	Machine	B	Library or Program	Reported Loss of Base-B Digits in	
				MRE	RMS
1	CDC 6400	2	Ours	1.00	0.00
	GP L3055	10	Ours	1.31	0.81
	IBM/370	16	Ours	1.00	0.19
	CDC 7600	2	FTN 4.7	2.00	0.09
	IBM/370	16	FTX 2.2	1.00	0.29
2	CDC 6400	2	Ours	1.67	0.00
	GP L3055	10	Ours	1.34	0.83
	IBM/370	16	Ours	0.99	0.57
	CDC 7600	2	FTN 4.7	1.74	0.02
	IBM/370	16	FTX 2.2	1.00	0.53
3	CDC 6400	2	Ours	3.28	1.29
	GP L3055	10	Ours	1.13	0.57
	IBM/370	16	Ours	1.07	0.59
	CDC 7600	2	FTN 4.7	2.53	0.56
	IBM/370	16	FTX 2.2	1.04	0.51
4	CDC 6400	2	Ours	0.97	0.00
	GP L3055	10	Ours	1.00	0.42
	IBM/370	16	Ours	0.53	0.10
	CDC 7600	2	FTN 4.7	0.98	0.00
	IBM/370	16	FTX 2.2	0.50	0.09

argument X' with the last four bits zeros. The Fortran statement

$$X = (X + 8.0E0) - 8.0E0 \quad ,$$

suitably modified to foil optimizing compilers, accomplishes the task on most contemporary computers for X's drawn from the primary interval.

The exceptions are those machines in which the active arithmetic registers carry more significance than the storage registers. It is necessary to force the storage and retrieval of intermediate results in this purification process on such machines (see Gentleman and Marovich

[1974]).   The four trailing zero bits in X' are enough to ensure that
$X' + X'/16 = 17X'/16$ is also an exact machine number.

The   second   source   of   contamination is   in   the   subtraction   of
ln(17/16).   This subtraction is   accomplished in a pseudo multiple
precision by expressing   ln(17/16)   as 31/512 (which   is exactly
representable in five bits or eight decimal places) plus a remainder
term and performing the subtraction in two steps.   These constants
should be adjusted appropriately on decimal machines carrying fewer than
eight digits of significance.   With these precautions,   the test
procedure is quite stable,   and a   good logarithm routine will return an
MRE = max$|E|$ close to machine precision.   On decimal machines the
division of X by 16 is not exact,   so for them the MRE will probably be
slightly larger.   We therefore expect our test program to report MRE
values for this test that are similar to those reported for the first
test.   The RMS values will probably be slightly greater.   Table 5.1
lists typical results.

The analogous   test for log(x), and our third test,   employs the
identity

$$log(x) = log(11x/10) - log(1.1)$$

over the range 1/sqrt(10) $\leq x \leq$ .9.   The auxiliary argument 11x/10 is
obtained   as $x + x$/10 after argument purification using   the Fortran
statement

$$X = (X + 8.0E0) - 8.0E0.$$

As before, the subtraction of log(1.1) is carried out in pseudo multiple
precision by expressing log(1.1) as 21/512 (expressible in eight decimal
places or five bits) plus a remainder term.   These constants should be
adjusted appropriately on decimal machines carrying fewer than eight
digits of significance.   A good implementation of ALOG10 on decimal
machines should return an MRE only slightly larger than the precision of
the machine.   For non-decimal machines larger errors may be found,
primarily because division by 10 is not exact even for purified
arguments on such machines.   Typical test results are again given in
Table 5.1.   Note in particular the expected increase in error for the
programs on binary machines.

For x outside the primary range we measure the relative error

$$E = [\ln(x^2) - 2 \ln(x)] / \ln(x^2)$$

in the identity

$$\ln(x^2) = 2 \ln(x).$$

In particular, we choose the interval $16 \le x \le 240$. In this argument range the machine representations of x and x^2 have different exponents, thus minimizing the possibility of undetected systematic error. Because the logarithm computation is insensitive to small argument perturbations for larger x, no argument purification is necessary. For the same reason, only gross errors in the handling of the exponents m and n are detectable by any identity test, and an implementation of ALOG that looked bad in the previous tests may even look good in this test (see Table 5.1).

```
C     PROGRAM TO TEST ALOG
C
C     DATA REQUIRED
C
C         NONE
C
C     SUBPROGRAMS REQUIRED FROM THIS PACKAGE
C
C         MACHAR - AN ENVIRONMENTAL INQUIRY PROGRAM PROVIDING
C                  INFORMATION ON THE FLOATING-POINT ARITHMETIC
C                  SYSTEM.  NOTE THAT THE CALL TO MACHAR CAN
C                  BE DELETED PROVIDED THE FOLLOWING FOUR
C                  PARAMETERS ARE ASSIGNED THE VALUES INDICATED
C
C                  IBETA - THE RADIX OF THE FLOATING-POINT SYSTEM
C                  IT    - THE NUMBER OF BASE-IBETA DIGITS IN THE
C                          SIGNIFICAND OF A FLOATING-POINT NUMBER
C                  XMIN  - THE SMALLEST NON-VANISHING FLOATING-POINT
C                          POWER OF THE RADIX
C                  XMAX  - THE LARGEST FINITE FLOATING-POINT NO.
C
C         RAN(K) - A FUNCTION SUBPROGRAM RETURNING RANDOM REAL
C                  NUMBERS UNIFORMLY DISTRIBUTED OVER (0,1)
C
C
C     STANDARD FORTRAN SUBPROGRAMS REQUIRED
C
C         ABS, ALOG, ALOG10, AMAX1, FLOAT, SIGN, SQRT
C
C
C     LATEST REVISION - DECEMBER 6, 1979
C
C     AUTHOR - W. J. CODY
C              ARGONNE NATIONAL LABORATORY
C
C
      INTEGER I,IBETA,IEXP,IOUT,IRND,IT,I1,J,K1,K2,K3,MACHEP,
     1        MAXEXP,MINEXP,N,NEGEP,NGRD
      REAL A,AIT,ALBETA,B,BETA,C,DEL,EIGHT,EPS,EPSNEG,HALF,ONE,
     1     RAN,R6,R7,TENTH,W,X,XL,XMAX,XMIN,XN,X1,Y,Z,ZERO,ZZ
C
      IOUT = 6
      CALL MACHAR(IBETA,IT,IRND,NGRD,MACHEP,NEGEP,IEXP,MINEXP,
```

```
      1                 MAXEXP,EPS,EPSNEG,XMIN,XMAX)
      BETA = FLOAT(IBETA)
      ALBETA = ALOG(BETA)
      AIT = FLOAT(IT)
      J = IT / 3
      ZERO = 0.0E0
      HALF = 0.5E0
      EIGHT = 8.0E0
      TENTH = 0.1E0
      ONE = 1.0E0
      C = ONE
C
      DO 50 I = 1, J
         C = C / BETA
   50 CONTINUE
C
      B = ONE + C
      A = ONE - C
      N = 2000
      XN = FLOAT(N)
      I1 = 0
C----------------------------------------------------------------
C     RANDOM ARGUMENT ACCURACY TESTS
C----------------------------------------------------------------
      DO 300 J = 1, 4
         K1 = 0
         K3 = 0
         X1 = ZERO
         R6 = ZERO
         R7 = ZERO
         DEL = (B - A) / XN
         XL = A
C
         DO 200 I = 1, N
            X = DEL * RAN(I1) + XL
            IF (J .NE. 1) GO TO 100
            Y = (X - HALF) - HALF
            ZZ = ALOG(X)
            Z = ONE / 3.0E0
            Z = Y * (Z - Y / 4.0E0)
            Z = (Z - HALF) * Y * Y + Y
            GO TO 150
  100       IF (J .NE. 2) GO TO 110
```

```
            X = (X + EIGHT) - EIGHT
            Y = X + X / 16.0E0
            Z = ALOG(X)
            ZZ = ALOG(Y) - 7.7746816434842581E-5
            ZZ = ZZ - 31.0E0/512.0E0
            GO TO 150
    110     IF (J .NE. 3) GO TO 120
            X = (X + EIGHT) - EIGHT
            Y = X + X * TENTH
            Z = ALOG10(X)
            ZZ = ALOG10(Y) - 3.7706015822504075E-4
            ZZ = ZZ - 21.0E0/512.0E0
            GO TO 150
    120     Z = ALOG(X*X)
            ZZ = ALOG(X)
            ZZ = ZZ + ZZ
    150     W = ONE
            IF (Z .NE. ZERO) W = (Z - ZZ) / Z
            Z = SIGN(W,Z)
            IF (Z .GT. ZERO) K1 = K1 + 1
            IF (Z .LT. ZERO) K3 = K3 + 1
            W = ABS(W)
            .IF (W .LE. R6) GO TO 160
            R6 = W
            X1 = X
    160     R7 = R7 + W*W
            XL = XL + DEL
    200  CONTINUE
C
            K2 = N - K3 - K1
            R7 = SQRT(R7/XN)
            IF (J .EQ. 1) WRITE (IOUT,1000)
            IF (J .EQ. 2) WRITE (IOUT,1001)
            IF (J .EQ. 3) WRITE (IOUT,1005)
            IF (J .EQ. 4) WRITE (IOUT,1002)
            IF (J .EQ. 1) WRITE (IOUT,1009) N,C
            IF (J .NE. 1) WRITE (IOUT,1010) N,A,B
            IF (J .NE. 3) WRITE (IOUT,1011) K1,K2,K3
            IF (J .EQ. 3) WRITE (IOUT,1012) K1,K2,K3
            WRITE (IOUT,1020) IT,IBETA
            W = -999.0E0
            IF (R6 .NE. ZERO) W = ALOG(ABS(R6))/ALBETA
            WRITE (IOUT,1021) R6,IBETA,W,X1
```

```
          W = AMAX1(AIT+W,ZERO)
          WRITE (IOUT,1022) IBETA,W
          W = -999.0E0
          IF (R7 .NE. ZERO) W = ALOG(ABS(R7))/ALBETA
          WRITE (IOUT,1023) R7,IBETA,W
          W = AMAX1(AIT+W,ZERO)
          WRITE (IOUT,1022) IBETA,W
          IF (J .GT. 1) GO TO 230
          A = SQRT(HALF)
          B = 15.0E0 / 16.0E0
          GO TO 300
  230     IF (J .GT. 2) GO TO 240
          A = SQRT(TENTH)
          B = 0.9E0
          GO TO 300
  240     A = 16.0E0
          B = 240.0E0
  300 CONTINUE
C-----------------------------------------------------------------
C     SPECIAL TESTS
C-----------------------------------------------------------------
      WRITE (IOUT,1025)
      WRITE (IOUT,1030)
C
      DO 320 I = 1, 5
          X = RAN(I1)
          X = X + X + 15.0E0
          Y = ONE / X
          Z = ALOG(X) + ALOG(Y)
          WRITE (IOUT,1060) X, Z
  320 CONTINUE
C
      WRITE (IOUT,1040)
      X = ONE
      Y = ALOG(X)
      WRITE (IOUT,1041) Y
      X = XMIN
      Y = ALOG(X)
      WRITE (IOUT,1042) X, Y
      X = XMAX
      Y = ALOG(X)
      WRITE (IOUT,1043) X, Y
C-----------------------------------------------------------------
```

```
C     TEST OF ERROR RETURNS
C--------------------------------------------------------------------
      WRITE (IOUT,1050)
      X = -2.0E0
      WRITE (IOUT,1052) X
      Y = ALOG(X)
      WRITE (IOUT,1055) Y
      X = ZERO
      WRITE (IOUT,1052) X
      Y = ALOG(X)
      WRITE (IOUT,1055) Y
      WRITE (IOUT,1100)
      STOP
 1000 FORMAT(47H1TEST OF ALOG(X) VS T.S. EXPANSION OF ALOG(1+Y)  //)
 1001 FORMAT(44H1TEST OF ALOG(X) VS ALOG(17X/16)-ALOG(17/16)    //)
 1002 FORMAT(32H1TEST OF ALOG(X*X) VS 2 * LOG(X)  //)
 1005 FORMAT(50H1TEST OF ALOG10(X) VS ALOG10(11X/10)-ALOG10(11/10) //)
 1009 FORMAT(I7,47H RANDOM ARGUMENTS WERE TESTED FROM THE INTERVAL /
     1 6X,26H(1-EPS,1+EPS), WHERE EPS =, E15.4//)
 1010 FORMAT(I7,47H RANDOM ARGUMENTS WERE TESTED FROM THE INTERVAL /
     1 6X,1H(,E15.4,1H,,E15.4,1H)//)
 1011 FORMAT(19H ALOG(X) WAS LARGER,I6,7H TIMES, /
     1      12X,7H AGREED,I6,11H TIMES, AND /
     2      8X,11HWAS SMALLER,I6,7H TIMES.//)
 1012 FORMAT(21H ALOG10(X) WAS LARGER,I6,7H TIMES, /
     1      14X,7H AGREED,I6,11H TIMES, AND /
     2      10X,11HWAS SMALLER,I6,7H TIMES.//)
 1020 FORMAT(10H THERE ARE,I4,5H BASE,I4,
     1      46H SIGNIFICANT DIGITS IN A FLOATING-POINT NUMBER  //)
 1021 FORMAT(30H THE MAXIMUM RELATIVE ERROR OF,E15.4,3H = ,I4,3H **,
     1 F7.2/4X,16HOCCURRED FOR X =,E17.6)
 1022 FORMAT(27H THE ESTIMATED LOSS OF BASE,I4,
     1 22H SIGNIFICANT DIGITS IS,F7.2//)
 1023 FORMAT(40H THE ROOT MEAN SQUARE RELATIVE ERROR WAS,E15.4,
     1      3H = ,I4,3H **,F7.2)
 1025 FORMAT(14H1SPECIAL TESTS//)
 1030 FORMAT(52H THE IDENTITY  ALOG(X) = -ALOG(1/X)  WILL BE TESTED.//
     1      8X,1HX,9X,13HF(X) + F(1/X)/)
 1040 FORMAT(//26H TEST OF SPECIAL ARGUMENTS //)
 1041 FORMAT(13H ALOG(1.0) = ,E15.7//)
 1042 FORMAT(19H ALOG(XMIN) = ALOG(,E15.7,4H) = ,E15.7//)
 1043 FORMAT(19H ALOG(XMAX) = ALOG(,E15.7,4H) = ,E15.7//)
 1050 FORMAT(22H1TEST OF ERROR RETURNS//)
```

```
 1052 FORMAT(38H ALOG WILL BE CALLED WITH THE ARGUMENT,E15.4/
    1          37H THIS SHOULD TRIGGER AN ERROR MESSAGE//)
 1055 FORMAT(24H ALOG RETURNED THE VALUE,E15.4///)
 1060 FORMAT(2E15.7/)
 1100 FORMAT(25H THIS CONCLUDES THE TESTS )
C       ---------- LAST CARD OF ALOG/ALOG10 TEST PROGRAM ----------
      END
```

6. EXP

a. General Discussion

We assume that the radix B of the floating-point number system (see Glossary) is either 10 or $2**k$, where k is an integer and $1 \leq k \leq 4$. Let $X = N \cdot \ln(C) + g$, $|g| \leq \ln(C)/2$, where ln denotes the natural logarithm, $C = $ sqrt(10) if $B = 10$, and $C = 2$ otherwise. Then

$$\exp(X) = \exp(g) \cdot C ** N.$$

The computation of the exponential thus involves three steps: the reduction of the given argument to a related argument in a small interval symmetric about the origin, the computation of the exponential for the reduced argument, and the reconstruction of the desired function from its components.

The accuracy of the function value depends critically upon the accuracy of g. Let

$$y = \exp(g).$$

Then

$$dy/y = dg;$$

i.e., the relative error in $\exp(g)$ is approximately the absolute error in g. Assuming that X is exact, this error is in turn proportional to the magnitude of X because of the finite word length of the computer. The only way to achieve small absolute error in g is to extend the effective precision of the computer during the computation of g. Higher precision floating-point arithmetic can be used on some machines, but in most cases the computation

$$g = [(X1 - N \cdot C1) + X2] - N \cdot C2$$

must be used, where $X1 + X2 = X$, $X1$ is the integer part of X, and $C1 + C2$ represents $\ln(C)$ to more than working precision. When N is small enough that $N \cdot C1$ is representable exactly in the machine, this scheme provides extra digits of precision equivalent to the number of extra digits in the representation of $\ln(C)$. If $N \cdot C1$ cannot be represented exactly, the computation is equivalent to not using extra precision. Thus there is a practical limit on the magnitude of N, and hence on the magnitude of X, for which this method should be used. But X is already subject to a much more severe limitation: There is a largest and smallest X such that $\exp(X)$ can be represented in the machine. To be precise, if $XMIN$ is the smallest positive floating-point number and $XMAX$ is the largest floating-point number short of overflow, then $\exp(X)$ can be represented only for X between $\ln(XMIN)$ and $\ln(XMAX)$. It is always possible to choose $C1$ so that $N \cdot C1$ will be representable exactly in the machine for any X within these bounds. As always, careful argument reduction cannot compensate for inaccuracies in X.

b.   Flow Chart for EXP(X)

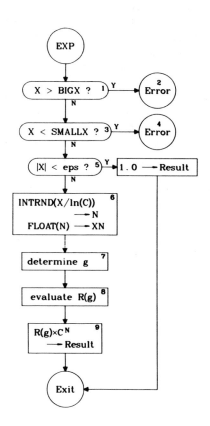

Note: Small integers indicate an implementation note.

c. Implementation Notes, Non-Decimal Fixed-Point Machines

1) Let *XMAX* be the largest positive finite floating-point number. Then *BIGX* should be slightly less than ln(*XMAX*). We suggest the largest machine number less than ln(*XMAX*).

2) If execution is to continue rather than terminate, then a default function value of *XMAX* can be provided in addition to an error message.

3) Let *XMIN* be the smallest positive floating-point number. Then *SMALLX* should be slightly greater than ln(*XMIN*). We suggest the smallest machine number greater than ln(*XMIN*).

4) If execution is to continue rather than terminate, then a default function value of 0 can be provided in addition to an error message.

5) *Eps* should be chosen so that $\exp(X) = 1.0$ to machine precision for $|X| < eps$, and so that $p1 \cdot X^2$ will not underflow for $|X| \geq eps$ (see Note 8). We suggest $eps = 2 \cdot \cdot (-b-1)$ where there are b bits in the floating-point significand (see Glossary).

6) $C = 2$ in this case (see Chapter 2 for definitions of INTRND and FLOAT). On some machines it may be more efficient to form *XN* with AINTRND and then use INT to obtain N. To avoid the expensive floating-point divide, form $X/\ln(2)$ by multiplication with the stored constant

$$1/\ln(2) = 1.4426\ 95040\ 88896\ 34074.$$

7) Let G denote the floating-point value obtained in this step. We assume that a multiple-step argument reduction scheme is to be used. On machines with a guard digit for floating-point addition (see Glossary), use the computation

$$G = (X - XN \cdot C1) - XN \cdot C2.$$

When that guard digit is not present, use

$$G = [(X1 - XN \cdot C1) + X2] - XN \cdot C2,$$

where, in terms of our operations (see Chapter 2),

        X1 = AINT(X)
and
        X2 = X - X1.

In either case use

        C1 =   355/512 = .543 (octal)
           =   0.69335 9375 (decimal)
        C2 = -2.1219 44400 54690 58277 E-4.

Exact representation of $C1$ is crucial, but $C2$ need only be represented to the precision of the machine. Let b be the number of bits in the floating-point significand (see Glossary) and assume $2**n$ bounds both $\ln(XMAX)/\ln(2)$ and $-\ln(XMIN)/\ln(2)$. Then $C1$ and $C2$ provide accurate argument reduction whenever $n + 10 \leq b$. For example, when $b = 20$, $XMAX$ may be as large as 10^{300}, and when $XMAX = 10^{76}$, b must be at least 18. On machines that do not meet these requirements, let

        C1 = 11/16 = .54 (octal)
           = 0.6875 (decimal)
        C2 = 5.6471 80560 E-3,

where $C2$ is appropriately rounded. $|G| \leq \ln(2)/2$ at this point.

8) Convert to fixed point here by letting $g = FIX(G)$ (see Chapter 2). The following fixed-point rational functions $R(g)$, derived especially for this work, approximate $\exp(g)/2$ (the scaling by $1/2$ is necessary here to avoid fixed-point overflow). Let b be the number of bits in the significand of a floating-point number (see Glossary). Then

                    for b $\leq$ 29

        p0 = 0.24999 99995 0
        p1 = 0.00416 02886 3
        q0 = 0.5
        q1 = 0.04998 71787 8

for $30 \leq b \leq 42$

p0 = 0.24999 99999 9992
p1 = 0.00595 04254 9776
q0 = 0.5
q1 = 0.05356 75176 4522
q2 = 0.00029 72936 3682

for $43 \leq b \leq 56$

p0 = 0.24999 99999 99999 993
p1 = 0.00694 36000 15117 929
p2 = 0.00001 65203 30026 828
q0 = 0.5
q1 = 0.05555 38666 96900 119
q2 = 0.00049 58628 84905 441

Evaluate $R(g)$ in fixed point. First form $z = g^2$. Then form $g \cdot P(z)$ and $Q(z)$ using nested multiplication. For example, for $43 \leq b \leq 56$,

g·P(z) = ((p2 · z + p1) · z + p0) · g

and

Q(z) = (q2 · z + q1) · z + q0.

Finally, form

r = .5 + g·P(z)/[Q(z)-g·P(z)]

in fixed point and convert back to floating point with $R(g)$ = REFLOAT(r) (see Chapter 2).

9) Because of the scaling in the previous step, add 1 to N. The details of the remainder of this step depend upon the radix of the floating-point representation, which we have assumed to be $2 \cdot \cdot k$. If $k = 1$, i.e., if the radix is 2, then in terms of our operations (see Chapter 2),

Result = ADX(R,N).

Otherwise, let $N = k \cdot m + n$, $0 \leq n < k$, and

    RES = R * (2**n)

where the powers of 2 may be stored in an array indexed by n.   Then

    Result = ADX(RES,m).

d. Implementation Notes, Non-Decimal Floating-Point Machines

1) Let *XMAX* be the largest positive finite floating-point number. Then *BIGX* should be slightly less than ln(*XMAX*). We suggest the largest machine number less than ln(*XMAX*).

2) If execution is to continue rather than terminate, then a default function value of *XMAX* can be provided in addition to an error message.

3) Let *XMIN* be the smallest positive floating-point number. Then *SMALLX* should be slightly greater than ln(*XMIN*). We suggest the smallest machine number greater than ln(*XMIN*).

4) If execution is to continue rather than terminate, then a default function value of 0 can be provided in addition to an error message.

5) *Eps* should be chosen so that $\exp(X) = 1.0$ to machine precision for $|X| < eps$, and so that $p1 \cdot X^2$ will not underflow for $|X| \geq eps$ (see Note 8). We suggest $eps = [B \cdot \cdot (-t)]/2$ where B is the radix of the floating-point representation and there are t base-B digits in the significand (see Glossary).

6) $C = 2$ in this case (see Chapter 2 for definitions of INTRND and FLOAT). On some machines it may be more efficient to form *XN* with AINTRND and then use INT to obtain N. To avoid the floating-point divide, form $X/\ln(2)$ by multiplication with the stored constant

$$1/\ln(2) = 1.4426\ 95040\ 88896\ 34074.$$

7) If higher precision floating point is available and reasonably efficient, consider converting both X and *XN* to the higher precision and using it to form

$$g = X - XN \cdot \ln(2),$$

where

$$\ln(2) = 0.69314\ 71805\ 59945\ 30941\ 72321$$

-67-

should also be represented in the higher precision.   Then convert g back to the working precision.

A multiple-step argument reduction must be used when use of higher precision floating point is impractical. Use the computation

    g = (X - XN*C1) - XN*C2

on machines with a guard digit for floating-point addition (see Glossary). When that guard digit is not present, use

    g = [(X1 - XN*C1) + X2] - XN*C2,

where, in terms of our operations (see Chapter 2),

        X1 = AINT(X)
and
        X2 = X - X1.

In either case use

    C1 =   355/512 = .543 (octal)
        = 0.69335 9375 (decimal)
    C2 = -2.1219 44400 54690 58277 E-4.

Exact representation of $C1$ is crucial, but $C2$ need only be represented to the precision of the machine. Let b be the number of bits in the floating-point significand (see Glossary), and assume $2**n$ bounds both $\ln(XMAX)/\ln(2)$ and $-\ln(XMIN)/\ln(2)$. Then $C1$ and $C2$ provide accurate argument reduction whenever $n + 10 \leq b$.   For example, when $b = 20$, $XMAX$ may be as large as 10^{300}, and when $XMAX = 10^{76}$, b must be at least 18.   On machines that do not meet these requirements, let

    C1 = 11/16 = .54 (octal)
        = 0.6875 (decimal)
    C2 = 5.6471 80560 E-3,

where $C2$ is appropriately rounded. $|g| \leq \ln(2)/2$ at this point.

8) The following rational functions $R(g)$,   derived especially for this work, approximate $\exp(g)/2$. The factor 1/2 is inserted here to

counteract wobbling precision (see Glossary)   in radices other than
2. We assume that the radix of the floating-point representation is
$2**k$ and that b is the number of bits in the significand (see
Glossary). Then

for b ≤ 29

```
p0 = 0.24999 99995 0 E+0
p1 = 0.41602 88626 8 E-2
q0 = 0.50000 00000 0 E+0
q1 = 0.49987 17877 8 E-1
```

for 30 ≤ b ≤ 42

```
p0 = 0.24999 99999 9992 E+0
p1 = 0.59504 25497 7591 E-2
q0 = 0.50000 00000 0000 E+0
q1 = 0.53567 51764 5222 E-1
q2 = 0.29729 36368 2238 E-3
```

for 43 ≤ b ≤ 56

```
p0 = 0.24999 99999 99999 993 E+0
p1 = 0.69436 00015 11792 852 E-2
p2 = 0.16520 33002 68279 130 E-4
q0 = 0.50000 00000 00000 000 E+0
q1 = 0.55553 86669 69001 188 E-1
q2 = 0.49586 28849 05441 294 E-3
```

for 57 ≤ b ≤ 65

```
p0 = 0.25000 00000 00000 00000 E+0
p1 = 0.75753 18015 94227 76666 E-2
p2 = 0.31555 19276 56846 46356 E-4
q0 = 0.50000 00000 00000 00000 E+0
q1 = 0.56817 30269 85512 21787 E-1
q2 = 0.63121 89437 43985 03557 E-3
q3 = 0.75104 02839 98700 46114 E-6
```

First form $z = g^2$. Then form $g \cdot P(z)$ and $Q(z)$ using nested
multiplication. For example, for 43 ≤ b ≤ 56,

$$g \cdot P(z) = ((p2 \cdot z + p1) \cdot z + p0) \cdot g$$

and

$$Q(z) = (q2 \cdot z + q1) \cdot z + q0.$$

Finally, form

$$R(g) = .5 + g \cdot P(z)/[Q(z) - g \cdot P(z)]$$

9) Because of the scaling in the previous step, add 1 to N. The details of the remainder of this step depend upon the radix of the floating-point representation, which we have assumed to be $2^{**}k$. If $k = 1$, i.e., if the radix is 2, then in terms of our operations (see Chapter 2),

$$\text{Result} = \text{ADX}(R, N).$$

Otherwise, let $N = k \cdot m + n$, $0 \leq n < k$, and

$$\text{RES} = R \cdot (2^{**}n)$$

where the powers of 2 may be stored in an array indexed by n. Then

$$\text{Result} = \text{ADX}(\text{RES}, m).$$

e. Implementation Notes, Decimal Floating-Point Machines

1) Let *XMAX* be the largest positive finite floating-point number. Then *BIGX* should be slightly less than ln(*XMAX*). We suggest the largest machine number less than ln(*XMAX*).

2) If execution is to continue rather than terminate, then a default function value of *XMAX* can be provided in addition to an error message.

3) Let *XMIN* be the smallest positive floating-point number. Then *SMALLX* should be slightly greater than ln(*XMIN*). We suggest the smallest machine number greater than ln(*XMIN*).

4) If execution is to continue rather than terminate, then a default function value of 0 can be provided in addition to an error message.

5) *Eps* should be chosen so that $\exp(X) = 1.0$ to machine precision for $|X| < eps$, and so that $p1 \cdot X^2$ will not underflow for $|X| \geq eps$ (see Note 8). We suggest $eps = [10 \cdot \cdot (-d)]/2$ where there are d digits in the floating-point significand (see Glossary).

6) $C = \text{sqrt}(10)$ in this case (see Chapter 2 for definitions of INTRND and FLOAT). On some machines it may be more efficient to form *XN* with AINTRND and then use INT to obtain N. To avoid the floating-point divide, form $X/\ln[\text{sqrt}(10)]$ by multiplication with the stored constant

   $$1/\ln[\text{sqrt}(10)] = 0.86858\ 89638\ 06503\ 65530.$$

7) If higher precision floating point is available and reasonably efficient, consider converting both X and *XN* to the higher precision and using it to form

   $$g = X - XN \cdot \ln(C),$$

where

ln(C) = 1.15129 25464 97022 84200 89957

should also be represented in the higher precision.   Then convert *g* back to the working precision.

A multiple-step argument reduction must be used when use of higher precision floating point is impractical.   Use the computation

g = (X − XN·C1) − XN·C2

on machines with a guard digit for floating-point addition (see Glossary).   When that guard digit is not present, use

g = [(X1 − XN·C1) + X2] − XN·C2,

where, in terms of our operations (see Chapter 2),

X1 = AINT(X)

and

X2 = X − X1.

In either case use

C1 = 1.151 E+0
C2 = 2.9254 64970 22842 009 E-4,

where *C*2 should be rounded to machine precision.   Let *d* be the number of digits in the floating-point significand (see Glossary) and assume $10^{**}n$ bounds both ln(*XMAX*)/ln(*C*)   and −ln(*XMIN*)/ln(*C*). Then *C*1 and *C*2 provide   accurate argument reduction whenever $n + 4 \leq d$.   For example, when $d = 8$, *XMAX* may be as large as 10^{500}, and when *XMAX* = 10^{99}, *d* must be at least 7.   On machines that do not meet these requirements, let

C1 = 1.15 E+0
C2 = 1.2925 46497 02284 2009 E-3,

where *C*2 is appropriately rounded. $|g| \leq$ ln(10)/4 at this point.

8) The following rational approximations $R(g)$ were derived especially for this work. Let d be the number of digits in the significand (see Glossary). Then

$$\text{for } d \leq 7$$

$p0 = 0.50034\ 9857\ \text{E}+1$
$p1 = 0.83046\ 5413\ \text{E}-1$
$q0 = 0.10006\ 9975\ \text{E}+2$
$q1 = 0.10000\ 0000\ \text{E}+1$

$$\text{for } 8 \leq d \leq 10$$

$p0 = 0.84249\ 03867\ 900\ \text{E}+3$
$p1 = 0.20041\ 43275\ 526\ \text{E}+2$
$q0 = 0.16849\ 80773\ 608\ \text{E}+4$
$q1 = 0.18049\ 79288\ 462\ \text{E}+3$
$q2 = 0.10000\ 00000\ 000\ \text{E}+1$

$$\text{for } 11 \leq d \leq 14$$

$p0 = 0.50446\ 48895\ 05869\ 7\ \text{E}+3$
$p1 = 0.14008\ 29975\ 62819\ 6\ \text{E}+2$
$p2 = 0.33287\ 36465\ 16410\ 3\ \text{E}-1$
$q0 = 0.10089\ 29779\ 01174\ 4\ \text{E}+4$
$q1 = 0.11209\ 40810\ 96616\ 0\ \text{E}+3$
$q2 = 0.10000\ 00000\ 00000\ 0\ \text{E}+1$

$$\text{for } 15 \leq d \leq 18$$

$p0 = 0.33326\ 70292\ 26801\ 61137\ \text{E}+6$
$p1 = 0.10097\ 41487\ 24273\ 91798\ \text{E}+5$
$p2 = 0.42041\ 42681\ 37450\ 31524\ \text{E}+2$
$q0 = 0.66653\ 40584\ 53603\ 22323\ \text{E}+6$
$q1 = 0.75739\ 33461\ 59883\ 44395\ \text{E}+5$
$q2 = 0.84124\ 35845\ 14154\ 54514\ \text{E}+3$
$q3 = 0.10000\ 00000\ 00000\ 00000\ \text{E}+1$

First form $z = g^2$. Then form $g \cdot P(z)$ and $Q(z)$ using nested multiplication. For example, for $11 \leq d \leq 14$,

$$g \cdot P(z) = ((p2 \cdot z + p1) \cdot z + p0) \cdot g$$

and

$$Q(z) = (z + q1) \cdot z + q0.$$

Note that because $q2 = 1.0$, $q2 \cdot z$ can be represented as z, saving one multiplication. Finally, form

$$R(g) = \{.5 + g \cdot P(z)/[Q(z)-g \cdot P(z)]\} \cdot 2.0.$$

This peculiar-looking construction avoids loss of significance when $R(g) < 1.0$. Indeed, the final multiplication by 2.0 is also best done by adding the intermediate result to itself.

9) If N is an odd integer, replace $R(g)$ by sqrt(10)$\cdot R(g)$ when N is positive and by $R(g)$/sqrt(10) when N is negative, where

$$sqrt(10) = 3.1622\ 77660\ 16837\ 93320.$$

Finally, using the integer representation of N, divide N by 2, where integer division is assumed to ignore remainders, and form (see Chapter 2)

$$Result = ADX(R,N).$$

f. Testing

The tests are divided into four major parts. First is a random
argument test of exp(x) for arguments in the primary range, checking the
accuracy of the computation of exp(g) for the reduced argument g.
Second are similar tests using large positive and negative arguments to
check the accuracy of the argument reduction scheme. Third is a cursory
check of the identity

$$\exp(x) \cdot \exp(-x) = 1$$

and several tests with special arguments, including some close to the
theoretically largest and smallest acceptable arguments.   Finally,   the
error returns are checked with arguments exceeding the theoretical
limits.

The exponential function is extremely sensitive to small errors in
arguments greater than one in magnitude.   Recall from the general
discussion earlier that the relative error in the exponential function
is roughly equal to the absolute error in the argument.   If there is a
rounding error in the machine number X, and if X is bounded in magnitude
between $B**(n-1)$ and $B**n$, where B is the radix of the floating-point
system, then the last n B-ary digits in the machine representation of
exp(X) are probably incorrect.   Poor argument reduction in the
exponential function can introduce errors that behave as if they were
rounding errors in the argument.   It is therefore essential that
arguments used in the test procedure be error-free if we are to
distinguish between good and bad argument reduction.

The most obvious identity to use in the random argument accuracy
tests,

$$\exp(x) = [\exp(x/2)]^2,$$

is unsatisfactory because it tends to magnify errors.   Squaring is an
expansion mapping,   carrying one machine   interval into a second
containing roughly twice as many floating-point numbers.   This means
that about half of all machine numbers cannot be generated by squaring
other machine numbers.   If the machine representation of exp(x) happens
to be one of these excluded numbers,   then the above identity cannot be
satisfied regardless of the quality of the exponential routine.   In

addition, because

$$[x*(1+e)]^2 = x^2*(1+2e)$$

to first order terms in e, squaring $\exp(x/2)$ doubles the corresponding relative error, further contaminating the error we want to measure.

A better possibility is an identity of the form

$$\exp(x-v) = \exp(x) * \exp(-v),$$

where v is an exact machine number and $\exp(-v)$ is known to more than machine precision. An appropriate choice of v guarantees that the arguments x and $x-v$ used in the test will always lead either to the same or to different values of N during argument reduction. Further, the extra error normally associated with multiplying by a rounded value of $\exp(-v)$ can be minimized by representing $\exp(-v)$ as a sum of constants and forming the product in two steps, i.e., by representing $\exp(-v)$ as $K1 + K2$ and forming $\exp(x)*\exp(-v)$ as $\exp(x)*K1 + \exp(x)*K2$.

The above identity with $v = 1/16$ forms the basis of the accuracy tests for arguments in the primary interval (by slight adjustment of the lower bound of the test interval, both x and $x-v$ are guaranteed to lie in the primary interval). Thus we measure

$$E = [\exp(x-v) - \exp(x)*\exp(-v)] / \exp(x-v).$$

Assume that relative errors of D and d are made in the evaluation of $\exp(x-v)$ and $\exp(x)$, respectively, and that the argument $x-v$ contains an absolute error of e. Then

$$E = \frac{\exp(x-v)*(1+e)*(1+D) - \exp(x)*\exp(-v)*(1+d)}{\exp(x-v)*(1+e)*(1+D)}.$$

Simplifying, and retaining only terms linear in d, D and e, we get

$$E = D + e - d,$$

where e is likely to dominate when $|x-v| > 1$, as explained above. Although that situation does not happen for the primary interval, we still prefer to use exact machine numbers for arguments. We assume, therefore, that X is already an exact machine number obtained from a random number generator. Then, because $v > 0$ in this case, $X-v$ is also exact if it is positive. If it is negative, the sequence of Fortran statements

```
Y = X - V
X = Y + V      ,
```

where V is the machine representation of v, leads to a pair of exact machine numbers differing by v; $e = 0$ in the above error analysis, and

```
E = D - d.
```

As with all argument purification schemes, the program must be modified to force storage of intermediate results on machines that ordinarily retain them in overlength arithmetic registers.

Accuracy tests outside of the primary interval use $v = 45/16$ but are otherwise analogous to the above procedure. This choice of v ensures that X and $X-V$ lead to different values of N in the argument reduction step. The intervals used are carefully chosen to ensure that arguments approach the largest and smallest that can be used in the exponential, while at the same time protecting against underflow in performing the subtraction in E.

A good implementation of EXP should return an MRE (see Chapter 3) only slightly greater than the precision of the machine for all argument ranges. The RMS error should be at, or slightly less than, machine precision. When the reported MRE is significantly larger than the machine precision, the distribution of the algebraic signs of the errors as reported on the output becomes important. Our experience indicates that when the MRE is large, there is a tendency for the errors D and d to be of the same sign and comparable in magnitude. Because $E = D - d$, the MRE value reported before conversion to units of base-B digits (see Chapter 3) may be conservative by up to an order of magnitude when this happens.

The test results reported in Table 6.1 are typical of good implementations of EXP. In all cases the MRE reports a loss of about one base-B digit (slightly larger for binary machines), and the RMS reports a loss of a small fraction of a digit. Further, the errors are comparable for a given program across all of the tests. The results

TABLE 6.1

Typical Results for EXP Tests

Test	Machine	B	Library or Program	Reported Loss of Base-B Digits in MRE	RMS
1	CDC 7600	2	Ours	1.50	0.00
	IBM/370	16	Ours	1.00	0.67
	CDC 7600	2	FTN 4.7	1.63	0.06
	IBM/370	16	FTX 2.2	1.00	0.68
2	CDC 7600	2	Ours	1.55	0.00
	IBM/370	16	Ours	1.00	0.55
	CDC 7600	2	FTN 4.7	1.37	0.00
	IBM/370	16	FTX 2.2	1.00	0.53
3	CDC 7600	2	Ours	1.55	0.05
	IBM/370	16	Ours	1.00	0.56
	CDC 7600	2	FTN 4.7	1.31	0.00
	IBM/370	16	FTX 2.2	1.00	0.55

quoted for our algorithm on the IBM equipment are for a fixed-point implementation. The MRE values for the corresponding floating-point implementation are slightly larger (by at most .2 digits), but the RMS values are almost identical to those reported here. We believe the slight increase in the MRE values is the result of wobbling precision encountered during evaluation of the rational approximation. This problem is almost impossible to overcome in any reasonable way; fortunately, it is not a serious problem.

The above tests will not detect a systematic error whereby the calculated function value is too large by a constant factor. The test program checks for this situation by evaluating the identity

$$\exp(x) = [\exp(x/2)]^2$$

for one argument.

```
C      PROGRAM TO TEST EXP
C
C      DATA REQUIRED
C
C         NONE
C
C      SUBPROGRAMS REQUIRED FROM THIS PACKAGE
C
C         MACHAR - AN ENVIRONMENTAL INQUIRY PROGRAM PROVIDING
C                  INFORMATION ON THE FLOATING-POINT ARITHMETIC
C                  SYSTEM.  NOTE THAT THE CALL TO MACHAR CAN
C                  BE DELETED PROVIDED THE FOLLOWING FOUR
C                  PARAMETERS ARE ASSIGNED THE VALUES INDICATED
C
C                     IBETA - THE RADIX OF THE FLOATING-POINT SYSTEM
C                     IT    - THE NUMBER OF BASE-IBETA DIGITS IN THE
C                             SIGNIFICAND OF A FLOATING-POINT NUMBER
C                     XMIN  - THE SMALLEST NON-VANISHING FLOATING-POINT
C                             POWER OF THE RADIX
C                     XMAX  - THE LARGEST FINITE FLOATING-POINT NO.
C
C         RAN(K) - A FUNCTION SUBPROGRAM RETURNING RANDOM REAL
C                  NUMBERS UNIFORMLY DISTRIBUTED OVER (0,1)
C
C
C      STANDARD FORTRAN SUBPROGRAMS REQUIRED
C
C         ABS, AINT, ALOG, AMAX1, EXP, FLOAT, SQRT
C
C
C      LATEST REVISION - DECEMBER 6, 1979
C
C      AUTHOR - W. J. CODY
C               ARGONNE NATIONAL LABORATORY
C
C
       INTEGER I,IBETA,IEXP,IOUT,IRND,IT,I1,J,K1,K2,K3,MACHEP,
      1         MAXEXP,MINEXP,N,NEGEP,NGRD
       REAL A,AIT,ALBETA,B,BETA,D,DEL,EPS,EPSNEG,ONE,RAN,R6,R7,
      1     TWO,TEN,V,W,X,XL,XMAX,XMIN,XN,X1,Y,Z,ZERO,ZZ
C
       IOUT = 6
       CALL MACHAR(IBETA,IT,IRND,NGRD,MACHEP,NEGEP,IEXP,MINEXP,
```

```
     1                    MAXEXP,EPS,EPSNEG,XMIN,XMAX)
      BETA = FLOAT(IBETA)
      ALBETA = ALOG(BETA)
      AIT = FLOAT(IT)
      ONE = 1.0E0
      TWO = 2.0E0
      TEN = 10.0E0
      ZERO = 0.0E0
      V = 0.0625E0
      A = TWO
      B = ALOG(A) * 0.5E0
      A = -B + V
      D = ALOG(0.9E0*XMAX)
      N = 2000
      XN = FLOAT(N)
      I1 = 0
C----------------------------------------------------------------------
C     RANDOM ARGUMENT ACCURACY TESTS
C----------------------------------------------------------------------
      DO 300 J = 1, 3
         K1 = 0
         K3 = 0
         X1 = ZERO
         R6 = ZERO
         R7 = ZERO
         DEL = (B - A) / XN
         XL = A
C
         DO 200 I = 1, N
            X = DEL * RAN(I1) + XL
C----------------------------------------------------------------------
C     PURIFY ARGUMENTS
C----------------------------------------------------------------------
            Y = X - V
            IF (Y .LT. ZERO) X = Y + V
            Z = EXP(X)
            ZZ = EXP(Y)
            IF (J .EQ. 1) GO TO 100
            IF (IBETA .NE. 10) Z = Z * .0625E0 -
     1                      Z * 2.44533210469205703B9E-3
            IF (IBETA .EQ. 10) Z = Z * 6.0E-2 +
     1                      Z * 5.466789530794296106E-5
            GO TO 110
```

```
  100        Z = Z - Z * 6.0586937186652421388E-2
  110        W = ONE
             IF (ZZ .NE. ZERO) W = (Z - ZZ) / ZZ
             IF (W .LT. ZERO) K1 = K1 + 1
             IF (W .GT. ZERO) K3 = K3 + 1
             W = ABS(W)
             IF (W .LE. R6) GO TO 120
             R6 = W
             X1 = X
  120        R7 = R7 + W*W
             XL = XL + DEL
  200    CONTINUE
C
         K2 = N - K3 - K1
         R7 = SQRT(R7/XN)
         WRITE (IOUT,1000) V, V
         WRITE (IOUT,1010) N,A,B
         WRITE (IOUT,1011) K1,K2,K3
         WRITE (IOUT,1020) IT,IBETA
         W = -999.0E0
         IF (R6 .NE. ZERO) W = ALOG(ABS(R6))/ALBETA
         WRITE (IOUT,1021) R6,IBETA,W,X1
         W = AMAX1(AIT+W,ZERO)
         WRITE (IOUT,1022) IBETA,W
         W = -999.0E0
         IF (R7 .NE. ZERO) W = ALOG(ABS(R7))/ALBETA
         WRITE (IOUT,1023) R7,IBETA,W
         W = AMAX1(AIT+W,ZERO)
         WRITE (IOUT,1022) IBETA,W
         IF (J .EQ. 2) GO TO 270
         V = 45.0E0 / 16.0E0
         A = -TEN * B
         B = 4.0E0 * XMIN * BETA ** IT
         B = ALOG(B)
         GO TO 300
  270    A = -TWO * A
         B = TEN * A
         IF (B .LT. D) B = D
  300 CONTINUE
C----------------------------------------------------------------------
C    SPECIAL TESTS
C----------------------------------------------------------------------
      WRITE (IOUT,1025)
```

```
      WRITE (IOUT,1030)
C
      DO 320 I = 1, 5
         X = RAN(I1) * BETA
         Y = -X
         Z = EXP(X) * EXP(Y) - ONE
         WRITE (IOUT,1060) X, Z
  320 CONTINUE
C
      WRITE (IOUT,1040)
      X = ZERO
      Y = EXP(X) - ONE
      WRITE (IOUT,1041) Y
      X = AINT(ALOG(XMIN))
      Y = EXP(X)
      WRITE (IOUT,1042) X, Y
      X = AINT(ALOG(XMAX))
      Y = EXP(X)
      WRITE (IOUT,1042) X, Y
      X = X / TWO
      V = X / TWO
      Y = EXP(X)
      Z = EXP (V)
      Z = Z * Z
      WRITE (IOUT,1043) X, Y, V, Z
C----------------------------------------------------------------------
C     TEST OF ERROR RETURNS
C----------------------------------------------------------------------
      WRITE (IOUT,1050)
      X = -ONE / SQRT(XMIN)
      WRITE (IOUT,1052) X
      Y = EXP(X)
      WRITE (IOUT,1061) Y
      X = -X
      WRITE (IOUT,1052) X
      Y = EXP(X)
      WRITE (IOUT,1061) Y
      WRITE (IOUT,1100)
      STOP
 1000 FORMAT(15H1TEST OF EXP(X-,F7.4,16H) VS EXP(X)/EXP(,F7.4,1H) //)
 1010 FORMAT(I7,47H RANDOM ARGUMENTS WERE TESTED FROM THE INTERVAL /
     1 6X,1H(,E15.4,1H,,E15.4,1H)//)
 1011 FORMAT(20H EXP(X-V) WAS LARGER,I6,7H TIMES, /
```

```
      1       13X,7H AGREED,I6,11H TIMES, AND /
      2     9X,11HWAS SMALLER,I6,7H TIMES.//)
 1020 FORMAT(10H THERE ARE,I4,5H BASE,I4,
      1      46H SIGNIFICANT DIGITS IN A FLOATING-POINT NUMBER  //)
 1021 FORMAT(30H THE MAXIMUM RELATIVE ERROR OF,E15.4,3H = ,I4,3H **,
      1  F7.2/4X,16HOCCURRED FOR X =,E17.6)
 1022 FORMAT(27H THE ESTIMATED LOSS OF BASE,I4,
      1  22H SIGNIFICANT DIGITS IS,F7.2//)
 1023 FORMAT(40H THE ROOT MEAN SQUARE RELATIVE ERROR WAS,E15.4,
      1      3H = ,I4,3H **,F7.2)
 1025 FORMAT(14H1SPECIAL TESTS//)
 1030 FORMAT(52H THE IDENTITY  EXP(X)*EXP(-X) = 1.0  WILL BE TESTED.//
      1      8X,1HX,9X,14HF(X)*F(-X) - 1 /)
 1040 FORMAT(//26H TEST OF SPECIAL ARGUMENTS //)
 1041 FORMAT(20H EXP(0.0) - 1.0E0 = ,E15.7/)
 1042 FORMAT(5H EXP(,E13.6,3H) =,E13.6/)
 1043 FORMAT(8H0IF EXP(,E13.6,4H) = ,E13.6,13H IS NOT ABOUT /
      1 5H EXP(,E13.6,7H)**2 = ,E13.6,26H THERE IS AN ARG RED ERROR)
 1050 FORMAT(22H1TEST OF ERROR RETURNS //)
 1052 FORMAT(37H0EXP WILL BE CALLED WITH THE ARGUMENT,E15.4/
      1      37H THIS SHOULD TRIGGER AN ERROR MESSAGE//)
 1060 FORMAT(2E15.7/)
 1061 FORMAT(23H EXP RETURNED THE VALUE,E15.4///)
 1100 FORMAT(25H THIS CONCLUDES THE TESTS )
C     ---------- LAST CARD OF EXP TEST PROGRAM ----------
      END
```

7.   POWER (**)

a.   General Discussion

The Fortran ** operator is defined mathematically as

$$x ** y = \exp(y \cdot \ln(x)).$$

The obvious implementation of this definition using existing software for the exponential and logarithm functions results in large errors independent of those associated with the elementary function software used (Clark and Cody [1969] and Clark, Cody and Kuki [1971]). To see this, let

$$w = y \cdot \ln(x)$$

and

$$z = \exp(w).$$

Then it is easily shown that

$$dz/z = dw,$$

that is, that the relative error (see Glossary) in $z = x ** y$ is approximately the absolute error in w, which, because of the finite word length of the computer, is proportional to the magnitude of w. Thus the finite word length, not the accuracy of either the exponential or logarithm computation, is the limiting factor. The only way to decrease the relative error in z is to extend the effective word length of the computer and determine $\ln(x)$, w and z in this "extended precision." On some machines either the greater significance in fixed-point arithmetic or higher precision floating point can be exploited for part of the computation, while on others a pseudo extended-precision floating-point computation must be used. In any case the power function becomes completely self-contained and independent of the software for the exponential and logarithm. The algorithms we present for this computation are far more complicated than any other algorithms presented in this manual. Despite this complexity our self-contained power function should be competitive in execution speed with the traditional power function and, in many cases, should be significantly faster.

We describe the floating-point version of the algorithm. The key to pseudo extended-precision arithmetic in this case is the representation of a floating-point number V, say, in the "reduced form"

$$V = V1 + V2,$$

where $V1$ and $V2$ are standard floating-point numbers, $V1$ is defined by

$$V1 = FLOAT(INTRND(C{\cdot}V))/C$$

(the definition varies slightly in the implementation notes), and C is a floating-point integer depending upon the radix of the number system (see Glossary). In general the computation of $X**Y$ will be carried out as

$$Z = n**W,$$
where
$$W = Y \cdot logn(X),$$

logn denotes the base-n logarithm, and n again depends upon the floating-point radix.

Let X be a positive floating-point number, $X = f{\cdot}B**(m)$ and $1/B \leq f < 1$, and assume $B = n**k$. Determine an odd integer $p < C$ and a non-negative integer $r < k$ such that

$$f = n**(-r-p/C) \cdot g/a,$$
where
$$a = n**(-p/C),$$

$$g = f \cdot n**r,$$

$$1/n \leq g < 1,$$
and
$$|logn(g/a)| \leq 1/C.$$

This last relation guarantees small absolute error in $\log n(X)$ when $\log n(g/a)$ is accurate to working precision. Then, in reduced form,

where
$$U = \log n(X) = U1 + U2,$$

$$U1 = k*m - r - p/C,$$

$$U2 = \log n(g/a) = \log n((1+s)/(1-s)),$$

and

$$s = (g-a)/(g+a).$$

The computation for $U2$ roughly parallels that for $\ln(g)$ described in the notes for ALOG/ALOG10. Because X is assumed to be exact, g is exact and full precision is retained in $g-a$ by expressing a as

$$a = a1 + a2$$

and forming

$$g - a = (g - a1) - a2.$$

A rational approximation generated especially for this work is used to evaluate $U2$. This approximation uses the auxiliary variable z, where z is an appropriate integer multiple of s.

$U1$, $U2$ and the reduced form of Y are then used to produce the reduced form of W. Finally, because

$$W1 = k*m' - r' - p'/C,$$

$$Z = B**(m') * n**(-r'-p'/C) * n**W2,$$

where $n**W2$ is evaluated by means of another rational approximation.

For non-decimal machines $C = 16$ and $n = 2$. The reduced form of the base-2 logarithm of X then guarantees that the absolute error in W is $2**(-4)$ times the normal rounding error in floating-point arithmetic. Theoretically, $|Y|$ must be greater than 16 before the error in W becomes important, but in practice the effects of the error in W are usually not seen until $|Y|$ exceeds 32.

For decimal machines $C = n = 10$, $r = r' = 0$ and $k = 1$.   The error in W is somewhat larger than before in this case,   but it is still acceptable, and the cost of further reduction is prohibitive.

For non-decimal fixed-point machines, the parameters are as for the non-decimal floating-point case.   Some, but not all, of the pseudo extended-precision computations are replaced by fixed-point computations under the assumption that fixed-point numbers carry at least four bits more precision than floating-point significands.

Error handling follows ANSI Fortran (American National Standards Institute [1966,   1978]) which forbids negative-valued floating-point numbers raised to floating-point powers, and zero raised to the zero power. Clearly zero cannot be raised to a negative power, either.

b. Flow Chart for POWER(X,Y)

(Assume $X = \pm f \times B^{**}e$, $1/B \leq f < 1$) [1]

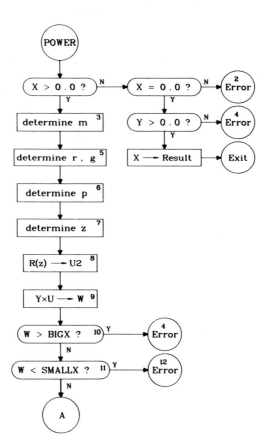

Note: Small integers indicate an implementation note.

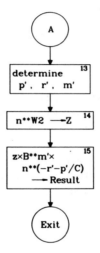

Note: Small integers indicate an implementation note.

c. Implementation Notes, Non-Decimal Fixed-Point Machines

1) In this case the radix for the floating-point number representation (see Glossary) is assumed to be $2^{**}k$. We also assume that fixed-point arithmetic carries at least four more bits of precision than floating-point arithmetic.

2) If execution is to continue rather than terminate, then a default function value should be provided in addition to the error message. The most obvious default is to continue the computation with $|X|$ after the error message.

3) In terms of our operations (see Chapter 2)

    m = INTXP(X)   .

4) If execution is to continue rather than terminate, then a default function value should be provided in addition to the error message. *XINF*, the largest floating-point number, is a reasonable default.

5) Form the fixed-point representation of $g' = g/2$, where $g = f \cdot 2^{**}r$, f is the floating-point significand and r is the number of leading zero bits in the first base-B digit of f (not g'). Thus $r < k$. First set

    g' = FIX(SETXP(X,0))/2

    (see Chapter 2), where the division by 2 may be accomplished with a shift operation. If bit manipulation instructions are available, then it may be more efficient to implement this whole operation directly without invoking the macros for SETXP and FIX.

    If $k = 1$, r is not needed, and we are done. If $k > 1$ and bit manipulation instructions are not available, set $r = 0$, test g', and repeatedly shift g' left one bit, replacing r by $r + 1$ each time, until $.25 \leq g' < .5$. Otherwise, extract the first $k+1$ bits of g', use them as an index to retrieve the proper value of r from an array of appropriate integers, and then shift g' left r bits.

6) Let $A1$ be an array of fixed-point values of the integer powers of $2^{**}(-1/16)$ scaled by 1/2. In particular,

$$A1(j) = (1/2) \cdot 2^{**}[(1-j)/16], \quad j = 1, \ldots, 17$$

rounded to fixed-point precision. The array may be constructed from the following octal values.

i	$(1/2) \cdot 2^{**} (-i/16)$ in octal
0	0.40000 00000 00000 00000 00000
1	0.36511 27642 51110 33141 30756
2	0.35260 14334 76722 20711 35501
3	0.34063 15735 41251 23410 42031
4	0.32721 17631 26551 65527 50347
5	0.31611 10602 50770 22007 07611
6	0.30531 62502 12520 33326 72371
7	0.27502 12163 72600 60665 75242
8	0.26501 17146 37635 71444 10546
9	0.25526 03735 22052 05126 14446
10	0.24577 55325 15425 04707 24163
11	0.23675 23114 04432 04215 33202
12	0.23015 77012 14333 42513 36433
13	0.22160 75156 35261 07031 54077
14	0.21345 34074 37250 57267 15760
15	0.20552 54154 76304 41730 51427
16	0.20000 00000 00000 00000 00000

Now the appropriate value of p may be found with the following algorithm (binary search):

```
set p = 1

if (g' ≤ A1(9)) then p = 9

if (g' ≤ al(p+4)) then p = p + 4

if (g' ≤ A1(p+2)) then p = p + 2
```

7) Let z be a scaled fixed-point value of s constructed as follows:

$$\frac{[g'-A1(p+1)]\cdot 16}{g' + A1(p+1)} \longrightarrow z,$$

where the multiplication by 16 may be accomplished with a shift operation. At this point $z = 16 \cdot s$, and $|z| < 0.35$. Save z for later use.

8) We evaluate $\log 2[g'/a1(j)]$ with a scaled minimax polynomial approximation $z \cdot P(z^2)$ derived especially for this work. Let b be the number of bits in the significand of a floating-point number. Then

for $b \leq 24$

p1 = 0.00130 24615 8

for $25 \leq b \leq 36$

p1 = 0.00130 20832 59758
p2 = 0.00000 30533 41066

for $37 \leq b \leq 50$

p1 = 0.00130 20833 33345 65
p2 = 0.00000 30517 57315 68
p3 = 0.00000 00085 21363 65

Form $v = z^2$ using fixed-point arithmetic. Then use nested multiplication to evaluate $P(v)$, the polynomial in v with coefficients $p1, p2, \ldots, pn$. For $37 \leq b \leq 50$, for example,

P(v) = (p3 • v + p2) • v + p1.

Note that $P(v) = p1$ for $b \leq 24$. Now form $8 \cdot R = z+z \cdot (v \cdot P(v))$ (note the scaling), and evaluate the unscaled quantity

U2 = [8•R] • [log2(e)/8] = log2[g'/a1(j)],

where

$\log 2(e)/8 = 0.18033\ 68801\ 11120\ 42592\ E+0.$

9) Efficiency and accuracy are crucial in this step. We must produce $W = U*Y$, where

$$U = (k*m-r) + p/16 + U2,$$

and decompose it into components $W1$ and $W2$, where $W1$ is the integer part of $16*W$, and $|W2| < 1/16$. Because the computation involves both integer and fractional quantities, it is very difficult to carry out in fixed point, and we must temporarily revert to floating point.

Begin by defining a new operation REDUCE(V) as either

FLOAT(INT(16.0*V)) * 0.0625

or

FLOAT(INTRND(16.0*V)) * 0.0625,

whichever can be implemented more efficiently. The main requirement is that

$|V\text{-REDUCE(V)}| < 1/16.$

When the definition is implemented directly, the final multiplication by 0.0625 often can be done with an appropriate ADX operation. But on many machines the most efficient implementation of REDUCE is to add a non-standard zero to V. Usually during floating-point addition the significand of the operand with the smaller exponent is downshifted in the arithmetic register by the difference in the exponents in order to properly align the digits. Digits shifted beyond the arithmetic register (which may retain more digits than those carried in the significand) are lost. After the addition, the significand of the result is again normalized. Thus, if $C0$ is a constant with zero significand and an exponent which will force precisely the unwanted bits of V to be lost,

REDUCE(V) = V + C0.

On octal machines the sequence must be

REDUCE(V) = [(V+V) + C0] * 0.5,

because shifts occur in multiples of three bits, and the first four bits of the fractional part of V must be saved.

This new operation is used to form the reduced representation of W given Y and the reduced representation of U. First find $U1$ with

FLOAT((k*m-r)*16-p) * 0.0625 --> U1.

Note the simplification of this computation on binary machines where $k = 1$ and $r = 0$.

Now find the reduced form of Y with

REDUCE(Y) --> Y1

Y-Y1 --> Y2

Then form the pseudo extended-precision product of U and Y with the following sequence of operations:

REFLOAT(U2)*Y + U1*Y2 --> W

REDUCE(W) --> W1

W-W1 --> W2

W1+U1*Y1 --> W

REDUCE(W) --> W1

W2+(W-W1) --> W2

REDUCE(W2) --> W

INT[16*(W1+W)] --> IW1

FIX(W2-W) --> w2

where $IW1$ is an integer and $w2$ is a fixed-point number.

10) We suggest trading a small loss in range for increased efficiency by comparing $IW1$ to the integer INT{16*log2(XMAX)-1}, where $XMAX$ is the largest positive finite floating-point number.

11) We suggest trading a small loss in range for increased efficiency by comparing $IW1$ to the integer $\text{INT}\{16 \cdot \log2(XMIN)+1\}$, where $XMIN$ is the smallest positive floating-point number.

12) If execution is to continue rather than terminate, then a default function value of 0 can be provided in addition to an error message.

13) The next step requires that $w2 \leq 0$. Therefore, add 1 to $IW1$ using integer arithmetic, and subtract $1/16$ from $w2$ in fixed point if $w2 > 0$. Then extract p', r' and m' as follows. First set $I = 0$ if $IW1 < 0$, and $I = 1$ otherwise. Then, using integer arithmetic,

$$|W1/16 + I \longrightarrow N$$

$$16 \cdot N - |W1 \longrightarrow p'.$$

Finally, for non-binary machines ($k \neq 1$) compute

$$N/k + I \longrightarrow m'$$

$$k \cdot m' - N \longrightarrow r',$$

but for binary machines ($k = 1$) compute only

$$N + I + 1 \longrightarrow m'.$$

14) $n = 2$ in this case. We evaluate $(2 \cdot \cdot w2)-1$ for $-0.625 \leq w2 \leq 0$ from a near-minimax polynomial approximation generated especially for this work:

for $b \leq 24$

q1 = 0.69314 675
q2 = 0.24018 510
q3 = 0.05436 038

for $25 \leq b \leq 45$

q1 = 0.69314 71805 56341
q2 = 0.24022 65061 44710
q3 = 0.05550 40488 ͺ3077
q4 = 0.00961 62065 95838
q5 = 0.00130 52551 59428

for $46 \leq b \leq 52$

$q1 = 0.69314\ 71805\ 59937\ 815$
$q2 = 0.24022\ 65069\ 56777\ 522$
$q3 = 0.05550\ 41084\ 24756\ 866$
$q4 = 0.00961\ 81176\ 91387\ 241$
$q5 = 0.00133\ 30810\ 11340\ 821$
$q6 = 0.00015\ 07740\ 61788\ 142$

Evaluate $z = w2 \cdot Q(w2)$ in fixed point, where $Q(w2)$ is a polynomial in $W2$ with coefficients $q1$, $q2$, $\ldots$, qn. Use nested multiplication. For $b \leq 24$, for example,

$z = ((q3 * w2 + q2) * w2 + q1) * w2.$

15) This computation is carried out in three steps. First, add 1 to z and multiply by $2**(-p'/16)$ with the following fixed-point computation:

A1(p'+1) + A1(p'+1)*z --> z.

The form $A1(p'+1) \cdot (1.0+z)$, which is mathematically equivalent, cannot be used in fixed point. Note that z is now scaled by $1/2$ because of the scaling on $A1$. This will be corrected with the factor $R1(r')$ for non-binary machines, and in the ADX operation below (using the m' constructed earlier) for binary machines.

Now convert back to floating point with

REFLOAT(z) --> Z.

For non-binary machines only ($k \neq 1$), let $R1$ be an array with $R1(i) = 2**(1-i)$, $i = 0, \ldots, k$, and form

Z*R1(r') --> Z.

Finally, for all machines,

ADX(Z,m') --> POWER.

d. Implementation Notes, Non-Decimal Floating-Point Machines

1) In this case the radix for the floating-point number representation (see Glossary) is assumed to be $2**k$.

2) If execution is to continue rather than terminate,   then a default function value should be provided in addition to the error message. The most obvious default is to continue the computation with $|X|$ after the error message.

3) In terms of our operations (see Chapter 2)

   $m = \text{INTXP}(X)$.

4) If execution is to continue rather than terminate,   then a default function value should be provided in addition to the error message. *XINF*, the largest floating-point number, is a reasonable default.

5) Let f be the floating-point significand and r the number of leading zero bits in the first base-B digit of f.   Then form $g = f * 2**r$ as follows:

If $k = 1$, r is not needed and

   $g = \text{SETXP}(X,0)$

(see Chapter 2).   When bit manipulation instructions are available, it may be more efficient to implement $\text{SETXP}(X,0)$ for $X > 0$ as a special case without invoking the full macro.

If $k > 1$ and bit manipulation instructions are not available, set

   $r = 0$

and

   $g = \text{SETXP}(X,0)$.

Then test g, and repeatedly replace g by $g + g$ and r by $r + 1$ until $.5 \leq g < 1$.

Otherwise $(k > 1$ and bit manipulation instructions available) extract the first base-B digit of f (the significand of X), and use it as an index to retrieve the proper value of r from an array of appropriate integers. Next use r as an index to extract $2**r$ from an array, scale X by $2**r$, and then set

g = SETXP(X,0)   ,

which again may best be implemented as a special case of the macro.

6) We require arrays of floating-point numbers $A1$ and $A2$ such that sums of appropriate array elements represent odd integer powers of $2**(-1/16)$ to beyond working precision. Because of later requirements (see Note 15) $A1$ includes the even integer powers of $2**(-1/16)$, as well, with all entries accurate to working precision. $A2$ then contains correction terms for the odd powers in $A1$. In particular,

A1(j) = 2**[(1-j)/16], j = 1, ..., 17,

rounded to working precision, and

A2(j) = 2**[(1-2j)/16] - A1(2j),   j = 1, ..., 8,

accurate to perhaps half of working precision. The arrays may be constructed from the following octal values:

i	$2**(-i/16)$ in octal
0	1.00000 00000 00000 00000 00000 00000
1	0.75222 57505 22220 66302 61734 72062
2	0.72540 30671 75644 41622 73201 32727
3	0.70146 33673 02522 47021 04062 61124
4	0.65642 37462 55323 53257 20715 15057
5	0.63422 21405 21760 44016 17421 53016
6	0.61263 45204 25240 66655 64761 25503
7	0.57204 24347 65401 41553 72504 02177
8	0.55202 36314 77473 63110 21313 73047
9	0.53254 07672 44124 12254 31114 01243

10   0.51377 32652 33052 11616 50345 72776
11   0.47572 46230 11064 10432 66404 42174
12   0.46033 76024 30667 05226 75065 32214
13   0.44341 72334 72542 16063 30176 55544
14   0.42712 70170 76521 36556 33737 10612

15   0.41325 30331 74611 03661 23056 22556
16   0.40000 00000 00000 00000 00000 00000

Now the appropriate value of p may be found with the following algorithm (binary search):

set p = 1

if (g $\leq$ A1(9)), then p = 9

if (g $\leq$ A1(p+4)), then p = p + 4

if (g $\leq$ A1(p+2)), then p = p + 2

7) We use the variable $z = 2s = 2[(g-a)/(g+a)]$. On non-binary machines the computation

$$\frac{[g-A1(p+1)] - A2((p+1)/2)}{g/2 + A1(p+1)/2} \dashrightarrow z,$$

where the order of operations implied by grouping is important, minimizes both the rounding error and the error associated with wobbling precision (see Glossary). On binary machines the computation can be simplified to

$$\frac{[g-A1(p+1)] - A2((p+1)/2)}{g + A1(p+1)} \dashrightarrow z$$

z + z --> z,

where the addition of z to itself could be accomplished with an ADX(z,1) operation when that is faster than the addition. At this point $|z| \leq .044$.

8) We use a minimax polynomial approximation $z \cdot P(z^2)$ derived especially for this work.   Let b be the number of bits in the significand of a floating-point number.   Then

for $b \leq 24$

p1 = 0.83357 541 E-1

for $25 \leq b \leq 36$

p1 = 0.83333 32862 45 E-1
p2 = 0.12506 48500 52 E-1

for $37 \leq b \leq 50$

p1 = 0.83333 33333 41213 6 E-1
p2 = 0.12499 99796 50060 8 E-1
p3 = 0.22338 24352 81541 8 E-2

for $51 \leq b \leq 64$

p1 = 0.83333 33333 33332 11405 E-1
p2 = 0.12500 00000 05037 99174 E-1
p3 = 0.22321 42128 59242 58967 E-2
p4 = 0.43445 77567 21631 19635 E-3

Form $v = z^2$ and evaluate $R = z \cdot v \cdot P(v)$, where $P(v)$ is a polynomial in v with coefficients $p1$, $p2$, ..., pn.   Use nested multiplication. For $37 \leq b \leq 50$, for example,

R(z) = [(p3 ⋅ v + p2) ⋅ v + p1] ⋅ v ⋅ z.

Now carefully evaluate

U2 = (z + R) ⋅ log2(e)

as follows.   First let

K = 0.44269 50408 88963 40736 E+0

to working precision, and form $R = R + K \cdot R$.   Then form

U2 = (R + z⋅K) + z,

where the order implied by parentheses is important.

9) This step is critical for both the accuracy and efficiency of the power function. Select carefully from the alternate methods suggested here so as to maximize the efficiency.

Begin by defining a new operation REDUCE(V) as either

> FLOAT(INT(16.0*V)) * 0.0625

or

> FLOAT(INTRND(16.0*V)) * 0.0625,

whichever can be implemented more efficiently. The main requirement is that

> |V-REDUCE(V)| < 1/16.

When the definition is implemented directly, the final multiplication by 0.0625 often can be done with an appropriate ADX operation. But on many machines the most efficient implementation of REDUCE is to add a non-standard zero to V. Usually during floating-point addition the significand of the operand with the smaller exponent is downshifted in the arithmetic register by the difference in the exponents in order to properly align the digits. Digits shifted beyond the arithmetic register (which may retain more digits than those carried in the significand) are lost. After the addition, the significand of the result is again normalized. Thus, if $C0$ is a constant with zero significand and an exponent which will force precisely the unwanted bits of V to be lost,

> REDUCE(V) = V + C0.

On octal machines the sequence must be

> REDUCE(V) = [(V+V) + C0] * 0.5,

because shifts occur in multiples of three bits, and the first four bits of the fractional part of V must be saved.

This new operation is used to form the reduced representation of W given Y and the reduced representation of U. First find $U1$ with

> FLOAT((k*m-r)*16-p) * 0.0625 --> U1.

Note the simplification of this computation on binary machines where
$k = 1$ and $r = 0$.

There are two options at this point. If higher precision
floating-point arithmetic is available and is reasonably efficient,
consider converting Y, $U1$ and $U2$ to the higher precision and then
using it to evaluate $W = Y \cdot (U1+U2)$. Then let $W1 = \text{REDUCE}(W)$,
$W2 - W-W1$ and $IW1 = \text{INT}(W1)$, where $W1$ and $W2$ are in the working
precision and $IW1$ is an integer.

Otherwise, proceed as follows. Find the reduced form of Y with

    REDUCE(Y) --> Y1

    Y-Y1 --> Y2

Then form the pseudo extended-precision product of U and Y with the
following sequence of operations:

    U2•Y + U1•Y2 --> W

    REDUCE(W) --> W1

    W-W1 --> W2

    W1+U1•Y1 --> W

    REDUCE(W) --> W1

    W2+(W-W1) --> W2

    REDUCE(W2) --> W

    INT(16•(W1+W)) --> IW1

    W2-W --> W2

10) We suggest trading a small loss in range for increased efficiency by
comparing $IW1$ to the integer $\text{INT}(16 \cdot \log2(XMAX)-1)$, where $XMAX$ is the
largest positive finite floating-point number.

11) We suggest trading a small loss in range for increased efficiency by comparing $IW1$ to the integer $INT\{16 \cdot \log2(XMIN)+1\}$, where $XMIN$ is the smallest positive floating-point number.

12) If execution is to continue rather than terminate, then a default function value of 0 can be provided in addition to an error message.

13) The next step requires that $W2 \leq 0$. Therefore, add 1 to $IW1$ using integer arithmetic, and subtract 1/16 from $W2$ if $W2 > 0$. Then extract p', r' and m' as follows. First set $I = 0$ if $IW1 < 0$, and $I = 1$ otherwise. For binary machines ($k = 1$) use integer arithmetic to form

> $|W1/16 + I \longrightarrow m'$
>
> $16 \cdot m' - |W1 \longrightarrow p'$

For non-binary machines ($k \neq 1$) use integer arithmetic to form

> $|W1/16 + I \longrightarrow N$
>
> $16 \cdot N - |W1 \longrightarrow p'$
>
> $N/k + I \longrightarrow m'$
>
> $k \cdot m' - N \longrightarrow r'$

14) $n = 2$ in this case. We evaluate $(2 \cdot \cdot W2)-1$ for $-.0625 \leq W2 \leq 0$ from a near-minimax polynomial approximation generated especially for this work. The interval and approximation form avoid possible wobbling precision when $k > 1$.

For $b \leq 24$

q1 = 0.69314 675 E+0
q2 = 0.24018 510 E+0
q3 = 0.54360 383 E-1

For $25 \leq b \leq 45$

q1 = 0.69314 71805 56341 E+0
q2 = 0.24022 65061 44710 E+0
q3 = 0.55504 04881 30765 E-1
q4 = 0.96162 06595 83789 E-2
q5 = 0.13052 55159 42810 E-2

For $46 \leq b \leq 52$

q1 = 0.69314 71805 59937 815 E+0
q2 = 0.24022 65069 56777 522 E+0
q3 = 0.55504 10842 47568 661 E-1
q4 = 0.96181 17691 38724 104 E-2
q5 = 0.13330 81011 34082 075 E-2
q6 = 0.15077 40617 88142 382 E-3

For $53 \leq b \leq 64$

q1 = 0.69314 71805 59945 29629 E+0
q2 = 0.24022 65069 59095 37056 E+0
q3 = 0.55504 10866 40855 95326 E-1
q4 = 0.96181 29059 51724 16964 E-2
q5 = 0.13333 54131 35857 84703 E-2
q6 = 0.15400 29044 09897 64601 E-3
q7 = 0.14928 85268 05956 08186 E-4

Evaluate $Z = W2 \cdot Q(W2)$, where $Q(W2)$ is a polynomial in $W2$ with coefficients $q1, q2, \ldots, qn$. Use nested multiplication. For $b \leq$ 24, for example,

$$Z = ((q3 * W2 + q2) * W2 + q1) * W2.$$

15) This computation is carried out in three steps. First, add 1 to Z and multiply by $2**(-p'/16)$ with the following computation:

$$A1(p'+1) + A1(p'+1) * Z \longrightarrow Z.$$

Do not use the form $A1(p'+1) * (1.0+Z)$, which is mathematically equivalent but often not as accurate.

For non-binary machines only, let $R1$ be an array with $R1(i) = 2**(-i)$, $i = 0, \ldots, k$, and form

    Z·R1(r') --> Z.

Finally, for all machines,

    ADX(Z,m') --> Result.

e. Implementation Notes, Decimal Floating-Point Machines

1) In this case the radix for the floating-point number representation (see Glossary) is 10.

2) If execution is to continue rather than terminate, then a default function value should be provided in addition to the error message. The most obvious default is to continue the computation with $|X|$ after the error message.

3) In terms of our operations (see Chapter 2)

$$m = \text{INTXP}(X) \quad .$$

4) If execution is to continue rather than terminate, then a default function value should be provided in addition to the error message. $XINF$, the largest floating-point number, is a reasonable default.

5) In this case r is not needed, and (see Chapter 2)

$$g = \text{SETXP}(X,0) \quad .$$

6) We require arrays of floating-point numbers $A1$ and $A2$ such that sums of appropriate array elements represent odd integer powers of $10**(-1/10)$ to beyond working precision. Because of later requirements (see Note 15), $A1$ includes the even integer powers of $10**(-1/10)$ as well with all entries accurate to working precision. $A2$ then contains correction terms for the odd powers in $A1$. In particular,

$$A1(j) = 10**[(1-j)/10], \quad j = 1, \ldots, 11$$

rounded to working precision, and

$$A2(j) = 10**[(1-2j)/10] - A1(2j), \quad j = 1, \ldots, 5,$$

accurate to perhaps half of working precision. The arrays may be constructed from the following decimal values:

i	10 ** (-i/10)
0	1.00000 00000 00000 00000 00000 000
1	0.79432 82347 24281 50206 59182 828
2	0.63095 73444 80193 24943 43601 366
3	0.50118 72336 27272 28500 15541 869
4	0.39810 71705 53497 25077 02523 051
5	0.31622 77660 16837 93319 98893 544
6	0.25118 86431 50958 01110 85032 068
7	0.19952 62314 96887 96013 52455 397
8	0.15848 93192 46111 34852 02101 373
9	0.12589 25411 79416 72104 23954 106
10	0.10000 00000 00000 00000 00000 000

Now the appropriate value of p may be found as follows. First set $p = 1$. Then repeatedly modify p with

if $(g \leq A1(p+2))$, then $p = p + 2$

until $g > a1(p+2)$.

7) Determine the variable $z = s = (g-a)/(g+a)$ as follows:

$$\frac{[g-A1(p+1)] - A2((p+1)/2)}{g + A1(p+1)} \longrightarrow z$$

At this point $|z| \leq .115$.

8) We use a minimax rational approximation $z \cdot R(z^2)$ derived especially for this work. Let d be the number of digits in the significand of a floating-point number. Then

for $d \leq 8$

$p0 = -0.48144\ 78516\ E+0$
$q0 = -0.16628\ 73334\ E+1$
$q1 = 0.10000\ 00000\ E+1$

for $9 \leq d \leq 14$

```
p0 =   0.12095 10556 17031 7 E+1
p1 = -0.62077 57571 87918 2 E+0
q0 =   0.41775 01464 74140 2 E+1
q1 = -0.46505 84419 61834 9 E+1
q2 =   0.10000 00000 00000 0 E+1
```

for $15 \leq d \leq 18$

```
p0 = -0.35184 51552 93711 75192 E+1
p1 =   0.35829 52156 67236 56966 E+1
p2 = -0.68650 74087 13682 76474 E+0
q0 = -0.12152 30114 43221 36016 E+2
q1 =   0.19666 45902 38905 35938 E+2
q2 = -0.89628 58940 90517 72560 E+1
q1 =   0.10000 00000 00000 00000 E+1
```

Form $v = z^2$ and evaluate $R = z \cdot [K + v \cdot P(v)/Q(v)]$, where P and Q are polynomials in v with coefficients $p0$, $p1$, ... pn and $q0$, $q1$, ..., qm, respectively, and

$$K = 2/\ln(10) = 0.86858\ 89638\ 06503\ 65530\ \text{E+0}$$

rounded to machine precision. Use nested multiplication. For $9 \leq d \leq 14$, for example,

$$v \cdot P(v) = (p1 \cdot v + p0) \cdot v,$$

and

$$Q(v) = (v + q1) \cdot v + q0.$$

Note that because $q2 = 1.0$, one multiplication is saved by representing $q2 \cdot v$ as v.

9) This step is critical for both the accuracy and efficiency of the power function. Select carefully from the alternate methods suggested here so as to maximize the efficiency.

Begin by defining a new operation REDUCE(V) as either

```
FLOAT( INT(10.0•V)) • 0.1
```

or

```
FLOAT( INTRND(10.0•V)) • 0.1      ,
```

whichever can be implemented more efficiently. The main requirement is that

$$|V-\text{REDUCE}(V)| < 1/10.$$

When the definition is implemented directly, the final multiplication by 0.1 often can be done with an ADX operation. But on many machines the most efficient implementation of REDUCE is to add a non-standard zero to V. Usually during floating-point addition the significand of the operand with the smaller exponent is downshifted in the arithmetic register by the difference in the exponents in order to properly align the digits. Digits shifted beyond the arithmetic register (which may retain more digits than those carried in the significand) are lost. After the addition, the significand of the result is again normalized. Thus, if $C0$ is a constant with zero significand and an exponent which will force precisely the unwanted digits of V to be lost,

$$\text{REDUCE}(V) = V + C0.$$

This new operation is used to form the reduced representation of W given Y and the reduced representation of U. First find $U1$ with

$$\text{FLOAT}(10*\text{m}-\text{p}) * 0.1 \text{ --> } U1.$$

There are two options at this point. If higher precision floating-point arithmetic is available and is reasonably efficient, consider converting Y, $U1$ and $U2$ to the higher precision and then using it to evaluate $W = Y*(U1+U2)$. Then let $W1 = \text{REDUCE}(W)$, $W2 = W-W1$ and $IW1 = \text{INT}(W1)$, where $W1$ and $W2$ are in the working precision and $IW1$ is an integer.

Otherwise, proceed as follows. Find the reduced form of Y with

$$\text{REDUCE}(Y) \text{ --> } Y1$$

$$Y-Y1 \text{ --> } Y2$$

Then form the pseudo extended-precision product of U and Y with the following sequence of operations:

$$U2*Y + U1*Y2 \text{ --> } W$$

REDUCE(W) --> W1

W-W1 --> W2

W1+U1*Y1 --> W

REDUCE(W) --> W1

W2+(W-W1) --> W2

REDUCE(W2) --> W

INT[10*(W1+W)] --> IW1

W2-W --> W2

10) We suggest trading a small loss in range for increased efficiency by comparing $IW1$ to the integer INT($10 * \log(XMAX)-1$), where $XMAX$ is the largest positive finite floating-point number.

11) We suggest trading a small loss in range for increased efficiency by comparing $IW1$ to the integer INT($10 * \log(XMIN)+1$), where $XMIN$ is the smallest positive floating-point number.

12) If execution is to continue rather than terminate, then a default function value of 0 can be provided in addition to an error message.

13) The next step requires that $W2 \leq 0$. Therefore, add 1 to $IW1$ using integer arithmetic and subtract 0.1 from $W2$ if $W2 > 0$. Then extract p', r' and m' as follows. First set $I = 0$ if $IW1 < 0$, and $I = 1$ otherwise. Then use integer arithmetic to form

IW1/10 + I --> m'

10*m' - IW1 --> p'

14) In this case $n = 10$. We evaluate $(10**W2)-1$ for $-.1 \leq W2 \leq 0$ from a near-minimax rational approximation generated especially for this work.

For d ≤ 7

pp0 = -0.38883 9832 E+1
pp1 = -0.21742 4847 E+1
pp2 = -0.78964 7014 E+0
qq0 = -0.16887 0925 E+1
qq1 = 0.10000 0000 E+1

For 8 ≤ d ≤ 10

pp0 = 0.82998 14853 06 E+1
pp1 = 0.17805 77775 84 E+1
pp2 = 0.68536 85048 84 E+0
qq0 = 0.36045 63799 45 E+1
qq1 = -0.33766 11203 26 E+1
qq2 = 0.10000 00000 00 E+1

For 11 ≤ d ≤ 14

pp0 = -0.37713 99188 31947 3 E+2
pp1 = -0.57975 91698 28398 6 E+1
pp2 = -0.46710 07431 07040 0 E+1
pp3 = -0.51359 30940 15587 9 E+0
qq0 = -0.16378 97856 54144 4 E+2
qq1 = 0.16339 13385 89750 1 E+2
qq2 = -0.63664 36505 45209 5 E+1
qq3 = 0.10000 00000 00000 0 E+1

For 15 ≤ d ≤ 18

pp0 = 0.23539 70807 49261 19272 E+3
pp1 = 0.28195 17958 42955 14217 E+2
pp2 = 0.34363 74379 23829 31895 E+2
pp3 = 0.35616 93889 90563 55495 E+1
pp4 = 0.41071 57590 70777 89734 E+0
qq0 = 0.10223 16532 25538 32434 E+3
qq1 = -0.10545 35294 64899 79088 E+3
qq2 = 0.45994 87860 33907 54883 E+2
qq3 = -0.10224 89787 60959 10327 E+2
qq4 = 0.10000 00000 00000 00000 E+1

Evaluate $Z = W2 \cdot PP(W2)/QQ(W2)$, where $pp(W2)$ and $QQ(W2)$ are polynomials in $W2$ with coefficients $pp0$, $pp1$, $\ldots$, ppn and $qq0$, $qq1$, $\ldots$, qqn, respectively. Use nested multiplication (see Note 8).

15) This computation is carried out in three steps. First, add 1 to Z and multiply by $10 ** (-p'/10)$ with the following computation:

       A1(p'+1) + A1(p'+1)∗Z --> Z.

Do not use the form $A1(p'+1) \cdot (1.0+Z)$, which is mathematically equivalent but often not as accurate.

Finally,

       ADX(Z,m') --> Result.

f.   Testing

The tests are divided into six major parts.   The first four are a
series of random argument tests with various identities and argument
ranges to check the accuracy of specific steps in the power computation.
The fifth is a short check of the relation

$$x**y = 1 / [x**(-y)].$$

Finally there is a series of computations with special arguments to
check the function near its argument limits and to check the error
returns.

As indicated in the general discussion above,   the power function
$x**y$ is essentially calculated as

$$z = \exp(w)$$

where

$$w = y * \ln(x).$$

The successive steps in this computation are the calculation of $\ln(x)$, w
and $\exp(w)$.   Because the relative error in the exponential function
approximately equals   the absolute error   in the   argument,   the
computations of $\ln(x)$ and the product $y*\ln(x)$ are especially critical
and require the care outlined in our algorithm.

The first test measures the relative error in the identity

$$x**(1.0) = x$$

for x drawn from the interval $[1/B,1]$ where B is the radix for the
floating-point number representation. Some implementations of the power
function detect the fact that the exponent is an integer and merely
multiply the base by itself the appropriate number of times.   This test
is vacuous for such programs but does have meaning for implementations
of algorithms similar to the one that we advocate.   For such
implementations we measure

$$E = [x - x**1.0] / x.$$

In this case $w = 1.0∗\ln(x)$.   Assume D is the relative error in z, d the absolute error in $\ln(x)$, e the absolute error in the multiplication to obtain w, and h the generated relative error in computing $\exp(w)$ (see Glossary).   Then it follows that

$$E = [x - x(1+D)] / x$$

$$= -D,$$

where

$$D = d + e∗\ln(x) + h,$$

and only terms linear in d, e and h have been kept.   On many machines floating-point multiplication by 1.0 is exact; hence $e = 0$.   For such machines this test checks the accuracy of the computation $\exp[\ln(x)]$ in the case where little or no argument reduction is needed for either $\ln(x)$ or $\exp(w)$. Even when multiplication by 1.0 is not exact, however, the term $e∗\ln(x)$ is a small multiple of the basic rounding error of the machine, and E is still a valuable estimate of the error in $\exp[\ln(x)]$. For good implementations of the power function this test should therefore report accuracies only slightly less than machine precision. Ideally the MRE (see Chapter 3) should report a loss of one base-B digit or less, and the RMS should report a loss of a small fraction of a digit.   These expectations are illustrated by the results in Table 7.1. There is no error for the Argonne routine on the IBM 370 because that routine detects the case $y = 1$ and immediately returns x.

The second test measures the relative error in the identity

$$(x^2)∗∗(1.5) = x^3$$

for x again drawn from $[1/B,B]$.   In this case

$$E = [x^3 - (x^2)∗∗(1.5)] / x^3,$$

and $w = 1.5∗\ln(x^2)$.   In addition to the errors D, d, e and h previously defined, there is now a relative error g in squaring x.   Thus

$$E = [x^3(1+g) - x^2∗∗(1.5)(1+D)] / [x^3(1+g)].$$

Keeping only terms linear in g and D, this simplifies to

$$E = g - D.$$

TABLE 7.1

Typical Results for POWER Tests

Test	Machine	B	Library or Program	Reported Loss of Base-B Digits in	
				MRE	RMS
1	CDC 6400	2	Ours	0.37	0.00
	IBM/370	16	Ours	0.99	0.43
	CDC 7600	2	FTN 4.6	1.00	0.00
	IBM/370	16	Argonne	0.00	0.00
2	CDC 6400	2	Ours	0.99	0.00
	IBM/370	16	Ours	1.00	0.21
	CDC 7600	2	FTN 4.6	2.23	0.18
	IBM/370	16	Argonne	1.00	0.48
3	CDC 6400	2	Ours	1.00	0.00
	IBM/370	16	Ours	1.00	0.20
	CDC 7600	2	FTN 4.6	9.92	8.58
	IBM/370	16	Argonne	1.00	0.48
4	CDC 6400	2	Ours	4.21	1.59
	IBM/370	16	Ours	0.99	0.45
	CDC 7600	2	FTN 4.6	10.00	6.69
	IBM/370	16	Argonne	1.00	0.26

Because the absolute transmitted error in the logarithm is approximately given by the relative error in the argument, we have

$$D = 1.5(g + d) + e \cdot \ln(x) + h$$

and

$$E = -[g/2 + 1.5 \cdot d + e \cdot \ln(x) + h].$$

The main difference between this expression for E and the previous one is the term involving g. While this term is usually only a small contribution to E for this test, it is possible to "purify" the argument x to guarantee that $g = 0$. This is accomplished by perturbing the original random argument x to a nearby argument x' with sufficient trailing zero digits to protect the accuracy in the squaring process.

If SCALE = B⋅⋅[(t+1)/2], then the Fortran statements

        Y = X ⋅ SCALE

        X = (X + Y) - Y

purify x on all machines except those where the active arithmetic
registers carry more significance than the storage registers. It is
necessary to force the storage of intermediate results here and in other
more critical steps in the test program on such machines (see Gentleman
and Marovich [1974]).

Using purified arguments, this second identity test should return
MRE and RMS values similar to those predicted for the first test. The
main difference between these two tests is that this one forces a
non-trivial multiplication in forming w, thus checking to see if that
multiplication is done carefully. Assuming that the MRE for the first
test was non-zero, and in particular that the power function does not
make a special case of the computation when $y = 1.0$, differences between
the error statistics for the first two tests are probably due to
inaccuracies in that multiplication. The increased error reported in
Table 7.1 for the FTN 4.6 routine on the CDC 7600 is probably of this
nature.

The third test is identical to the second except that x is chosen
such that $1 \leq x^3 < XMAX$, where $XMAX$ is the largest machine-representable
floating-point number. This test differs from the previous two in
requiring significant argument reduction in the $\ln(x)$ and $\exp(w)$
computations. The exponent y is still relatively simple so the reported
MRE and RMS values for good implementations of the power function should
be similar to those predicted for the previous tests. Errors in the
multiplication to form w will dominate all other errors in this test and
larger than expected values of MRE and RMS probably mean a problem in
forming that product. If the multiplication is carefully done, then any
increased error is primarily due to the computation of $\ln(x)$ or $\exp(w)$
for large arguments. The results reported for this test in Table 7.1
are almost identical to those for previous tests except for the FTN 4.6
routine where the larger error strengthens our belief that the
multiplication to form w is done in working precision.

The final random argument accuracy test is the most demanding.   It checks the identity

$$(x^2)**(y/2) = x**y$$

by evaluating

$$E = [x**y - (x^2)**(y/2)] / x**y$$

for x drawn randomly from $[.01,10]$ and y drawn randomly from $[-C,C]$, where C is the largest floating-point number such that $x**C$ will neither underflow nor overflow for any of the selected x. At most the first two base-B digits of the exponent were non-zero in the previous tests (the case $y = 1.5$), but here all digits in y may be non-zero.   This test therefore requires more from the product to form w than the previous tests, in addition to requiring significant argument reduction in computing $\ln(x)$ and $\exp(w)$.

Let D be the relative error in producing $x**y$, and D' be the relative error in producing $(x^2)**(y/2)$.   Then the above expression for E becomes

$$E = [x**y(1+D) - x**Y(1+D')] / [x**y(1+D)]$$

$$= D - D',$$

where higher order terms in D and D' are neglected.   Define d, e, h and the corresponding primed quantities analogous to the previous definitions.   Let g' be the relative error in squaring x and c' be the relative error in evaluating $y/2$ given an exact y.   Then it is easily shown that

$$D = d + e \cdot \ln(x) + h$$

and

$$D' = (y/2)[g' + c' \cdot \ln(x^2)] + d' + e' \cdot \ln(x^2) + h'.$$

Because y can be large in magnitude, the small errors g' and c' can be magnified until they dominate the measured error.   Purification of x thus becomes important in this case, but it is equally important to purify y.   Given a random y, the following sequence of Fortran statements

        Y2 = Y / 2.0

        Y2 = (Y2 + Y) - Y

        Y = Y2 + Y2

produces a possibly perturbed value of y and a corresponding error-free value of $y/2$.   Again it is necessary to force the storage of intermediate results here on machines in which the active arithmetic registers carry more significance than the storage registers.

        Using purified arguments, both g' and c' vanish, and the above expression for D' becomes

        D' = d' + e'*ln(x²) + h'.

Unless higher precision arithmetic is used to evaluate $y \cdot \ln(x)$, e and e' will dominate E for sufficiently large y.   The algorithm we propose provides four extra bits for the product on binary machines,   for example, and e and e' then become important for $y > 16$ and $y > 32$, respectively.   In general the MRE value for even a good implementation of the power function will report the loss of about n base-B digits in this test, where n is the smallest integer such that $B**(n+m-1)$ bounds C and where there are m extra digits used in forming the product $y \cdot \ln(x)$. The RMS value should be much smaller,   but may still be larger than the error reported in the earlier tests.   The test results reported in Table 7.1 for our algorithm on the CDC 6400 illustrate this type of error.

```
C      PROGRAM TO TEST POWER FUNCTION (∗∗)
C
C      DATA REQUIRED
C
C         NONE
C
C      SUBPROGRAMS REQUIRED FROM THIS PACKAGE
C
C         MACHAR - AN ENVIRONMENTAL INQUIRY PROGRAM PROVIDING
C                  INFORMATION ON THE FLOATING-POINT ARITHMETIC
C                  SYSTEM.  NOTE THAT THE CALL TO MACHAR CAN
C                  BE DELETED PROVIDED THE FOLLOWING SIX
C                  PARAMETERS ARE ASSIGNED THE VALUES INDICATED
C
C                  IBETA  - THE RADIX OF THE FLOATING-POINT SYSTEM
C                  IT     - THE NUMBER OF BASE-IBETA DIGITS IN THE
C                           SIGNIFICAND OF A FLOATING-POINT NUMBER
C                  MINEXP - THE LARGEST IN MAGNITUDE NEGATIVE
C                           INTEGER SUCH THAT  FLOAT(IBETA)∗∗MINEXP
C                           IS A POSITIVE FLOATING-POINT NUMBER
C                  MAXEXP - THE LARGEST POSITIVE INTEGER EXPONENT
C                           FOR A FINITE FLOATING-POINT NUMBER
C                  XMIN   - THE SMALLEST NON-VANISHING FLOATING-POINT
C                           POWER OF THE RADIX
C                  XMAX   - THE LARGEST FINITE FLOATING-POINT
C                           NUMBER
C
C         RAN(K) - A FUNCTION SUBPROGRAM RETURNING RANDOM REAL
C                  NUMBERS UNIFORMLY DISTRIBUTED OVER (0,1)
C
C
C      STANDARD FORTRAN SUBPROGRAMS REQUIRED
C
C         ABS, ALOG, AMAX1, EXP, FLOAT, SQRT
C
C
C      LATEST REVISION - DECEMBER 6, 1979
C
C      AUTHOR - W. J. CODY
C               ARGONNE NATIONAL LABORATORY
C
C
       INTEGER I,IBETA,IEXP,IOUT,IRND,IT,I1,J,K1,K2,K3,MACHEP,
```

```
     1          MAXEXP,MINEXP,N,NEGEP,NGRD
     REAL A,AIT,ALBETA,B,BETA,C,DEL,DELY,EPS,EPSNEG,ONE,
     1     ONEP5,RAN,R6,R7,SCALE,TWO,W,X,XL,XMAX,XMIN,XN,
     2     XSQ,X1,Y,Y1,Y2,Z,ZERO,ZZ
C
     IOUT = 6
     CALL MACHAR(IBETA,IT,IRND,NGRD,MACHEP,NEGEP,IEXP,MINEXP,
     1            MAXEXP,EPS,EPSNEG,XMIN,XMAX)
     BETA = FLOAT(IBETA)
     ALBETA = ALOG(BETA)
     AIT = FLOAT(IT)
     ALXMAX = ALOG(XMAX)
     ZERO = 0.0E0
     ONE = FLOAT(1)
     TWO = ONE + ONE
     ONEP5 = (TWO + ONE) / TWO
     SCALE = ONE
     J = (IT+1) / 2
C
     DO 20 I = 1, J
        SCALE = SCALE * BETA
  20 CONTINUE
C
     A = ONE / BETA
     B = ONE
     C = -AMAX1(ALXMAX,-ALOG(XMIN))/ALOG(100E0)
     DELY = -C - C
     N = 2000
     XN = FLOAT(N)
     I1 = 0
     Y1 = ZERO
C-------------------------------------------------------------------
C    RANDOM ARGUMENT ACCURACY TESTS
C-------------------------------------------------------------------
     DO 300 J = 1, 4
        K1 = 0
        K3 = 0
        X1 = ZERO
        R6 = ZERO
        R7 = ZERO
        DEL = (B - A) / XN
        XL = A
C
```

```
          DO 200 I = 1, N
             X = DEL * RAN(I1) + XL
             IF (J .NE. 1) GO TO 50
             ZZ = X ** ONE
             Z = X
             GO TO 110
   50        W = SCALE * X
             X = (X + W) - W
             XSQ = X * X
             IF (J .EQ. 4) GO TO 70
             ZZ = XSQ ** ONEP5
             Z = X * XSQ
             GO TO 110
   70        Y = DELY * RAN(I1) + C
             Y2 = (Y/TWO + Y) - Y
             Y = Y2 + Y2
             Z = X ** Y
             ZZ = XSQ ** Y2
  110        W = ONE
             IF (Z .NE. ZERO) W = (Z - ZZ) / Z
             IF (W .GT. ZERO) K1 = K1 + 1
             IF (W .LT. ZERO) K3 = K3 + 1
             W = ABS(W)
             IF (W .LE. R6) GO TO 120
             R6 = W
             X1 = X
             IF (J .EQ. 4) Y1 = Y
  120        R7 = R7 + W * W
             XL = XL + DEL
  200     CONTINUE
C
          K2 = N - K3 - K1
          R7 = SQRT(R7/XN)
          IF (J .GT. 1) GO TO 210
          WRITE (IOUT,1000)
          WRITE (IOUT,1010) N,A,B
          WRITE (IOUT,1011) K1,K2,K3
          GO TO 220
  210     IF (J .EQ. 4) GO TO 215
          WRITE (IOUT,1001)
          WRITE (IOUT,1010) N,A,B
          WRITE (IOUT,1012) K1,K2,K3
          GO TO 220
```

```
  215     WRITE (IOUT,1002)
          W = C + DELY
          WRITE (IOUT,1014) N,A,B,C,W
          WRITE (IOUT,1013) K1,K2,K3
  220     WRITE (IOUT,1020) IT,IBETA
          W = -999.0E0
          IF (R6 .NE. ZERO) W = ALOG(ABS(R6))/ALBETA
          IF (J .NE. 4) WRITE (IOUT,1021) R6,IBETA,W,X1
          IF (J .EQ. 4) WRITE (IOUT,1024) R6,IBETA,W,X1,Y1
          W = AMAX1(AIT+W,ZERO)
          WRITE (IOUT,1022) IBETA,W
          W = -999.0E0
          IF (R7 .NE. ZERO) W = ALOG(ABS(R7))/ALBETA
          WRITE (IOUT,1023) R7,IBETA,W
          W = AMAX1(AIT+W,ZERO)
          WRITE (IOUT,1022) IBETA,W
          IF (J .EQ. 1) GO TO 300
          B = 10.0E0
          A = 0.01E0
          IF (J .EQ. 3) GO TO 300
          A = ONE
          B = EXP(ALXMAX/3.0E0)
  300 CONTINUE
C----------------------------------------------------------------
C     SPECIAL TESTS
C----------------------------------------------------------------
      WRITE (IOUT,1025)
      WRITE (IOUT,1030)
      B = 10.0E0
C
      DO 320 I = 1, 5
         X = RAN(I1) * B + ONE
         Y = RAN(I1) * B + ONE
         Z = X ** Y
         ZZ = (ONE/X) ** (-Y)
         W = (Z - ZZ) / Z
         WRITE (IOUT,1060) X, Y, W
  320 CONTINUE
C----------------------------------------------------------------
C     TEST OF ERROR RETURNS
C----------------------------------------------------------------
      WRITE (IOUT,1050)
      X = BETA
```

```
      Y = FLOAT(MINEXP)
      WRITE (IOUT,1051) X, Y
      Z = X ∗∗ Y
      WRITE (IOUT,1055) Z
      Y = FLOAT(MAXEXP-1)
      WRITE (IOUT,1051) X, Y
      Z = X ∗∗ Y
      WRITE (IOUT,1055) Z
      X = ZERO
      Y = TWO
      WRITE (IOUT,1051) X, Y
      Z = X ∗∗ Y
      WRITE (IOUT,1055) Z
      X = -Y
      Y = ZERO
      WRITE (IOUT,1052) X, Y
      Z = X ∗∗ Y
      WRITE (IOUT,1055) Z
      Y = TWO
      WRITE (IOUT,1052) X, Y
      Z = X ∗∗ Y
      WRITE (IOUT,1055) Z
      X = ZERO
      Y = ZERO
      WRITE (IOUT,1052) X, Y
      Z = X ∗∗ Y
      WRITE (IOUT,1055) Z
      WRITE (IOUT,1100)
      STOP
 1000 FORMAT(20H1TEST OF X∗∗1.0 VS X  //)
 1001 FORMAT(26H1TEST OF XSQ∗∗1.5 VS XSQ∗X  //)
 1002 FORMAT(27H1TEST OF X∗∗Y VS XSQ∗∗(Y/2)  //)
 1010 FORMAT(I7,47H RANDOM ARGUMENTS WERE TESTED FROM THE INTERVAL /
     1 6X,1H(,E15.4,1H,,E15.4,1H))//)
 1011 FORMAT(18H X∗∗1.0 WAS LARGER,I6,7H TIMES, /
     1     11X,7H AGREED,I6,11H TIMES, AND /
     2     7X,11HWAS SMALLER,I6,7H TIMES.//)
 1012 FORMAT(18H X∗∗1.5 WAS LARGER,I6,7H TIMES, /
     1     11X,7H AGREED,I6,11H TIMES, AND /
     2     7X,11HWAS SMALLER,I6,7H TIMES.//)
 1013 FORMAT(18H  X∗∗Y  WAS LARGER,I6,7H TIMES, /
     1     11X,7H AGREED,I6,11H TIMES, AND /
     2     7X,11HWAS SMALLER,I6,7H TIMES.//)
```

```
1014 FORMAT(I7,45H RANDOM ARGUMENTS WERE TESTED FROM THE REGION /
    1 6X,6HX IN (,E15.4,1H,,E15.4,9H), Y IN (,E15.4,1H,,E15.4,1H)//)
1020 FORMAT(10H THERE ARE,I4,5H BASE,I4,
    1    46H SIGNIFICANT DIGITS IN A FLOATING-POINT NUMBER  //)
1021 FORMAT(30H THE MAXIMUM RELATIVE ERROR OF,E15.4,3H = ,I4,3H **,
    1 F7.2/4X,16HOCCURRED FOR X =,E17.6)
1022 FORMAT(27H THE ESTIMATED LOSS OF BASE,I4,
    1 22H SIGNIFICANT DIGITS IS,F7.2//)
1023 FORMAT(40H THE ROOT MEAN SQUARE RELATIVE ERROR WAS,E15.4,
    1    3H = ,I4,3H **,F7.2)
1024 FORMAT(30H THE MAXIMUM RELATIVE ERROR OF,E15.4,3H = ,I4,3H **,
    1 F7.2/4X,16HOCCURRED FOR X =,E17.6,4H Y =,E17.6)
1025 FORMAT(14H1SPECIAL TESTS//)
1030 FORMAT(54H THE IDENTITY  X ** Y = (1/X) ** (-Y)  WILL BE TESTED.
    1   //8X,1HX,14X,1HY,9X,24H(X**Y-(1/X)**(-Y) / X**Y /)
1050 FORMAT(22H1TEST OF ERROR RETURNS//)
1051 FORMAT(2H (,E14.7,7H ) ** (,E14.7,20H ) WILL BE COMPUTED.,/
    1        41H THIS SHOULD NOT TRIGGER AN ERROR MESSAGE//)
1052 FORMAT(2H (,E14.7,7H ) ** (,E14.7,20H ) WILL BE COMPUTED.,/
    1        37H THIS SHOULD TRIGGER AN ERROR MESSAGE//)
1055 FORMAT(22H THE VALUE RETURNED IS,E15.4///)
1060 FORMAT(2E15.7,6X,E15.7/)
1100 FORMAT(25H THIS CONCLUDES THE TESTS )
C     ---------- LAST CARD OF POWER TEST PROGRAM ----------
      END
```

8. SIN/COS

a. General Discussion

Let $|X| = N*\text{pi}+f$, where $|f| \leq \text{pi}/2$. Then

$$\sin(X) = \text{sign}(X) * \sin(f) * (-1) ** N$$

and

$$\cos(X) = \sin(X+\text{pi}/2).$$

The computation of sin or cos thus involves three numerically distinct steps: the reduction of the given argument X to a related argument f, the evaluation of $\sin(f)$ over a small interval symmetric about the origin, and the reconstruction of the desired function value from these results. Sin(f) can be evaluated in a variety of ways.   Here we use a minimax polynomial approximation derived from one in the collection of Hart et al. [1968].

The accuracy of the function values depends critically upon the accuracy of the argument reduction. Under the assumption that X is free of rounding or other errors, there is a possibility of loss of significance in f unless the difference $|X|-N*\text{pi}$ is evaluated using extra precision. Higher precision floating-point arithmetic can be used on some machines. When this is not practical, the computation

$$f = [(X1-N*C1) + X2] - N*C2,$$

where $X1 + X2 = |X|$ and $C1 + C2$ represents pi to more than working precision, preserves significance in f even though several leading significant figures may be lost in the subtraction.   The protection afforded, however,   is limited to the number of extra digits in this representation of pi.   Should $|X|$ agree with an integer multiple of pi to more than this number of extra digits, the reduced argument f will lose a corresponding number of digits of precision. The precision also degenerates to that of the unaltered computation $|X| - N \cdot pi$ whenever $N \cdot C1$ cannot be represented *exactly* in the machine, e.g., when N becomes too large. Indeed, there will be a quantum drop in the precision of the function value as N passes this threshold. Note also that there is no way to compensate for inaccuracies in X.

For $|X|$ sufficiently large, $|X|$ and $N \cdot pi$ agree to full machine precision. In that extreme case there is no precision in $SIN(X)$ and an error condition exists. Clearly there is a general erosion of the precision of $SIN(X)$ for smaller $|X|$ despite the careful argument reduction just outlined. The algorithm presented here suggests an error return before the quantum loss in significance in f associated with the threshold on N mentioned above. This seems reasonable because the function is "grainy" for larger $|X|$; i.e., even the correct function values for neighboring floating-point arguments beyond this point probably disagree by more than half of the machine precision.

b.   Flow Chart for SIN(X)/COS(X)

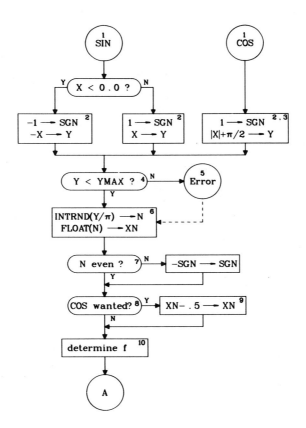

Note: Small integers indicate an implementation note.

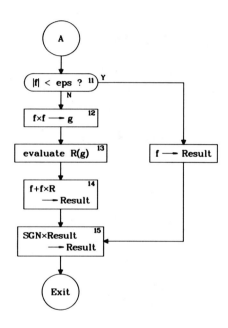

Note: Small integers indicate an implementation note.

c. Implementation Notes, Non-Decimal Fixed-Point Machines

1) These may be alternate entries to one subroutine or entries to two different subroutines if multiple entries are not supported. See Note 4.

2) Using *SGN* as a flag may be more efficient than assigning a floating-point value to it. See Note 15.

3) Use of $|X|$ here guarantees that the identity $COS(-X) = COS(X)$ will hold. Use the following constant to machine precision:

   pi/2 = 1.57079 63267 94896 61923

4) On machines that do not support multiple entry points, this is a natural point at which to begin a new subroutine. The parameters to be passed in that case are X, Y and *SGN*.

   The value of *YMAX* depends upon the number of bits b in the representation of the floating-point significand (see Glossary) and the number of bits in an integer. *YMAX* must satisfy the following conditions:

   a) $XN \cdot C1$ and $(XN-.5) \cdot C1$ (see Notes 9 and 10) must both be exactly representable for $Y < YMAX$;
   b) a rounding error in the last bit of Y should not lead to a relative error in $sin(Y)$ much greater in magnitude than $2 \cdot \cdot (b/2)$ for $Y < YMAX$; and
   c) N (see Notes 6 and 7) should be representable as an integer.

   A reasonable choice for *YMAX*, subject to condition (c), is the integer part of $pi \cdot 2 \cdot \cdot (b/2)$.

5) If execution is to continue rather than terminate, then a default function value should be provided in addition to an error message. Two possibilities exist: A default value of 0.0 can be returned (especially appropriate for extremely large arguments), or processing can continue normally, provided N is still representable as an integer. The latter alternative may produce a few significant figures in the function value if the argument is not too large in

magnitude, but returns essentially random results for very large
arguments. In either case the error message should be returned
first.

6) This rounds Y/pi to the nearest integer (see Chapter 2 for
definitions of INTRND and FLOAT). On some machines it may be more
efficient to form XN with AINTRND and then use INT to obtain N. To
avoid the expensive floating-point divide, form Y/pi by
multiplication with the stored constant $1/\text{pi}$. Use the following
value to machine precision:

$1/\text{pi} = 0.31830\ 98861\ 83790\ 67154.$

The computation of N may impose a restriction on $YMAX$ (see Note 4)
when there are fewer than b bits available for the representation of
an integer.

7) N is a positive integer. If machine instructions for testing
specific bits are available, then the parity of N can be determined
from its low-order bit; i.e., N is even if the bit is 0 and odd if
the bit is 1.

8) The condition 'COS wanted' is equivalent to the condition $|X| \neq Y$.

9) This is equivalent to adding pi/2 to X for the COS entry but leads
to greater accuracy in f when done at this point. Note that XN is
no longer integer.

10) We assume that the multiple-step argument reduction scheme is to be
used. On machines with a floating-point guard digit for addition
(see Glossary), the computation becomes

$f = (|X|-XN \cdot C1) - XN \cdot C2.$

Special care must be taken on machines that lack the guard digit, or
the argument reduction may lose significance for arguments slightly
less than an integer power of the radix B. Full precision is
retained on such machines with the computation

$f = [(X1-XN \cdot C1) + X2] - XN \cdot C2,$

where, in terms of our operations (see Chapter 2),

        X1 = AINT(|X|)
and
        X2 = |X| - X1.

Recall that b is the number of bits in the significand of a floating-point number. For $b \leq 32$ the constants

        C1 = 201/64
           = 3.11 (octal)
           = 3.140625 (decimal),
        C2 = 96765 35897 93 E-4

provide an extra 8 bits of precision in the argument reduction. For $b \geq 33$ the constants

        C1 = 3217/1024
           = 3.1104 (octal)
           = 3.14160 15625 (decimal),
        C2 = -8.9089 10206 76153 73566 17 E-6

provide an extra 12 bits of precision. *Exact* representation of $C1$ is crucial, but $C2$ need only be represented to the significance of the machine. At this point $|f| \leq$ pi/2.

11) Fixed-point underflow will not hurt here, but we want to be efficient. *Eps* should be chosen small enough that $\sin(f) = f$ to machine precision for $|f| < eps$, but large enough that the shorter computational path ordinarily will be followed whenever $r1 \cdot f^3$ would underflow (see Note 13). We suggest $eps = 2 \cdot \cdot (-b/2)$.

12) We convert to fixed point here, scaling as we go to avoid overflow. Let $h = FIX(f/2)$ (see Chapter 2), and form $g = h \cdot h$ in fixed point. Then

        $g = (f/2)^2 < pi^2/16 < .62.$

13) The following fixed-point polynomial approximations, $R(g)$, were derived from approximations in Hart et al. [1968]:

for $b \leq 24$

r1 = -0.66666 62674
r2 = 0.13332 84022
r3 = -0.01267 67480
r4 = 0.00066 60872

for $25 \leq b \leq 32$

r1 = -0.66666 66643 530
r2 = 0.13333 32915 289
r3 = -0.01269 81330 068
r4 = 0.00070 46136 593
r5 = -0.00002 44411 867

for $33 \leq b \leq 50$

r1 = -0.66666 66666 66638 613
r2 = 0.13333 33333 32414 742
r3 = -0.01269 84126 86862 404
r4 = 0.00070 54673 00385 092
r5 = -0.00002 56531 15784 674
r6 = 0.00000 06573 19716 142
r7 = -0.00000 00120 76093 891

for $51 \leq b \leq 60$

r1 = -0.66666 66666 66666 60209
r2 = 0.13333 33333 33330 64050
r3 = -0.01269 84126 98369 17789
r4 = 0.00070 54673 71779 91056
r5 = -0.00002 56533 57361 43317
r6 = 0.00000 06577 74038 64562
r7 = -0.00000 00125 22156 53481
r8 = 0.00000 00001 78289 31802

Evaluate $R(g) = g \cdot P(g)$,   where P is a polynomial, in fixed point using nested multiplication. For example, for $b \leq 24$,

R(g) = (((r4 • g + r3) • g + r2) • g + r1) • g.

14) We now convert back to floating point.   Let R = REFLOAT$[R(g)]$ (see Chapter 2),   and   form $f+f \cdot R$ in floating   point.   The algebraically equivalent form $f \cdot (1+R)$ may be less accurate and should be avoided.

15) Because floating-point multiplies are expensive,   the more efficient approach may be to use *SGN* earlier as a flag and to change the sign of *Result* here if the flag is set.

d. Implementation Notes, All Floating-Point Machines

1) These may be alternate entries to one subroutine, or entries to two different subroutines if multiple entries are not supported. See Note 4.

2) Assigning a floating-point value to *SGN* will probably be more efficient than using it as a flag. See Note 15.

3) Use of $|X|$ here guarantees that the identity $\cos(-X) = \cos(X)$ will hold. Use the following constant to machine precision:

   pi/2 = 1.57079 63267 94896 61923.

4) On machines that do not support multiple entry points, this is a natural point at which to begin a new routine. The parameters to be passed in that case are X, Y and *SGN*.

   The value of *YMAX* depends upon the number t of base B digits in the representation of the floating-point significand (see Glossary) and the number of digits in an integer. *YMAX* must satisfy the following conditions:

   a) $XN \cdot C1$ and $(XN-.5) \cdot C1$ (see Notes 9 and 10) must both be exactly representable for $Y < YMAX$;
   b) a rounding error in the last digit of Y should not lead to a relative error in $\sin(Y)$ much greater in magnitude than $B^{**}(t/2)$ for $Y < YMAX$;
   c) N (see Notes 6 and 7) should be representable as an integer.

   A reasonable choice for *YMAX*, subject to condition (c), is the integer part of $pi \cdot B^{**}(t/2)$.

5) If execution is to continue rather than terminate, then a default function value should be provided in addition to an error message. Two possibilities exist: A default value of 0.0 can be returned (especially appropriate for extremely large arguments), or processing can continue normally, provided N is still representable as an integer. The latter alternative may produce a few significant figures in the function value if the argument is not too large in

magnitude, but returns essentially random results for very large arguments. In either case the error message should be returned first.

6) This rounds Y/pi to the nearest integer (see Chapter 2 for definitions of INTRND and FLOAT). On some machines it may be more efficient to form XN with AINTRND and then use INT to obtain N. To avoid the floating-point divide, form Y/pi by multiplication with the stored constant 1/pi. Use the following value to machine precision:

　　　1/pi = 0.31830 98861 83790 67154.

The computation of N may impose a restriction on $YMAX$ (see Note 4) when there are fewer than t digits available for the representation of an integer.

7) N is a positive integer. If machine instructions for testing specific bits are available on non-decimal machines, then the parity of N can be determined from its low-order bit; i.e., N is even if the bit is 0 and odd if the bit is 1.

8) The condition 'COS wanted' is equivalent to the condition $|X| \neq Y$.

9) This is equivalent to adding pi/2 to X for the COS entry but leads to greater accuracy in f when done at this point. Note that XN is no longer integer.

10) If higher precision floating point is available and reasonably efficient, consider converting X and XN to the higher precision and using it to form

　　　$f = |X| - XN*pi$,

where

　　　pi = 3.14159 26535 89793 23846

is also given in the higher precision. Then convert f back to the working precision.

The multiple-step argument reduction scheme is used when the above scheme is impractical. On machines with a floating-point guard digit for addition (see Glossary), the computation becomes

$$f = (|X|-XN \cdot C1) - XN \cdot C2.$$

Special care must be taken on machines that lack the guard digit, or the argument reduction may lose significance for arguments slightly less than an integer power of the radix B. Full precision is retained on such machines with the computation

$$f = [(X1-XN \cdot C1) + X2] - XN \cdot C2,$$

where, in terms of our operations (see Chapter 2),

$$X1 = AINT(|X|)$$

and

$$X2 = |X| - X1.$$

Let b be the number of significant bits in the floating-point significand on a non-decimal machine. For $b \le 32$ the constants

$$C1 = 201/64$$
$$\quad = 3.11 \text{ (octal)}$$
$$\quad = 3.140625 \text{ (decimal)},$$
$$C2 = 9.6765\ 35897\ 93\ E-4.$$

provide an extra 8 bits of precision in the argument reduction. For $b \ge 33$ the constants

$$C1 = 3217/1024$$
$$\quad = 3.1104 \text{ (octal)}$$
$$\quad = 3.14160\ 15625 \text{ (decimal)},$$
$$C2 = -8.9089\ 10206\ 76153\ 73566\ 17\ E-6$$

provide an extra 12 bits of precision. On decimal machines $C1$ should be the first 3 or 4 significant decimal figures of pi, and $C2$ should be determined so that $C1 + C2$ represents pi to 3 or 4 decimal places beyond machine precision. *Exact* representation of $C1$ is crucial, but $C2$ need only be represented to the significance of the machine. At this point $|f| \le$ pi/2.

11) *Eps* should be chosen so that $\sin(f) = f$ to machine precision for $|f| < eps$, and so that $r1 \cdot f^3$ will not underflow for $|f| \geq eps$ (see Note 13). We suggest $eps = B**(-t/2)$.

12) There is no possibility of underflow or overflow at this point.

13) The following polynomial approximations, $R(g)$, were derived from approximations in Hart et al. [1968]. Let b be the number of bits in the significand of a floating-point number on a non-decimal machine, and d be the number of digits in the significand on a decimal machine. Then

for $b \leq 24$, or $d \leq 8$

$r1 = -0.16666\ 65668\ E+0$
$r2 = \ \ 0.83330\ 25139\ E-2$
$r3 = -0.19807\ 41872\ E-3$
$r4 = \ \ 0.26019\ 03036\ E-5$

for $25 \leq b \leq 32$, or
$9 \leq d \leq 10$

$r1 = -0.16666\ 66660\ 883\ E+0$
$r2 = \ \ 0.83333\ 30720\ 556\ E-2$
$r3 = -0.19840\ 83282\ 313\ E-3$
$r4 = \ \ 0.27523\ 97106\ 775\ E-5$
$r5 = -0.23868\ 34640\ 601\ E-7$

for $33 \leq b \leq 50$, or
$11 \leq d \leq 15$

$r1 = -0.16666\ 66666\ 66659\ 653\ E+0$
$r2 = \ \ 0.83333\ 33333\ 27592\ 139\ E-2$
$r3 = -0.19841\ 26982\ 32225\ 068\ E-3$
$r4 = \ \ 0.27557\ 31642\ 12926\ 457\ E-5$
$r5 = -0.25051\ 87088\ 34705\ 760\ E-7$
$r6 = \ \ 0.16047\ 84463\ 23816\ 900\ E-9$
$r7 = -0.73706\ 62775\ 07114\ 174\ E-12$

for $51 \leq b \leq 60$, or
$16 \leq d \leq 18$

$r1 = -0.16666\ 66666\ 66666\ 65052$ E+0
$r2 =\ \ \ 0.83333\ 33333\ 33316\ 50314$ E-2
$r3 = -0.19841\ 26984\ 12018\ 40457$ E-3
$r4 =\ \ \ 0.27557\ 31921\ 01527\ 56119$ E-5
$r5 = -0.25052\ 10679\ 82745\ 84544$ E-7
$r6 =\ \ \ 0.16058\ 93649\ 03715\ 89114$ E-9
$r7 = -0.76429\ 17806\ 89104\ 67734$ E-12
$r8 =\ \ \ 0.27204\ 79095\ 78888\ 46175$ E-14

Evaluate $R(g) = g{\cdot}P(g)$, where P is a polynomial, using nested multiplication. For example, for $b \leq 24$,

$$R(g) = (((r4\ \ast\ g + r3)\ \ast\ g + r2)\ \ast\ g + r1)\ \ast\ g.$$

14) The algebraically equivalent form $f{\cdot}(1+R)$ may be less accurate and should be avoided.

15) Multiplying by a floating-point value of *SGN* is probably more efficient than using *SGN* as a flag.

e. Testing

The tests are divided into four major parts. First is a random argument test to determine the accuracy of the basic computation, i.e., the evaluation of $\sin(x)$ where no argument reduction is needed. Second are similar tests of both $\sin(x)$ and $\cos(x)$ but using arguments which require that argument reduction be performed. Third is a series of short tests with special arguments. These include cursory checks of the three properties

$$\sin(-x) = -\sin(x),$$

$$\cos(-x) = \cos(x),$$

and

$$\sin(x) = x$$

to machine precision for $|x| \ll 1$. In addition, there is a check for underflow during the evaluation of $\sin(x)$ for very small x and a demonstration of the "granularity" of the function values for large x, that is, of the large changes induced in the function values by small changes in large arguments. Finally, there is a test for an error return when x is so large that there is no significance in the reduced argument f.

The random argument tests for $\sin(x)$ use the identity

$$\sin(x) = \sin(x/3)[3 - 4 \sin^2(x/3)].$$

It is important that the subtraction not introduce a loss in significance from cancellation of leading significant digits. This can be assured by proper selection of arguments. When x is drawn from the interval $[3m \cdot \mathrm{pi}, (3m+1/2) \cdot \mathrm{pi}]$, $x/3$ is in the interval $[m \cdot \mathrm{pi}, (m+1/6) \cdot \mathrm{pi}]$, $4 \sin^2(x/3) \leq 1$, and there is no cancellation. We henceforth assume these limitations on the arguments.

The tests measure the relative difference between the two sides of the identity. Thus we measure

$$E = \{\sin(x) - \sin(x/3)[3 - 4 \sin^2(x/3)]\} / \sin(x).$$

Assume for the moment that $|x| \leq$ pi/2.   Because x is a random argument manufactured in the machine, we can safely assume that it is error free. However, there may be an error e in evaluating $x/3$. Now

$$\sin(x/3 + e) = \sin(x/3) \cos(e) + \cos(x/3) \sin(e).$$

Noting that

$$\sin(e) = e$$

and

$$\cos(e) = 1$$

to machine precision for e small, and that

$$|\cos(x/3)| < 1,$$

we can estimate

$$\sin(x/3+e) = \sin(x/3) + e.$$

Assume that relative errors of D and d are made in the evaluations of $\sin(x)$ and $\sin(x/3)$, respectively.   Then

$$E = \frac{\sin(x)(1+D)-\sin(x/3+e)(1+d)[3-4 \sin^2(x/3+e)(1+d)^2]}{\sin(x) \ (1+D)}.$$

Using the identity and estimate for $\sin(x/3+e)$,   and keeping only terms linear in e, d and D, we can write

$$E = D - d[1-8 \frac{\sin^3(x/3)}{\sin(x)}] + e[\frac{1}{\sin(x/3)} - 8 \frac{\sin^2(x/3)}{\sin(x)}].$$

Because $\sin^3(x/3)/\sin(x)$ is bounded above by 1/8 for the interval under consideration,   the coefficient of d is crudely bounded between 0 and 1. However,   the coefficient of e is unbounded and could dominate the measured error, especially when x lies outside the primary interval.   It is therefore necessary to "purify" the test arguments to ensure that $e = 0$,   i.e.,   to perturb the original random argument x to a nearby x' such that both x' and $x'/3$ are *exactly* representable in the machine.

The following Fortran statements do the job on most computers:

    Y = X / 3.0E0

    Y = (Y + X) - X

    X = 3.0E0 * Y   .

The exceptions are those machines where the active arithmetic registers carry more significance than the storage registers. On such machines it is necessary to force the storage and retrieval of intermediate results (see Gentleman and Marovich [1974]).

If purified arguments are used, the error measured in our tests is given by

    E = D - c*d,

where $0 \leq c \leq 1$. Crude bounds indicate $0 \leq |E| \leq |D|+|d|$. In practice E turns out to be a reasonable estimate of D. The significant statistic obtained from the tests is MRE = $\max|E|$ (see Chapter 3). A large value of MRE indicates a large value of D and/or d. The converse is not necessarily true; there may be a cancellation of leading digits in forming E from D and d. Our experience has been that this first test reports accuracies only slightly less than machine precision for good implementations of the basic computation of $\sin(x)$ (see Table 8.1). Typically the MRE reports a loss of about $k+1$ bits of precision on machines with a radix of $B = 2^{**}k$, and a little over one digit on decimal machines. The tabulated loss of 1.18 digits on the IBM machine, for example, is a loss of between four and five bits, three of which are probably due to "wobbling precision" (see Glossary). The RMS typically reports a loss of a small fraction of a base-B digit.

Our second test draws x from [6*pi, 6.5*pi]. Assuming that the first test gave a small MRE, the MRE in the second test measures the accuracy of the argument reduction scheme. A good implementation should return MRE and RMS values comparable to those obtained in the first test. The large errors reported in Table 8.1 for the Varian 72, for example, probably indicate trouble in argument reduction. On the other hand, the unexpectedly large MRE reported for our program on the GP L3055 occurred for an argument which agreed with 6*pi to five decimal places. The extra precision in our multistep argument reduction was

TABLE 8.1

Typical Results for SIN/COS Tests

Test	Machine	B	Library or Program	Reported Loss of Base-B Digits in	
				MRE	RMS
1	CDC 6400	2	Ours	2.00	0.73
	GP L3055	10	Ours	1.07	0.51
	IBM/370	16	Ours	1.08	0.71
	PDP/11	2	DOS 8.02	1.99	0.10
	Varian 72	2	Fort E3	1.87	0.00
	IBM/370	16	Argonne	1.18	0.69
2	CDC 6400	2	Ours	2.20	0.80
	GP L3055	10	Ours	2.28	0.77
	IBM/370	16	Ours	1.16	0.72
	PDP/11	2	DOS 8.02	1.74	0.09
	Varian 72	2	Fort E3	13.54	8.55
	IBM/370	16	Argonne	1.16	0.70
3	CDC 6400	2	Ours	2.39	0.68
	GP L3055	10	Ours	1.38	0.58
	IBM/370	16	Ours	1.11	0.70
	PDP/11	2	DOS 8.02	12.63	7.66
	Varian 72	2	Fort E3	12.69	7.31
	IBM/370	16	Argonne	1.16	0.69

insufficient to protect the precision of the reduced argument in this case. Note that the corresponding RMS value is reassurance that a programming error has not occurred and that the large MRE is an isolated occurrence.

The third test checks the accuracy of $\cos(x)$ with the identity

$$\cos(x) = \cos(x/3)[4 \cos^2(x/3) - 3].$$

Analysis similar to that for $\sin(x)$ shows that x should be drawn from the interval $[(3m+1) \cdot pi, (3m+3/2) \cdot pi]$ to preserve significance in the right-hand side. (Our test uses $m=2$.) Similarly, when the arguments are purified, the error measured is

$$E = D - c \cdot d,$$

where E, D and d are defined analogously to the $\sin(x)$ case and where $0 \leq c \leq 2$. A good implementation should again return MRE and RMS values comparable to those of the first test (see Table 8.1). Errors significantly larger than those reported for the previous test are usually due to carelessness in adjusting the argument by pi/2 for the COS entry. The results reported in Table 8.1 for the program on the PDP/11, for example, suggest that the argument reduction has been carefully done for the SIN entry, but not for the COS entry.

The above tests do not detect gross errors in the period of the function because the identities used are also satisfied by $\sin(kx)$ for arbitrary k. Our test program verifies that $k=1$ by making a finite difference approximation to the derivative near $x = 6 \cdot pi$.

```
C     PROGRAM TO TEST SIN/COS
C
C     DATA REQUIRED
C
C         NONE
C
C     SUBPROGRAMS REQUIRED FROM THIS PACKAGE
C
C         MACHAR - AN ENVIRONMENTAL INQUIRY PROGRAM PROVIDING
C                  INFORMATION ON THE FLOATING-POINT ARITHMETIC
C                  SYSTEM.  NOTE THAT THE CALL TO MACHAR CAN
C                  BE DELETED PROVIDED THE FOLLOWING FIVE
C                  PARAMETERS ARE ASSIGNED THE VALUES INDICATED
C
C                  IBETA  - THE RADIX OF THE FLOATING-POINT SYSTEM
C                  IT     - THE NUMBER OF BASE-IBETA DIGITS IN THE
C                           SIGNIFICAND OF A FLOATING-POINT NUMBER
C                  MINEXP - THE LARGEST IN MAGNITUDE NEGATIVE
C                           INTEGER SUCH THAT  FLOAT(IBETA)**MINEXP
C                           IS A POSITIVE FLOATING-POINT NUMBER
C                  EPS    - THE SMALLEST POSITIVE FLOATING-POINT
C                           NUMBER SUCH THAT 1.0+EPS .NE. 1.0
C                  EPSNEG - THE SMALLEST POSITIVE FLOATING-POINT
C                           NUMBER SUCH THAT 1.0-EPSNEG .NE. 1.0
C
C         RAN(K) - A FUNCTION SUBPROGRAM RETURNING RANDOM REAL
C                  NUMBERS UNIFORMLY DISTRIBUTED OVER (0,1)
C
C
C     STANDARD FORTRAN SUBPROGRAMS REQUIRED
C
C         ABS, ALOG, AMAX1, COS, FLOAT, SIN, SQRT
C
C
C     LATEST REVISION - DECEMBER 6, 1979
C
C     AUTHOR - W. J. CODY
C              ARGONNE NATIONAL LABORATORY
C
C
      INTEGER I,IBETA,IEXP,IOUT,IRND,IT,I1,J,K1,K2,K3,MACHEP,
     1        MAXEXP,MINEXP,N,NEGEP,NGRD
```

```
      REAL  A,AIT,ALBETA,B,BETA,BETAP,C,DEL,EPS,EPSNEG,EXPON,ONE,RAN,
     1      R6,R7,THREE,W,X,XL,XMAX,XMIN,XN,X1,Y,Z,ZERO,ZZ
C
      IOUT = 6
      CALL MACHAR(IBETA,IT,IRND,NGRD,MACHEP,NEGEP,IEXP,MINEXP,
     1            MAXEXP,EPS,EPSNEG,XMIN,XMAX)
      BETA = FLOAT(IBETA)
      ALBETA = ALOG(BETA)
      AIT = FLOAT(IT)
      ONE = 1.0E0
      ZERO = 0.0E0
      THREE = 3.0E0
      A = ZERO
      B = 1.570796327E0
      C = B
      N = 2000
      XN = FLOAT(N)
      I1 = 0
C---------------------------------------------------------------
C     RANDOM ARGUMENT ACCURACY TESTS
C---------------------------------------------------------------
      DO 300 J = 1, 3
         K1 = 0
         K3 = 0
         X1 = ZERO
         R6 = ZERO
         R7 = ZERO
         DEL = (B - A) / XN
         XL = A
C
         DO 200 I = 1, N
            X = DEL * RAN(I1) + XL
            Y = X / THREE
            Y = (X + Y) - X
            X = THREE * Y
            IF (J .EQ. 3) GO TO 100
            Z = SIN(X)
            ZZ = SIN(Y)
            W = ONE
            IF (Z .NE. ZERO) W = (Z - ZZ*(THREE-4.0E0*ZZ*ZZ)) / Z
            GO TO 110
  100       Z = COS(X)
            ZZ = COS(Y)
```

```
              W = ONE
              IF (Z .NE. ZERO) W = (Z + ZZ*(THREE-4.0E0*ZZ*ZZ)) / Z
  110         IF (W .GT. ZERO) K1 = K1 + 1
              IF (W .LT. ZERO) K3 = K3 + 1
              W = ABS(W)
              IF (W .LE. R6) GO TO 120
              R6 = W
              X1 = X
  120         R7 = R7 + W * W
              XL = XL + DEL
  200     CONTINUE
C
          K2 = N - K3 - K1
          R7 = SQRT(R7/XN)
          IF (J .EQ. 3) GO TO 210
          WRITE (IOUT,1000)
          WRITE (IOUT,1010) N,A,B
          WRITE (IOUT,1011) K1,K2,K3
          GO TO 220
  210     WRITE (IOUT,1005)
          WRITE (IOUT,1010) N,A,B
          WRITE (IOUT,1012) K1,K2,K3
  220     WRITE (IOUT,1020) IT,IBETA
          W = -999.0E0
          IF (R6 .NE. ZERO) W = ALOG(ABS(R6))/ALBETA
          WRITE (IOUT,1021) R6,IBETA,W,X1
          W = AMAX1(AIT+W,ZERO)
          WRITE (IOUT,1022) IBETA,W
          W = -999.0E0
          IF (R7 .NE. ZERO) W = ALOG(ABS(R7))/ALBETA
          WRITE (IOUT,1023) R7,IBETA,W
          W = AMAX1(AIT+W,ZERO)
          WRITE (IOUT,1022) IBETA,W
          A = 18.84955592E0
          IF (J .EQ. 2) A = B + C
          B = A + C
  300 CONTINUE
C------------------------------------------------------------------
C     SPECIAL TESTS
C------------------------------------------------------------------
      WRITE (IOUT,1025)
      C = ONE / BETA ** (IT/2)
      Z = (SIN(A+C) - SIN(A-C)) / (C + C)
```

```
      WRITE (IOUT,1026) Z
C
      WRITE (IOUT,1030)
C
      DO 320 I = 1, 5
         X = RAN(I1) * A
         Z = SIN(X) + SIN(-X)
         WRITE (IOUT,1060) X, Z
  320 CONTINUE
C
      WRITE (IOUT,1031)
      BETAP = BETA ** IT
      X = RAN(I1) / BETAP
C
      DO 330 I = 1, 5
         Z = X - SIN(X)
         WRITE (IOUT,1060) X, Z
         X = X / BETA
  330 CONTINUE
C
      WRITE (IOUT,1032)
C
      DO 340 I = 1, 5
         X = RAN(I1) * A
         Z = COS(X) - COS(-X)
         WRITE (IOUT,1060) X, Z
  340 CONTINUE
C
      WRITE (IOUT,1035)
      EXPON = FLOAT(MINEXP) * 0.75E0
      X = BETA ** EXPON
      Y = SIN(X)
      WRITE (IOUT,1061) X, Y
      WRITE (IOUT,1040)
      Z = SQRT(BETAP)
      X = Z * (ONE - EPSNEG)
      Y = SIN(X)
      WRITE (IOUT,1061) X, Y
      Y = SIN(Z)
      WRITE (IOUT,1061) Z, Y
      X = Z * (ONE + EPS)
      Y = SIN(X)
      WRITE (IOUT,1061) X, Y
```

```
C-------------------------------------------------------------------
C      TEST OF ERROR RETURNS
C-------------------------------------------------------------------
       WRITE (IOUT,1050)
       X = BETAP
       WRITE (IOUT,1052) X
       Y = SIN(X)
       WRITE (IOUT,1055) Y
       WRITE (IOUT,1100)
       STOP
 1000 FORMAT(43H1TEST OF SIN(X) VS 3*SIN(X/3)-4*SIN(X/3)**3  //)
 1005 FORMAT(43H1TEST OF COS(X) VS 4*COS(X/3)**3-3*COS(X/3)  //)
 1010 FORMAT(I7,47H RANDOM ARGUMENTS WERE TESTED FROM THE INTERVAL /
      1 6X,1H(,E15.4,1H,,E15.4,1H)//)
 1011 FORMAT(18H SIN(X) WAS LARGER,I6,7H TIMES, /
      1     11X,7H AGREED,I6,11H TIMES, AND /
      1    7X,11HWAS SMALLER,I6,7H TIMES.//)
 1012 FORMAT(18H COS(X) WAS LARGER,I6,7H TIMES, /
      1     11X,7H AGREED,I6,11H TIMES, AND /
      1    7X,11HWAS SMALLER,I6,7H TIMES.//)
 1020 FORMAT(10H THERE ARE,I4,5H BASE,I4,
      1     46H SIGNIFICANT DIGITS IN A FLOATING-POINT NUMBER  //)
 1021 FORMAT(30H THE MAXIMUM RELATIVE ERROR OF,E15.4,3H = ,I4,3H **,
      1 F7.2/4X,16HOCCURRED FOR X =,E17.6)
 1022 FORMAT(27H THE ESTIMATED LOSS OF BASE,I4,
      1 22H SIGNIFICANT DIGITS IS,F7.2//)
 1023 FORMAT(40H THE ROOT MEAN SQUARE RELATIVE ERROR WAS,E15.4,
      1    3H = ,I4,3H **,F7.2)
 1025 FORMAT(14H1SPECIAL TESTS//)
 1026 FORMAT(4H IF ,E13.6,21H IS NOT ALMOST 1.0E0,,
      1    4X,25HSIN HAS THE WRONG PERIOD.  //)
 1030 FORMAT(51H THE IDENTITY   SIN(-X) = -SIN(X)   WILL BE TESTED.//
      1     8X,1HX,9X,12HF(X) + F(-X)/)
 1031 FORMAT(51H THE IDENTITY SIN(X) = X , X SMALL, WILL BE TESTED.//
      1     8X,1HX,9X,8HX - F(X)/)
 1032 FORMAT(50H THE IDENTITY   COS(-X) = COS(X)   WILL BE TESTED.//
      1     8X,1HX,9X,12HF(X) - F(-X)/)
 1035 FORMAT(43H TEST OF UNDERFLOW FOR VERY SMALL ARGUMENT.)
 1040 FORMAT(49H THE FOLLOWING THREE LINES ILLUSTRATE THE LOSS IN,
      1 13H SIGNIFICANCE/36H FOR LARGE ARGUMENTS.  THE ARGUMENTS,
      2 17H ARE CONSECUTIVE.)
 1050 FORMAT(22H1TEST OF ERROR RETURNS//)
 1052 FORMAT(37H SIN WILL BE CALLED WITH THE ARGUMENT,E15.4/
```

```
      1        37H THIS SHOULD TRIGGER AN ERROR MESSAGE//)
 1055 FORMAT(23H SIN RETURNED THE VALUE,E15.4///)
 1060 FORMAT(2E15.7/)
 1061 FORMAT(/6X,5H SIN(,E13.6,3H) =,E13.6)
 1100 FORMAT(25H THIS CONCLUDES THE TESTS )
C     ---------- LAST CARD OF SIN/COS TEST PROGRAM ----------
      END
```

9. TAN/COTAN

a. General Discussion

Let $X = N \cdot (\text{pi}/2) + f$, where $|f| \leq \text{pi}/4$. Then

$$\tan(X) = \tan(f), \quad N \text{ even,}$$

$$= -1/\tan(f), \quad N \text{ odd,}$$

and

$$\cotan(X) = 1/\tan(X).$$

The computation of $\tan(X)$ or $\cotan(X)$ thus involves three numerically distinct steps: the reduction of the given argument X to a related argument f, the evaluation of $\tan(f)$ over a small interval symmetric about the origin, and the reconstruction of the desired function from these results. The calculation of $\tan(f)$ can be accomplished in a number of different ways. Here we use a minimax polynomial approximation derived especially for this work.

The tangent and cotangent functions are very sensitive to small errors in the argument over most of their domain. If

$$y = \tan(X),$$

then

$$dy/y = 2X \csc(2X) \, dX/X,$$

and the relative error in $\tan(X)$ is approximately the relative error in the argument magnified by $M(X) = 2X \csc(2X)$. Because $M(X)$ is large in magnitude for X close to half integer multiples of pi, $\tan(X)$ is sensitive to small argument errors near its zeros and singularities. The same analysis holds for the cotangent function except that $M(X)$ changes sign.

Assuming that X is exact, the critical step in this computation is the argument reduction. X and $N \cdot (pi/2)$ agree to the first few significant digits as X becomes larger in magnitude. Unless the difference $X - N \cdot (pi/2)$ is evaluated using extra precision, the loss of leading digits through subtraction will introduce inaccurate low-order digits in f which will propagate as if they were errors in the original argument X. Higher precision floating point provides the extra precision for this computation on some machines, but usually a pseudo extended-precision computation must be used. The computation

$$f = [(X1 - N \cdot C1) + X2] - N \cdot C2,$$

where $X1 + X2 = X$ and $C1 + C2$ represents pi/2 to more than working precision, preserves significance in f most of the time. Error will be introduced into f only when the number of digits lost in the subtraction exceeds the number of extra digits in the representation of pi/2, or when N becomes so large that $N \cdot C1$ cannot be represented *exactly* in the machine. In the first case the error is introduced gradually. The number of erroneous low-order digits of f roughly agrees with the excess loss of digits in the subtraction. In the second case the loss is abrupt and large. As N passes the threshold where $N \cdot C1$ is no longer exact, the computation reduces essentially to that of $X - N \cdot (pi/2)$, and the number of erroneous low-order digits in f suddenly agrees with the number of digits lost in the subtraction.

For $|X|$ sufficiently large, X and $N \cdot (pi/2)$ agree to full machine precision. In that extreme case there is no precision in TAN(X), and an error condition exists. We have just seen that there is a general loss of precision in TAN(X) for smaller $|X|$ despite careful argument reduction. The algorithm presented here suggests an error return before the quantum loss in significance in f associated with the threshold on N mentioned above. This is a reasonable action because the function is "grainy" for larger $|X|$; i.e., even the correct function values for neighboring floating-point arguments beyond this point probably agree to less than half of the machine precision.

b. Flow Chart for TAN(X)/COTAN(X)

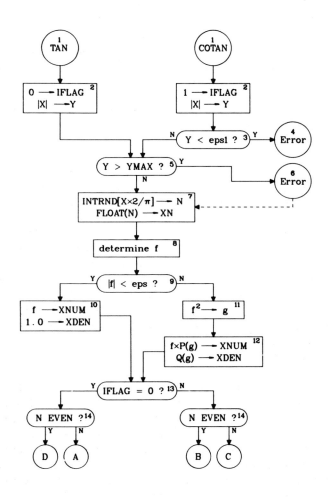

Note: Small integers indicate an implementation note.

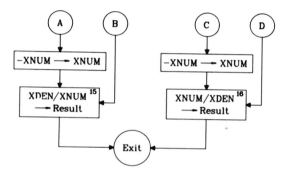

Note: Small integers indicate an implementation note.

c. Implementation Notes, Non-Decimal Fixed-Point Machines

1) These may be alternate entries to one subroutine if multiple entries are supported. Otherwise TAN and COTAN must be separate subroutines. They can either be written as self-contained subroutines by following the obvious paths in the flow chart and ignoring those operations involving *IFLAG* (see Notes 2 and 13), or they can each pass the parameters X, Y and *IFLAG* to a separate computational subroutine starting at the test against *YMAX* (see Note 5).

2) *IFLAG* need not be set if TAN and COTAN are each self-contained subroutines (see Note 1).

3) *Eps*1 should be the smallest positive floating-point number such that both *eps*1 and *-eps*1 can be reciprocated without causing an arithmetic exception.

4) If execution is to continue rather than terminate, then a default function value of ±*XMAX* should be provided in addition to an error message. Here *XMAX* is the largest positive floating-point number on the machine, and the algebraic sign should agree with that of X (we suggest a "+" sign when X is 0).

5) On machines that do not support multiple entry points this is a natural point at which to begin a new subroutine callable by TAN and COTAN (see Note 1). The parameters to be passed in that case are X, Y and *IFLAG*.

   The value of *YMAX* depends upon the number t of base-B digits in the representation of the floating-point significand (see Glossary) and the number of digits in an integer. *YMAX* must satisfy the following conditions:

   a) $XN \cdot C1$ (see Notes 7 and 8) must be exactly representable in the machine for $Y < YMAX$;
   b) N should be representable as an integer.

   A reasonable choice for *YMAX*, subject to condition (b), is the integer part of $B ** (t/2) \cdot pi/2$.

6) If execution is to continue rather than terminate, then a default function value should be provided in addition to an error message. Two possibilities exist. Either a value of 0.0 can be returned (especially appropriate for arguments that are extremely large in magnitude), or processing can continue normally, provided N is still representable as an integer. The latter alternative may return a few significant figures in the function value if the argument is not too large in magnitude, but returns essentially random numbers for large arguments. In either case an error message should be returned first.

7) See Chapter 2 for definitions of INTRND and FLOAT. On some machines it may be more efficient to form XN first using AINTRND, and then to obtain N using INT. Use the following constant to machine precision:

$$2/\text{pi} = 0.63661\ 97723\ 67581\ 34308$$

8) We assume that a multiple-step argument reduction scheme is to be used instead of higher precision floating point. On machines with a floating-point guard digit for addition (see Glossary) this computation becomes

$$f = (X-XN*C1)-XN*C2.$$

Otherwise, protect against loss of significance for arguments slightly less than an integer power of the radix B with

$$f = [(X1-XN*C1) + X2] - XN*C2,$$

where, in terms of our operations (see Chapter 2),

$$X1 = AINT(X)$$
and
$$X2 = X - X1.$$

Let b be the number of significant bits in the floating-point significand. For $b \leq 32$, the constants

$$
\begin{aligned}
C1 &= 201/128 \\
   &= 1.444 \quad \text{(octal)} \\
   &= 1.5703\ 125 \text{ (decimal)}
\end{aligned}
$$

and

C2 = 4.8382 67948 97 E-4

provide eight extra bits of precision in the argument reduction.
For $b > 32$, the constants

C1 = 3217/2048
   = 1.4442   (octal)
   = 1.57080 07812 5 (decimal)

and

C2 = -4.4544 55103 38076 86783 08 E-6

provide twelve bits of extra precision. *Exact* representation of C1
is crucial, but C2 need be represented only to the significance of
the machine. At this point $|f| \leq \text{pi}/4$.

9) Fixed-point underflow will not hurt in what follows, but for
   efficiency *eps* should be chosen so that $\tan(f) = f$ to machine
   precision for $|f| < eps$. We suggest $eps = B**(-t/2)$.

10) Store f as a floating-point number and ignore *XDEN* (see Notes 15 and
    16).

11) Set $h = \text{FIX}(f)$ (see Chapter 2), and evaluate $g = h \cdot h$ in fixed point.
    We assume there are more than b bits available for the
    representation of fixed-point numbers. There is no possibility of
    underflow or overflow at this point if *eps* is chosen as suggested.

12) The following rational approximations were derived especially for
    this work. Let b be the number of bits in the significand of a
    floating-point number. Then

             for b $\leq$ 22

         p1 =   0.16666 75142
         p2 = -0.00083 48534
         q0 =   0.50000 00000
         q1 = -0.20248 56694

for $23 \leq b \leq 32$

p1 =   0.16666 66658 406
p2 = -0.00744 91186 974
q0 =   0.50000 00000 000
q1 = -0.22234 73860 140
q2 =   0.00798 66960 665

for $33 \leq b \leq 52$

p1 =   0.16666 66666 66665 2540
p2 = -0.01026 94672 90449 3698
p3 =   0.00010 04822 04626 8875
q0 =   0.50000 00000 00000 0000
q1 = -0.23080 84018 71452 4420
q2 =   0.01167 24264 11034 3640
q3 = -0.00010 42240 22110 1935

We modify the flow chart at this point.   Ignore *XDEN* (see Notes 15 and 16), and evaluate $R = h \cdot P(g)/Q(g)$ using nested multiplication and fixed-point arithmetic. For example, for $25 \leq b \leq 32$,

$$h \cdot P(g) = (p2 \cdot g + p1) \cdot g \cdot h$$

and

$$Q(g) = (q2 \cdot g + q1) \cdot g + q0$$

Finally, set *XNUM* = REFLOAT(R)+f (see Chapter 2), where the final addition is done in floating point. This strategy minimizes the number of floating-point operations while retaining maximum significance for small $|f|$. Although this strategy does not specifically attempt to counteract the effects of wobbling precision (see Glossary) on non-binary machines when *XNUM* must be reciprocated (see Note 15), the statistical distribution of computational error in this scheme is comparable to that in the floating-point algorithm that follows.

13) This test may be ignored if TAN and COTAN are separate, self-contained subroutines (see Note 1).

14) When instructions are available for testing specific bits in an integer,   the parity of N can be determined from its integer representation.   On machines with either sign-magnitude or 2's

complement representation, the low-order bit is 0 for even numbers
and 1 for odd numbers. On machines with 1's complement
representation, the sign and low-order bits agree for even numbers
and disagree for odd numbers.

15) Set *Result* = 1.0/*XNUM* (see Notes 10 and 12).

16) Set *Result* = *XNUM* (see Notes 10 and 12).

d. Implementation Notes, All Floating-Point Machines

1) These may be alternate entries to one subroutine if multiple entries are supported. Otherwise TAN and COTAN must be separate subroutines. They can either be written as self-contained subroutines by following the obvious paths in the flow chart and ignoring those operations involving *IFLAG* (see Notes 2 and 13), or they can each pass the parameters X, Y and *IFLAG* to a separate computational subroutine starting at the test against *YMAX* (see Note 5).

2) *IFLAG* need not be set if TAN and COTAN are each self-contained subroutines (see Note 1).

3) *Eps*1 should be the smallest positive floating-point number such that both *eps*1 and *-eps*1 can be reciprocated without causing an arithmetic exception.

4) If execution is to continue rather than terminate, then a default function value of ±*XMAX* should be provided in addition to an error message. Here *XMAX* is the largest positive floating-point number on the machine, and the algebraic sign should agree with that of X (we suggest a "+" sign when X is 0).

5) On machines that do not support multiple entry points this is a natural point at which to begin a new subroutine callable by TAN and COTAN (see Note 1). The parameters to be passed in that case are X, Y and *IFLAG*.

The value of *YMAX* depends upon the number t of base-B digits in the representation of the floating-point significand (see Glossary) and the number of digits in an integer. *YMAX* must satisfy the following conditions:

a) $XN \cdot C1$ (see Notes 7 and 8) must be exactly representable in the machine for $Y < YMAX$;
b) N should be representable as an integer.

A reasonable choice for *YMAX*, subject to condition (b), is the integer part of $B**(t/2) \cdot pi/2$.

6) If execution is to continue rather than terminate, then a default function value should be provided in addition to an error message. Two possibilities exist. Either a value of 0.0 can be returned (especially appropriate for arguments that are extremely large in magnitude), or processing can continue normally, provided N is still representable as an integer. The latter alternative may return a few significant figures in the function value if the argument is not too large in magnitude, but returns essentially random numbers for large arguments. In either case an error message should be returned first.

7) See Chapter 2 for definitions of INTRND and FLOAT. On some machines it may be more efficient to form XN first using AINTRND, and then to obtain N using INT. Use the following constant to machine precision:

    2/pi = 0.63661 97723 67581 34308

8) If higher precision floating point is available and reasonably efficient, consider converting X and XN to the higher precision and using it to form

    f = X - XN*(pi/2),
where
    pi/2 = 1.57079 63267 94896 61923 132

is also given in the higher precision. Finally, convert f back to the working precision.

A multiple-step argument reduction must be used when the above scheme is impractical. On machines with a floating-point guard digit for addition (see Glossary) this computation becomes

    f = (X-XN*C1)-XN*C2.

Otherwise, protect against loss of significance for arguments slightly less than an integer power of the radix B with

    f = [(X1-XN*C1) + X2] - XN*C2,

where, in terms of our operations (see Chapter 2),

            X1 = AINT(X)
    and
            X2 = X - X1.

On a non-decimal machine let b be the number of significant bits in
the floating-point significand. For $b \leq 32$ the constants

        C1 = 201/128
           = 1.444   (octal)
           = 1.5703 125 (decimal)
    and
        C2 = 4.8382 67948 97 E-4

provide eight extra bits of precision in the   argument reduction.
For $b > 32$ the constants

        C1 = 3217/2048
           = 1.4442   (octal)
           = 1.57080 07812 5 (decimal)
    and
        C2 = -4.4544 55103 38076 86783 08 E-6

provide twelve bits of extra precision.

On decimal machines C1 should be the first 3 or 4 significant
decimal figures of pi/2, and C2 should be determined so that C1 + C2
represents pi/2 to 3 or 4 decimal places beyond machine precision.
Exact representation of C1 is crucial, but C2 need be represented
only to the significance of the machine. At this point $|f| \leq$ pi/4.

9) *Eps* should be chosen so that tan(f) = f to machine precision for
   $|f| <$ *eps*, and so that $p1 \cdot f^3$ (see Note 11) will not underflow for
   $|f| \geq$ *eps*. We suggest *eps* = $B**(-t/2)$.

10) No special comment for floating point.

11) There is no possibility of underflow or overflow at this point.

12) The following rational approximations $f \cdot R(g)$ were derived especially
    for this work.   Let b be the number of bits in the significand of a
    floating-point number on a non-decimal machine, and d be the number
    of decimal digits in the significand on a decimal machine. Then

for $b \leq 24$, or $d \leq 7$

p0 =   0.10000 0000 E+1
p1 = -0.95801 7723 E-1
q0 =   0.10000 0000 E+1
q1 = -0.42913 5777 E+0
q2 =   0.97168 5835 E-2

for $25 \leq b \leq 32$, or
$8 \leq d \leq 10$

p0 =   0.10000 00000 000 E+1
p1 = -0.11136 14403 566 E+0
p2 =   0.10751 54738 488 E-2
q0 =   0.10000 00000 000 E+1
q1 = -0.44469 47720 281 E+0
q2 =   0.15973 39213 300 E-1

for $33 \leq b \leq 52$, or
$11 \leq d \leq 16$

p0 =   0.10000 00000 00000 0000 E+1
p1 = -0.12828 34704 09574 3847 E+0
p2 =   0.28059 18241 16998 8906 E-2
p3 = -0.74836 34966 61206 5149 E-5
q0 =   0.10000 00000 00000 0000 E+1
q1 = -0.46161 68037 42904 8840 E+0
q2 =   0.23344 85282 20687 2802 E-1
q3 = -0.20844 80442 20387 0948 E-3

for $53 \leq b \leq 60$, or
$17 \leq d \leq 18$

p0 =   0.10000 00000 00000 00000 E+1
p1 = -0.13338 35000 64219 60681 E+0
p2 =   0.34248 87823 58905 89960 E-2
p3 = -0.17861 70734 22544 26711 E-4
q0 =   0.10000 00000 00000 00000 E+1
q1 = -0.46671 68333 97552 94240 E+0
q2 =   0.25663 83228 94401 12864 E-1
q3 = -0.31181 53190 70100 27307 E-3
q4 =   0.49819 43399 37865 12270 E-6

Form $f \cdot P(g)$ and $Q(g)$ using nested multiplication.   For example, for $25 \leq b \leq 32$,

$$f \cdot P(g) = (p2 \cdot g + p1) \cdot g \cdot f + f$$

and

$$Q(g) = (q2 \cdot g + q1) \cdot g + q0$$

Note that avoiding the explicit multiplication of f by $p0 = 1.0$ preserves accuracy in the evaluation of $f \cdot P(g)$. Similarly, on machines lacking a guard digit for floating-point addition (see Glossary), up to one base-B digit of precision can be saved in the final function value by replacing the addition of $q0 = 1.0$ in the evaluation of $Q(g)$ with successive additions of 0.5.

13) This test may be ignored if TAN and COTAN are separate self-contained subroutines (see Note 1).

14) When instructions are available on non-decimal machines for testing specific bits in an integer, the parity of N can be determined from its integer representation. On machines with either sign-magnitude or 2's complement representation, the low-order bit is 0 for even numbers and 1 for odd numbers. On machines with 1's complement representation, the sign and low-order bits agree for even numbers and disagree for odd numbers.

15) No special comment for floating point.

16) No special comment for floating point.

e. Testing

The test program for TAN/COTAN may require modification before it can be used to test existing libraries supplied with standard Fortran compilers. The problem arises because the 1966 Fortran standard (ANSI [1966]) did not include either TAN or COTAN among the required functions. Thus standard-conforming compilers and accompanying libraries were free to include or omit subprograms for the tangent and cotangent functions and were free to select names for the subprograms when they were included. The new 1978 standard (ANSI [1978]) requires a TAN program, but still fails to mention a subprogram for the cotangent. The confusion of existence and names for this function can be expected to persist, with either the name COTAN or COT frequently being used when the subroutine is supplied. The test program may require modification to either delete references to COTAN or replace them with references to COT, but the required modifications should be obvious in either case. Alternatively, when the cotangent subroutine does not exist, the test program can be run without alteration by providing a COTAN subprogram which takes the reciprocal of TAN when $X \neq 0$, and returns a default value when $X = 0$.

Tests are divided into four major parts. First is a random argument test to determine the accuracy of the computation of $\tan(x)$ when no argument reduction is necessary, thus checking the accuracy of the approximation used over the reduced argument range. Next is a series of random argument tests to determine the accuracy of both $\tan(x)$ and $\cot(x)$ when argument reduction is used. Third is a quick check of the properties

$$\tan(-x) = -\tan(x),$$

$$\cot(x) = 1/\tan(x)$$

and

$$\tan(x) = x$$

to machine precision for $|x| \ll 1$. There are also several short tests with specific arguments to detect underflow in TAN for very small $|x|$ and to recheck the argument reduction computation. Finally, there is a check for an error return for very large arguments.

The random argument tests for $\tan(x)$ use the identity

$$\tan(x) = 2 \tan(x/2) \ / \ [1-\tan^2(x/2)].$$

Thus we measure

$$E = \{\tan(x)-2\ \tan(x/2)/[1-\tan^2(x/2)]\}/\tan(x).$$

This expression must be evaluated carefully if it is to produce useful estimates of the error in $\tan(x)$. We saw in the general discussion of $\tan(x)$ above that a small relative error in the argument was transmitted to the function value with a magnification of

$$M(x) = 2x\ \csc(2x).$$

It is therefore important that both x and $x/2$ be error-free for the evaluation of E. By assumption the random argument x is exact and error-free, but the division of x by 2.0 on the computer may introduce rounding error into $x/2$. The arguments must be "purified" to eliminate this error. In some cases purification requires that x be perturbed to a nearby value, x', such that both x' and $x'/2$ are *exactly* represented in the machine. The Fortran statements

```
Y = X * 0.5E0
```

```
X = Y + Y
```

accomplish this on all machines except those which carry more significance in active arithmetic registers than in storage. It is necessary to force the storage and retrieval of intermediate results on such machines (see Gentleman and Marovich [1974]).

Even with purified arguments the expression E can greatly distort the error in $\tan(x)$. Assume that both x and $x/2$ are error-free but that errors of D and d are made in the evaluation of $\tan(x)$ and $\tan(x/2)$, respectively. Then

$$E = \frac{\tan(x)(1+D)-\{2\ \tan(x/2)(1+d)\}/\{1-\tan^2(x/2)(1+d)^2\}}{\tan(x)(1+D)}.$$

Let $c = 1/\cos(x)$ and assume that $|c|$ is bounded, i.e., that x is bounded away from $(n+1/2)\cdot\text{pi}$ where n is an integer. This restriction is reasonable because $\tan^2(x/2)$ approaches 1.0 for such x, which introduces an obvious numerical instability into the evaluation of E. Keeping only terms linear in D and d, E then reduces to

$$E = D - cd.$$

Restricting x to an interval $[(n-1/4) \cdot pi, (n+1/4) \cdot pi]$ for any integer n implies that $1 \leq |c| \leq \text{sqrt}(2)$, and E is a linear combination of D and d with small coefficients.

The first test uses $n = 0$. This test, in which neither x nor $x/2$ require argument reduction, checks the accuracy of the approximation used in the primary range. The significant statistic obtained is $\text{MRE} = \max|E|$ (see Chapter 3). A large value of MRE indicates a large value of D and/or d, but the converse may not be true; cancellation of leading digits in D and cd may cause the MRE to appear small even though D and d are large. The MRE should report a loss of a little more than $k+1$ bits of precision on machines with a radix of $B = 2 \cdot \cdot k$, and a little more than one digit on decimal machines for good implementations of $\tan(x)$. The corresponding RMS should report a loss of a fraction of a base-B digit. Table 9.1 illustrates this for several implementations of our algorithm and for typical existing library programs (the IBM FTX 2.2 program tested was for a double precision function).

Both $\tan(x)$ and $\tan(x/2)$ are bounded in magnitude by 1.0 for the first test. The second test, which is intended to check accuracy when function values become large, draws arguments from the interval $[7 \cdot pi/8, 9 \cdot pi/8]$ where $|\tan(x/2)| \geq 1.0$ and there is some argument reduction. The MRE and RMS values in this case should be consistent with those for the first test for good implementations of $\tan(x)$. The errors reported for the IBM FTX 2.2 routine in Table 9.1 are significantly greater than expected. Because the MRE value was obtained for an argument that agreed with pi to almost five decimal places, we suspect that the argument reduction scheme was at fault.

A third test draws x from the interval $(6 \cdot pi, 25 \cdot pi/4)$ where both function values are again bounded in magnitude by 1.0, but argument reduction is necessary. Differences between the error statistics for this test and the first test are therefore indicative of the quality of the argument reduction scheme used. Careful argument reduction in implementations of our algorithm results in almost identical error statistics for the first and third tests in Table 9.1. However, both the CDC FTN 4.6 and IBM FTX 2.2 programs apparently have problems with argument reduction.

TABLE 9.1

Typical Results for TAN/COTAN Tests

Test	Machine	B	Library or Program	Reported Loss of Base-B Digits in MRE	RMS
1	CDC 6400	2	Ours	2.48	0.69
	IBM/370	16	Ours	1.17	0.67
	CDC 6400	2	FTN 4.6	2.70	1.06
	IBM/370	16	FTX 2.2	1.25	0.73
2	CDC 6400	2	Ours	2.39	0.62
	IBM/370	16	Ours	1.30	0.88
	CDC 6400	2	FTN 4.6	2.52	0.87
	IBM/370	16	FTX 2.2	4.10	2.75
3	CDC 6400	2	Ours	2.48	0.69
	IBM/370	16	Ours	1.38	0.74
	CDC 6400	2	FTN 4.6	15.93	10.53
	IBM/370	16	FTX 2.2	4.97	3.61
4	CDC 6400	2	Ours	2.49	0.67
	IBM/370	16	Ours	1.29	0.82
	IBM/370	16	FTX 2.2	4.82	3.48

The fourth test checks $\cot(x)$ with the identity

$$\cot(x) = [\cot^2(x/2)-1]/[2 \cot(x/2)].$$

Defining E in the obvious way, restricting x as before, and letting D and d be the relative errors in the evaluation of $\cot(x)$ and $\cot(x/2)$, respectively, an analysis similar to that for the tangent case shows that again

$$E = D - cd,$$

where $c = 1/\cos(x)$. Random arguments for this test are again drawn from the interval $(6{\cdot}pi, 25{\cdot}pi/4)$ where $1 \le |c| < \sqrt{2}$. The interpretation of the error statistics for this test is similar to that for the third test. Good implementations of $\cotan(x)$ should return MRE and RMS values

comparable to those in the first test; larger values probably indicate
argument reduction problems. The complete agreement between the results
for the third and fourth tests in Table 9.1 is typical [note that there
was no cotan(x) program in the CDC FTN 4.6 library].

```
C       PROGRAM TO TEST TAN/COTAN
C
C       DATA REQUIRED
C
C          NONE
C
C       SUBPROGRAMS REQUIRED FROM THIS PACKAGE
C
C          MACHAR - AN ENVIRONMENTAL INQUIRY PROGRAM PROVIDING
C                   INFORMATION ON THE FLOATING-POINT ARITHMETIC
C                   SYSTEM.  NOTE THAT THE CALL TO MACHAR CAN
C                   BE DELETED PROVIDED THE FOLLOWING THREE
C                   PARAMETERS ARE ASSIGNED THE VALUES INDICATED
C
C                      IBETA  - THE RADIX OF THE FLOATING-POINT SYSTEM
C                      IT     - THE NUMBER OF BASE-IBETA DIGITS IN THE
C                               SIGNIFICAND OF A FLOATING-POINT NUMBER
C                      MINEXP - THE LARGEST IN MAGNITUDE NEGATIVE
C                               INTEGER SUCH THAT FLOAT(IBETA)**MINEXP
C                               IS A POSITIVE FLOATING-POINT NUMBER
C
C          RAN(K) - A FUNCTION SUBPROGRAM RETURNING RANDOM REAL
C                   NUMBERS UNIFORMLY DISTRIBUTED OVER (0,1)
C
C
C       STANDARD FORTRAN SUBPROGRAMS REQUIRED
C
C          ABS, ALOG, AMAX1, COTAN, FLOAT, TAN, SQRT
C
C
C       LATEST REVISION - DECEMBER 6, 1979
C
C       AUTHOR - W. J. CODY
C                ARGONNE NATIONAL LABORATORY
C
C
        INTEGER I,IBETA,IEXP,IOUT,IRND,IT,I1,J,K1,K2,K3,MACHEP,
       1        MAXEXP,MINEXP,N,NEGEP,NGRD
        REAL A,AIT,ALBETA,B,BETA,BETAP,C1,C2,DEL,EPS,EPSNEG,HALF,
       1     PI,RAN,R6,R7,W,X,XL,XMAX,XMIN,XN,X1,Y,Z,ZERO,ZZ
C
        IOUT = 6
        CALL MACHAR(IBETA,IT,IRND,NGRD,MACHEP,NEGEP,IEXP,MINEXP,
```

```
    1                 MAXEXP,EPS,EPSNEG,XMIN,XMAX)
      BETA = FLOAT(IBETA)
      ALBETA = ALOG(BETA)
      ZERO = 0.0E0
      HALF = 0.5E0
      AIT = FLOAT(IT)
      PI = 3.14159265E0
      A = ZERO
      B = PI * 0.25E0
      N = 2000
      XN = FLOAT(N)
      I1 = 0
C-----------------------------------------------------------------
C     RANDOM ARGUMENT ACCURACY TESTS
C-----------------------------------------------------------------
      DO 300 J = 1, 4
         K1 = 0
         K3 = 0
         X1 = ZERO
         R6 = ZERO
         R7 = ZERO
         DEL = (B - A) / XN
         XL = A
C
         DO 200 I = 1, N
            X = DEL * RAN(I1) + XL
            Y = X * HALF
            X = Y + Y
            IF (J .EQ. 4) GO TO 80
            Z = TAN(X)
            ZZ = TAN(Y)
            W = 1.0E0
            IF (Z .EQ. ZERO) GO TO 110
            W = ((HALF-ZZ)+HALF)*((HALF+ZZ)+HALF)
            W = (Z - (ZZ+ZZ)/W) / Z
            GO TO 110
   80       Z = COTAN(X)
            ZZ = COTAN(Y)
            W = 1.0E0
            IF (Z .EQ. ZERO) GO TO 110
            W = ((HALF-ZZ)+HALF)*((HALF+ZZ)+HALF)
            W = (Z+W/(ZZ+ZZ))/Z
  110       IF (W .GT. ZERO) K1 = K1 + 1
```

```
                 IF (W .LT. ZERO) K3 = K3 + 1
                 W = ABS(W)
                 IF (W .LE. R6) GO TO 120
                 R6 = W
                 X1 = X
   120           R7 = R7 + W * W
                 XL = XL + DEL
   200     CONTINUE
C
           K2 = N - K3 - K1
           R7 = SQRT(R7/XN)
           IF (J .NE. 4) WRITE (IOUT,1000)
           IF (J .EQ. 4) WRITE (IOUT,1005)
           WRITE (IOUT,1010) N,A,B
           IF (J .NE. 4) WRITE (IOUT,1011) K1,K2,K3
           IF (J .EQ. 4) WRITE (IOUT,1012) K1,K2,K3
           WRITE (IOUT,1020) IT,IBETA
           W = -999.0E0
           IF (R6 .NE. ZERO) W = ALOG(ABS(R6))/ALBETA
           WRITE (IOUT,1021) R6,IBETA,W,X1
           W = AMAX1(AIT+W,ZERO)
           WRITE (IOUT,1022) IBETA,W
           W = -999.0E0
           IF (R7 .NE. ZERO) W = ALOG(ABS(R7))/ALBETA
           WRITE (IOUT,1023) R7,IBETA,W
           W = AMAX1(AIT+W,ZERO)
           WRITE (IOUT,1022) IBETA,W
       IF (J .NE. 1) GO TO 250
           A = PI * 0.875E0
           B = PI * 1.125E0
           GO TO 300
   250     A = PI * 6.0E0
           B = A + PI * 0.25E0
   300 CONTINUE
C----------------------------------------------------------------
C     SPECIAL TESTS
C----------------------------------------------------------------
       WRITE (IOUT,1025)
       WRITE (IOUT,1030)
C
       DO 320 I = 1, 5
           X = RAN(I1) * A
           Z = TAN(X) + TAN(-X)
```

```
          WRITE (IOUT,1060) X, Z
  320 CONTINUE
C
      WRITE (IOUT,1031)
      BETAP = BETA ** IT
      X = RAN(I1) / BETAP
C
      DO 330 I = 1, 5
         Z = X - TAN(X)
         WRITE (IOUT,1060) X, Z
         X = X / BETA
  330 CONTINUE
C
      WRITE (IOUT,1035)
      X = BETA ** (FLOAT(MINEXP)*0.75E0)
      Y = TAN(X)
      WRITE (IOUT,1061) X, Y
      C1 = -225.0E0
      C2 = -.950846454195142026E0
      X = 11.0E0
      Y = TAN(X)
      W = ((C1-Y)+C2)/(C1+C2)
      Z = ALOG(ABS(W))/ALBETA
      WRITE (IOUT,1040) W, IBETA, Z
      WRITE (IOUT,1061) X, Y
      W = AMAX1(AIT+Z,ZERO)
      WRITE (IOUT,1022) IBETA, W
C----------------------------------------------------------------
C     TEST OF ERROR RETURNS
C----------------------------------------------------------------
      WRITE (IOUT,1050)
      X = BETA ** (IT/2)
      WRITE (IOUT,1051) X
      Y = TAN(X)
      WRITE (IOUT,1055) Y
      X = BETAP
      WRITE (IOUT,1052) X
      Y = TAN(X)
      WRITE (IOUT,1055) Y
      WRITE (IOUT,1100)
      STOP
 1000 FORMAT(45H1TEST OF TAN(X) VS 2*TAN(X/2)/(1-TAN(X/2)**2) //)
 1005 FORMAT(47H1TEST OF COT(X) VS (COT(X/2)**2-1)/(2*COT(X/2)) //)
```

```
1010 FORMAT(I7,47H RANDOM ARGUMENTS WERE TESTED FROM THE INTERVAL /
    1 6X,1H(,E15.4,1H,,E15.4,1H)//)
1011 FORMAT(18H TAN(X) WAS LARGER,I6,7H TIMES, /
    1      11X,7H AGREED,I6,11H TIMES, AND /
    1      7X,11HWAS SMALLER,I6,7H TIMES.//)
1012 FORMAT(18H COT(X) WAS LARGER,I6,7H TIMES, /
    1      11X,7H AGREED,I6,11H TIMES, AND /
    1      7X,11HWAS SMALLER,I6,7H TIMES.//)
1020 FORMAT(10H THERE ARE,I4,5H BASE,I4,
    1      46H SIGNIFICANT DIGITS IN A FLOATING-POINT NUMBER  //)
1021 FORMAT(30H THE MAXIMUM RELATIVE ERROR OF,E15.4,3H = ,I4,3H **,
    1 F7.2/4X,16HOCCURRED FOR X =,E17.6)
1022 FORMAT(27H THE ESTIMATED LOSS OF BASE,I4,
    1 22H SIGNIFICANT DIGITS IS,F7.2//)
1023 FORMAT(40H THE ROOT MEAN SQUARE RELATIVE ERROR WAS,E15.4,
    1      3H = ,I4,3H **,F7.2)
1025 FORMAT(14H1SPECIAL TESTS//)
1030 FORMAT(49H THE IDENTITY  TAN(-X) = -TAN(X)  WILL BE TESTED.//
    1      8X,1HX,9X,12HF(X) + F(-X)/)
1031 FORMAT(51H THE IDENTITY TAN(X) = X , X SMALL, WILL BE TESTED.//
    1      8X,1HX,9X,8HX - F(X)/)
1035 FORMAT(43H TEST OF UNDERFLOW FOR VERY SMALL ARGUMENT. /)
1040 FORMAT(33H THE RELATIVE ERROR IN TAN(11) IS  ,E15.7,3H = ,
    1      I4,3H **,F7.2,6H WHERE /)
1050 FORMAT(22H1TEST OF ERROR RETURNS//)
1051 FORMAT(37H TAN WILL BE CALLED WITH THE ARGUMENT,E15.4/
    1      41H THIS SHOULD NOT TRIGGER AN ERROR MESSAGE//)
1052 FORMAT(37H0TAN WILL BE CALLED WITH THE ARGUMENT,E15.4/
    1      37H THIS SHOULD TRIGGER AN ERROR MESSAGE//)
1055 FORMAT(23H TAN RETURNED THE VALUE,E15.4///)
1060 FORMAT(2E15.7/)
1061 FORMAT(6X,5H TAN(,E13.6,3H) =,E13.6/)
1100 FORMAT(25H THIS CONCLUDES THE TESTS )
C    ---------- LAST CARD OF TAN/COTAN TEST PROGRAM ----------
     END
```

10. ASIN/ACOS

a. General Discussion

The computation of the arcsine requires three steps: the reduction of an arbitrary argument X, subject to the condition $|X| \leq 1$, to a related argument Y such that $0 \leq Y \leq 1/2$; the evaluation of $\sin^{-1}(Y)$; and the reconstruction of $\sin^{-1}(X)$ from the results of the first two steps. The argument reduction step uses the identities

$$\sin^{-1}(X) = pi/2 - 2 \sin^{-1}\{sqrt[(1-X)/2]\}$$

and

$$\sin^{-1}(-X) = -\sin^{-1}(X)$$

as needed. Having found Y, we evaluate $\sin^{-1}(Y)$ using a minimax rational approximation generated especially for this work. Finally, the above identities are reapplied as needed to reconstruct $\sin^{-1}(X)$. The arccosine computation is reduced to that for the arcsine through the identity

$$\cos^{-1}(X) = pi/2 - \sin^{-1}(X).$$

The final value of $\sin^{-1}(X)$ is sensitive to small argument errors only for $|X|$ close to 1.0. Let $w = \sin^{-1}(X)$. Then from elementary calculus

$$dw/w = M(X) \, dX/X,$$

where

$$M(X) = X/[\sin^{-1}(X)sqrt(1-X^2)].$$

Thus the relative error in w is about $M(X)$ times the relative error in X. Because $X/\sin^{-1}(X)$ approaches 1 as X approaches 0, $M(0) = 1$. It is easy to show that $M(X) \geq 1$ for all $|X| \leq 1$. Although $M(X)$ is unbounded as $|X|$ approaches 1, it is not overly large for moderate $|X|$, becoming about 1.1 for $|X| = 0.5$, for example, and about 1.8 for $|X| = 0.9$. Even when X is error-free, small errors introduced into the computation during argument reduction will be magnified by $M(X)$ and distort the final function value. Careful argument reduction is therefore critical, especially for arguments close to 1.0 in magnitude.

The computation of $\cos^{-1}(X)$ is potentially more sensitive. Direct application of the identities above for arguments close to 1.0 could introduce severe loss of significance in taking the difference of two numbers close to pi/2. This error can be avoided for $X > 1/2$ by using the numerically stable representation

$$\cos^{-1}(X) = 2\ \sin^{-1}\{sqrt[(1-X)/2]\}$$

obtained by algebraically combining the first and third identities above. Similarly, the representation

$$\cos^{-1}(X) = pi - 2\ \sin^{-1}\{sqrt[(1+X)/2]\}$$

is used for the case $X < -1/2$.

b. Flow Chart for ASIN(X)/ACOS(X)

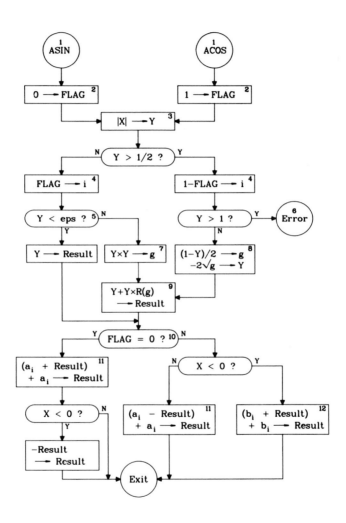

Note: Small integers indicate an implementation note.

c. Implementation Notes, Non-Decimal Fixed-Point Machines

1) These may be alternate entries to one subroutine if multiple entries are supported. Otherwise ASIN and ACOS must be separate subroutines. They can either be written as self-contained subroutines by following the obvious paths in the flow chart and making appropriate modifications to the steps involving *FLAG* (see Notes 2, 4, and 10), or they can each pass the parameters X and *FLAG* to a separate computational subroutine starting with the initial assignment to Y and ending at the test on *FLAG* (see Notes 3 and 10).

2) *FLAG* need not be set if ASIN and ACOS are each self-contained subroutines (see Note 1). Otherwise *FLAG* should be an integer.

3) On machines that do not support multiple entry points, this is a natural point at which to begin a new subroutine callable by ASIN and ACOS (see Note 1). The parameters to be passed in that case are X and *FLAG*.

4) If ASIN and ACOS are self-contained subroutines, then *FLAG* was not set earlier (see Notes 1 and 2). In that case the values *FLAG* would have assumed can be used to determine whether 0 or 1 should be assigned to i here.

5) Fixed-point underflow will not hurt in what follows, but for efficiency *eps* should be chosen so that $\sin^{-1}(Y) = Y$ to machine precision for $Y < eps$. We suggest $eps = B**(-t/2)$, where B is the radix of the floating-point representation and there are t base-B digits in the significand (see Glossary).

6) If execution is to continue rather than terminate, then a default function value should be provided in addition to an error message. We suggest *XMAX*, the largest positive floating-point number on the machine.

7) Set $f = FIX(Y)$ (see Chapter 2), and form $g = f \cdot f$ using fixed-point arithmetic. Fixed-point underflow will not hurt here or below.

8) Most of this step must be carried out in floating-point arithmetic because we need the final value of Y to full floating-point

significance. Revise the flow chart to read

   (1-Y)/2 --> f   in floating point

   -2 SQRT(f) --> Y   in floating point

   FIX(f) --> g

The strategy to be followed in the floating-point computations
depends upon the availability of guard digits (see Glossary) for
floating-point multiplication and addition and upon the radix B.
The quantity $1-Y$ can be evaluated accurately as it stands if chop
mode addition with guard digits is available. In all other cases
evaluate $((0.5-Y)+0.5)$, where the order of operations is important.
The subsequent division by 2.0 will generally be slow, and an
alternate operation should be used where possible. The division can
be replaced by a multiplication by 0.5, for example, but this
operation will often lose significance and should be avoided when
there are no guard digits for multiplication. On binary machines,
especially those supporting exponent modification in the instruction
set, the division could be replaced by an ADX operation with $N = -1$
(see Chapter 2).

Once f is determined, use the standard SQRT routine to find the new
value of Y. To increase speed and preserve accuracy, we suggest
doubling SQRT(f) either by adding it to itself or by using an ADX
operation on binary machines as above, but with $N = 1$.

9) We will use fixed-point arithmetic to evaluate a rational
   approximation $R(g)$ derived especially for this work. The final
   operations involving Y will be done in floating-point arithmetic to
   maximize the accuracy for small $|Y|$. Let b be the number of bits in
   the significand of a floating-point number. Then

                     for b $\leq$ 24

         p1 =   0.08333 31098
         p2 = -0.04500 65898
         q0 =   0.50000 00000
         q1 = -0.49507 79396
         q2 =   0.08922 78749

for $25 \leq b \leq 36$

```
p1 =   0.08333 33331 91669
p2 =  -0.08800 38762 68233
p3 =   0.01800 43563 66662
q0 =   0.50000 00000 00000
q1 =  -0.75302 33061 60715
q2 =   0.31295 90818 27048
q3 =  -0.03028 47984 82806
```

for $37 \leq b \leq 48$

```
p1 =   0.04166 66666 66628 83
p2 =  -0.06554 00387 86926 70
p3 =   0.02912 89116 60093 97
p4 =  -0.00319 21054 85259 50
q0 =   0.25000 00000 00000 00
q1 =  -0.50574 02327 43102 17
q2 =   0.33539 22897 63774 92
q3 =  -0.08018 59602 95834 55
q4 =   0.00488 05915 81071 13
```

Evaluate $R(g) = g \cdot P(g)/Q(g)$, where P and Q are polynomials with coefficients $p1$, $p2$, ..., pN, and $q0$, $q1$, ..., qN, respectively, as follows. First form $g \cdot P(g)$ and $Q(g)$ using nested multiplication and fixed-point arithmetic. For example, for $25 \leq b \leq 36$,

$$g \cdot P(g) = [(p3 \cdot g + p2) \cdot g + p1] \cdot g$$
and
$$Q(g) = [(q3 \cdot g + q2) \cdot g + q1] \cdot g + q0.$$

Form $r = g \cdot P(g)/Q(g)$ in fixed-point, and then set $R(g) = \text{REFLOAT}(r)$ (see Chapter 2). Finally evaluate $Y + Y \cdot R(g)$ in floating-point. Avoid the form $Y \cdot [1 + R(g)]$ which is numerically less stable on non-binary machines and machines lacking guard digits.

10) Omit this step if ASIN and ACOS are separate subroutines (see Note 1). If they share a computational subprogram beginning at the initial assignment to Y (see Note 3), then return control to ASIN or ACOS passing the parameters i and $Result$. From this point on the separate ASIN routine contains the path for $FLAG = 0$, and the ACOS routine contains the path for $FLAG = 1$.

11) Use the following constants to machine precision:

>   a(0) = 0.0
>   a(1) = pi/4
>   = 0.78539 81633 97448 30962 (decimal)
>   = 0.62207 73250 42055 06043 (octal)

The mathematically equivalent single addition/subtraction using stored constants that are twice these should be avoided because it may be numerically less accurate.

12) Use the following constants to machine precision:

>   b(0) = pi/2
>   = 1.57079 63267 94896 61923 (decimal)
>   = 1.44417 66521 04132 14107 (octal)
>   b(1) = a(1)

The mathematically equivalent single addition using stored constants that are twice these should be avoided because it may be numerically less accurate.

d. Implementation Notes, All Floating-Point Machines

1) These may be alternate entries to one subroutine if multiple entries are supported. Otherwise ASIN and ACOS must be separate subroutines. They can either be written as self-contained subroutines by following the obvious paths in the flow chart and making appropriate modifications to the steps involving *FLAG* (see Notes 2, 4, and 10), or they can each pass the parameters X and *FLAG* to a separate computational subroutine starting with the initial assignment to Y and ending at the test on *FLAG* (see Notes 3 and 10).

2) *FLAG* need not be set if ASIN and ACOS are each self-contained subroutines (see Note 1). Otherwise *FLAG* should be an integer.

3) On machines that do not support multiple entry points, this is a natural point at which to begin a new subroutine callable by ASIN and ACOS (see Note 1). The parameters to be passed in that case are X and *FLAG*.

4) If ASIN and ACOS are self-contained subroutines, then *FLAG* was not set earlier (see Notes 1 and 2). In that case the values *FLAG* would have assumed can be used to determine whether 0 or 1 should be assigned to i here.

5) Choose *eps* so that $\sin^{-1}(Y) = Y$ to machine precision for $Y < eps$, and so that $p1 \cdot Y^3$ (see Note 9) will not underflow for $Y \geq eps$. We suggest $eps = B^{**}(-t/2)$, where B is the radix of the floating-point representation and there are t base-B digits in the significand (see Glossary).

6) If execution is to continue rather than terminate, then a default function value should be provided in addition to an error message. We suggest *XMAX*, the largest positive floating-point number on the machine.

7) Underflow is not possible here if *eps* has been set as suggested above.

8) The strategy to be followed here depends upon the availability of guard digits (see Glossary) for floating-point multiplication and

addition, and upon the radix B. The quantity $1-Y$ can be evaluated accurately as it stands if chop mode addition with guard digits is available (see Glossary). In all other cases evaluate $((0.5-Y)+0.5)$, where the order of operations is important. The subsequent division by 2.0 will generally be slow, and an alternate operation should be used where possible. The division can be replaced by a multiplication by 0.5, for example, but this operation will often lose significance and should be avoided when there are no guard digits for multiplication. On binary machines, especially those supporting exponent modification in the instruction set, the division could be replaced by an ADX operation with $N = -1$ (see Chapter 2).

Once g is determined, use the standard SQRT routine to find the new value of Y. To increase speed and preserve accuracy we suggest doubling SQRT(g) either by adding it to itself or by using an ADX operation on binary machines as above, but with $N = 1$.

9) We will use a rational approximation $R(g)$ derived especially for this work. Let b be the number of bits in the significand of a floating-point number on a non-decimal machine, and d be the number of decimal digits in the significand on a decimal machine. Then

for $b \leq 24$, or $d \leq 7$

$$p1 = 0.93393\ 5835\ E+0$$
$$p2 = -0.50440\ 0557\ E+0$$
$$q0 = 0.56036\ 3004\ E+1$$
$$q1 = -0.55484\ 6723\ E+1$$
$$q2 = 0.10000\ 0000\ E+1$$

for $25 \leq b \leq 36$, or
$8 \leq d \leq 11$

$$p1 = -0.27516\ 55529\ 0596\ E+1$$
$$p2 = 0.29058\ 76237\ 4859\ E+1$$
$$p3 = -0.59450\ 14419\ 3246\ E+0$$
$$q0 = -0.16509\ 93320\ 2424\ E+2$$
$$q1 = 0.24864\ 72896\ 9164\ E+2$$
$$q2 = -0.10333\ 86707\ 2113\ E+2$$
$$q3 = 0.10000\ 00000\ 0000\ E+1$$

for $37 \leq b \leq 48$, or
$12 \leq d \leq 14$

p1 =   0.85372 16436 67719 50 E+1
p2 = -0.13428 70791 34253 12 E+2
p3 =   0.59683 15761 77515 34 E+1
p4 = -0.65404 06899 93350 09 E+0
q0 =   0.51223 29862 01096 91 E+2
q1 = -0.10362 27318 64014 80 E+3
q2 =   0.68719 59765 38088 06 E+2
q3 = -0.16429 55755 74951 70 E+2
q4 =   0.10000 00000 00000 00 E+1

for $49 \leq b \leq 60$, or
$15 \leq d \leq 18$

p1 = -0.27368 49452 41642 55994 E+2
p2 =   0.57208 22787 78917 31407 E+2
p3 = -0.39688 86299 75048 77339 E+2
p4 =   0.10152 52223 38064 63645 E+2
p5 = -0.69674 57344 73506 46411 E+0
q0 = -0.16421 09671 44985 60795 E+3
q1 =   0.41714 43024 82604 12556 E+3
q2 = -0.38186 30336 17501 49284 E+3
q3 =   0.15095 27084 10306 04719 E+3
q4 = -0.23823 85915 36702 38830 E+2
q5 =   0.10000 00000 00000 00000 E+1

Evaluate $R(g) = g \cdot P(g)/Q(g)$, where P and Q are polynomials with coefficients $p1$, $p2$, ..., $p\text{N}$, and $q0$, $q1$, ..., $q\text{N}$, respectively, using nested multiplication. For example, for $25 \leq b \leq 36$,

$$g \cdot P(g) = [(p3 \cdot g + p2) \cdot g + p1] \cdot g$$
and
$$Q(g) = [(g + q2) \cdot g + q1] \cdot g + q0,$$

which avoids explicit multiplication by $q3 = 1.0$. Finally, evaluate $Y + Y \cdot R(g)$. Avoid the form $Y \cdot [1 + R(g)]$ which is numerically less stable on non-binary machines and machines lacking guard digits.

10) Omit this step if ASIN and ACOS are separate subroutines (see Note 1). If they share a computational subprogram beginning at the

initial assignment to Y (see Note 3), then return control to ASIN or ACOS passing the parameters i and *Result*. From this point on the separate ASIN routine contains the path for *FLAG* = 0, and the ACOS routine contains the path for *FLAG* = 1.

11) Use the following constants to machine precision:

> a(0) = 0.0
> a(1) = pi/4
>   = 0.78539 81633 97448 30962 (decimal)
>   = 0.62207 73250 42055 06043 (octal)

The mathematically equivalent single addition/subtraction using stored constants that are twice these should be avoided because it may be numerically less accurate.

12) Use the following constants to machine precision:

> b(0) = pi/2
>   = 1.57079 63267 94896 61923 (decimal)
>   = 1.44417 66521 04132 14107 (octal)
> b(1) = a(1)

The mathematically equivalent single addition using stored constants that are twice these should be avoided because it may be numerically less accurate.

e. Testing

The test program for ASIN/ACOS may require modification before it can be used to test existing libraries supplied with some compilers. The 1966 Fortran standard (ANSI [1966]) specified neither of these functions but left standard-conforming compilers and accompanying libraries free to include them and to choose appropriate names as desired. The new 1978 Fortran standard (ANSI [1978]) does include these functions and specifies that the names shall be ASIN/ACOS. Our test programs follow this specification although some existing libraries use the names ARSIN/ARCOS.

The tests are divided into four major parts. First is a pair of random argument accuracy tests of the computation of $\sin^{-1}(x)$ and $\cos^{-1}(x)$ with small arguments. Second is a trio of random argument tests with large arguments. Third is a cursory check of the properties

$$\sin^{-1}(-x) = -\sin^{-1}(x)$$

and

$$\sin^{-1}(x) = x$$

to machine precision for $|x| \ll 1$, and a check for underflow during the evaluation of $\sin^{-1}(x)$ for very small x. Finally, the error return is tested with the argument $x = 1.2$.

Subprograms for the computation of $\sin^{-1}(x)$ and $\cos^{-1}(x)$ are often very accurate, and test programs must be written carefully if they are to measure that accuracy reliably. The few available identities involving $\sin^{-1}(x)$ and $\cos^{-1}(x)$ are not suitable for accuracy testing because they introduce excessive error which cannot be eliminated by the usual process of argument purification. Therefore, the accuracy tests used here compare $\sin^{-1}(x)$ or $\cos^{-1}(x)$ against Taylor series expansions truncated so as to provide accuracy over the test interval to at least the working precision of the machine. The final evaluation of the series is usually correct to within rounding error and is frequently correctly rounded even on computers with truncating arithmetic. These tests should be almost as discriminating as direct comparisons against higher precision computations, except possibly in cases where the program being tested implements the same Taylor series. In that case systematic error might go undetected. This is normally not the case, however, and is certainly not the case for implementations of the algorithms recommended here.

-185-

TABLE 10.1

Typical Results for ASIN/ACOS Tests

Test	Machine	B	Library or Program	Reported Loss of Base-B Digits in MRE	RMS
1	CDC 6400	2	Ours	0.99	0.00
	IBM/370	16	Ours	1.00	0.64
	CDC 6400	2	FTN 4.7	1.00	0.00
	IBM/370	16	FTX 2.2	1.00	0.38
2	CDC 6400	2	Ours	0.47	0.00
	IBM/370	16	Ours	0.87	0.69
	CDC 6400	2	FTN 4.7	0.47	0.00
	IBM/370	16	FTX 2.2	0.87	0.75
3	CDC 6400	2	Ours	1.24	0.03
	IBM/370	16	Ours	1.00	0.72
	CDC 6400	2	FTN 4.7	1.24	0.00
	IBM/370	16	FTX 2.2	1.00	0.75
4	CDC 6400	2	Ours	1.00	0.00
	IBM/370	16	Ours	0.99	0.29
	CDC 6400	2	FTN 4.7	1.90	0.00
	IBM/370	16	FTX 2.2	0.99	0.30
5	CDC 6400	2	Ours	0.66	0.00
	IBM/370	16	Ours	0.93	0.71
	CDC 6400	2	FTN 4.7	0.72	0.00
	IBM/370	16	FTX 2.2	0.68	0.34

The first test checks $\sin^{-1}(x)$ over the interval $[-0.125,0.125]$; the second checks $\cos^{-1}(x)$ over the same interval; the third checks $\sin^{-1}(x)$ over $[0.75,1.0]$; the fourth checks $\cos^{-1}(x)$ over that interval; and the last checks $\cos^{-1}(x)$ over the interval $[-1.0,-0.75]$. Satisfactory programs for either $\sin^{-1}(x)$ or $\cos^{-1}(x)$ should result in a loss of one base-B digit or less in the measured MRE (see Chapter 3) for all tests on non-binary machines. The MRE may be slightly larger on binary machines but should not exceed 1.5 bits. The RMS errors should indicate a loss of no more than 0.75 digits on non-binary machines for all but the fourth test, which should lose at most 0.5 digits. The measured RMS errors on binary machines should indicate essentially no loss of digits.

Table 10.1 lists results for these tests applied to typical implementations of our algorithm and to selected existing library programs. These results generally follow expectations except for the MRE for the CDC FTN 4.7 program in the fourth test, and even that error is not large enough to cause alarm.

```
C     PROGRAM TO TEST ASIN/ACOS
C
C     DATA REQUIRED
C
C         NONE
C
C     SUBPROGRAMS REQUIRED FROM THIS PACKAGE
C
C         MACHAR - AN ENVIRONMENTAL INQUIRY PROGRAM PROVIDING
C                  INFORMATION ON THE FLOATING-POINT ARITHMETIC
C                  SYSTEM.  NOTE THAT THE CALL TO MACHAR CAN
C                  BE DELETED PROVIDED THE FOLLOWING FOUR
C                  PARAMETERS ARE ASSIGNED THE VALUES INDICATED
C
C                  IBETA  - THE RADIX OF THE FLOATING-POINT SYSTEM
C                  IT     - THE NUMBER OF BASE-IBETA DIGITS IN THE
C                           SIGNIFICAND OF A FLOATING-POINT NUMBER
C                  IRND   - 0 IF FLOATING-POINT ADDITION CHOPS,
C                           1 IF FLOATING-POINT ADDITION ROUNDS
C                  MINEXP - THE LARGEST IN MAGNITUDE NEGATIVE
C                           INTEGER SUCH THAT FLOAT(IBETA)**MINEXP
C                           IS A POSITIVE FLOATING-POINT NUMBER
C
C         RAN(K) - A FUNCTION SUBPROGRAM RETURNING RANDOM REAL
C                  NUMBERS UNIFORMLY DISTRIBUTED OVER (0,1)
C
C
C     STANDARD FORTRAN SUBPROGRAMS REQUIRED
C
C         ABS, ACOS, ALOG, ALOG10, AMAX1, ASIN, FLOAT, INT, SQRT
C
C
C     LATEST REVISION - DECEMBER 6, 1979
C
C     AUTHOR - W. J. CODY
C              ARGONNE NATIONAL LABORATORY
C
C
      INTEGER I,IBETA,IEXP,IOUT,IRND,IT,I1,J,K,K1,K2,K3,L,M,
     1        MACHEP,MAXEXP,MINEXP,N,NEGEP,NGRD
      REAL A,AIT,ALBETA,B,BETA,BETAP,C1,C2,DEL,EPS,EPSNEG,HALF,RAN,
     1     R6,R7,S,SUM,W,X,XL,XM,XMAX,XMIN,XN,X1,Y,YSQ,Z,ZERO,ZZ
C
```

```
      IOUT = 6
      CALL MACHAR(IBETA,IT,IRND,NGRD,MACHEP,NEGEP,IEXP,MINEXP,
     1                MAXEXP,EPS,EPSNEG,XMIN,XMAX)
      BETA = FLOAT(IBETA)
      ALBETA = ALOG(BETA)
      ZERO = 0.0E0
      HALF = 0.5E0
      AIT = FLOAT(IT)
      K = INT(ALOG10(BETA**IT)) + 1
      IF (IBETA .NE. 10) GO TO 20
      C1 = 1.57E0
      C2 = 7.96326794896619231132E-4
      GO TO 30
   20 C1 = 201.0E0/128.0E0
      C2 = 4.83826794896619231132E-4
   30 A = -0.125E0
      B = -A
      N = 2000
      XN = FLOAT(N)
      I1 = 0
      L = -1
C-----------------------------------------------------------------
C     RANDOM ARGUMENT ACCURACY TESTS
C-----------------------------------------------------------------
      DO 300 J = 1, 5
         K1 = 0
         K3 = 0
         L = -L
         X1 = ZERO
         R6 = ZERO
         R7 = ZERO
         DEL = (B - A) / XN
         XL = A
C
         DO 200 I = 1, N
            X = DEL*RAN(I1) + XL
            IF (J .LE. 2) GO TO 40
            YSQ = HALF - HALF*ABS(X)
            X = (HALF - (YSQ+YSQ)) + HALF
            IF (J .EQ. 5) X = -X
            Y = SQRT(YSQ)
            Y = Y + Y
            GO TO 50
```

```
40        Y = X
          YSQ = Y*Y
50        SUM = ZERO
          XM = FLOAT(K+K+1)
          IF (L .GT. 0) Z = ASIN(X)
          IF (L .LT. 0) Z = ACOS(X)
C
          DO 60 M = 1, K
             SUM = YSQ*(SUM + 1.0E0/XM)
             XM = XM - 2.0E0
             SUM = SUM*(XM/(XM+1.0E0))
60        CONTINUE
C
          SUM = SUM*Y
          IF ((J .NE. 1) .AND. (J .NE. 4)) GO TO 70
          ZZ = Y + SUM
          SUM = (Y - ZZ) + SUM
          IF (IRND .NE. 1) ZZ = ZZ + (SUM+SUM)
          GO TO 110
70        S = C1 + C2
          SUM = ((C1 - S) + C2) - SUM
          ZZ = S + SUM
          SUM = ((S - ZZ) + SUM) - Y
          S = ZZ
          ZZ = S + SUM
          SUM = (S - ZZ) + SUM
          IF (IRND .NE. 1) ZZ = ZZ + (SUM+SUM)
110       W = 1.0E0
          IF (Z .NE. ZERO) W = (Z-ZZ)/Z
          IF (W .GT. ZERO) K1 = K1 + 1
          IF (W .LT. ZERO) K3 = K3 + 1
          W = ABS(W)
          IF (W .LE. R6) GO TO 120
          R6 = W
          X1 = X
120       R7 = R7 + W*W
          XL = XL + DEL
200       CONTINUE
C
          K2 = N - K3 - K1
          R7 = SQRT(R7/XN)
          IF (L .LT. 0) GO TO 210
          WRITE (IOUT,1000)
```

```
              WRITE (IOUT,I010) N,A,B
              WRITE (IOUT,1011) K1,K2,K3
              GO TO 220
    210       WRITE (IOUT,1005)
              WRITE (IOUT,1010) N,A,B
              WRITE (IOUT,1012) K1,K2,K3
    220       WRITE (IOUT,1020) IT,IBETA
              W = -999.0E0
              IF (R6 .NE. ZERO) W = ALOG(ABS(R6))/ALBETA
              WRITE (IOUT,1021) R6,IBETA,W,X1
              W = AMAX1(AIT+W,ZERO)
              WRITE (IOUT,1022) IBETA,W
              W = -999.0E0
              IF (R7 .NE. ZERO) W = ALOG(ABS(R7))/ALBETA
              WRITE (IOUT,1023) R7,IBETA,W
              W = AMAX1(AIT+W,ZERO)
              WRITE (IOUT,1022) IBETA,W
              IF (J .NE. 2) GO TO 250
              A = 0.75E0
              B = 1.0E0
    250       IF (J .NE. 4) GO TO 300
              B = -A
              A = -1.0E0
              C1 = C1 + C1
              C2 = C2 + C2
              L = -L
    300 CONTINUE
C-----------------------------------------------------------------
C     SPECIAL TESTS
C-----------------------------------------------------------------
      WRITE (IOUT,1025)
      WRITE (IOUT,1030)
C
      DO 320 I = 1, 5
          X = RAN(I1)*A
          Z = ASIN(X) + ASIN(-X)
          WRITE (IOUT,1060) X, Z
    320 CONTINUE
C
      WRITE (IOUT,1031)
      BETAP = BETA ** IT
      X = RAN(I1) / BETAP
C
```

```
      DO 330 I = 1, 5
         Z = X - ASIN(X)
         WRITE (IOUT,1060) X, Z
         X = X / BETA
  330 CONTINUE
C
      WRITE (IOUT,1035)
      X = BETA ** (FLOAT(MINEXP)*0.75E0)
      Y = ASIN(X)
      WRITE (IOUT,1061) X, Y
C-----------------------------------------------------------------
C     TEST OF ERROR RETURNS
C-----------------------------------------------------------------
      WRITE (IOUT,1050)
      X = 1.2E0
      WRITE (IOUT,1052) X
      Y = ASIN(X)
      WRITE (IOUT,1055) Y
      WRITE (IOUT,1100)
      STOP
 1000 FORMAT(33H1TEST OF ASIN(X) VS TAYLOR SERIES //)
 1005 FORMAT(33H1TEST OF ACOS(X) VS TAYLOR SERIES //)
 1010 FORMAT(I7,47H RANDOM ARGUMENTS WERE TESTED FROM THE INTERVAL /
     1 6X,1H(,E15.4,1H,,E15.4,1H))//)
 1011 FORMAT(19H ASIN(X) WAS LARGER,I6,7H TIMES, /
     1      12X,7H AGREED,I6,11H TIMES, AND /
     2    8X,11HWAS SMALLER,I6,7H TIMES.//)
 1012 FORMAT(19H ACOS(X) WAS LARGER,I6,7H TIMES, /
     1      12X,7H AGREED,I6,11H TIMES, AND /
     2    8X,11HWAS SMALLER,I6,7H TIMES.//)
 1020 FORMAT(10H THERE ARE,I4,5H BASE,I4,
     1    46H SIGNIFICANT DIGITS IN A FLOATING-POINT NUMBER  //)
 1021 FORMAT(30H THE MAXIMUM RELATIVE ERROR OF,E15.4,3H = ,I4,3H **,
     1 F7.2/4X,16HOCCURRED FOR X =,Z15)
C    1 F7.2/4X,16HOCCURRED FOR X =,E17.6)
 1022 FORMAT(27H THE ESTIMATED LOSS OF BASE,I4,
     1 22H SIGNIFICANT DIGITS IS,F7.2//)
 1023 FORMAT(40H THE ROOT MEAN SQUARE RELATIVE ERROR WAS,E15.4,
     1    3H = ,I4,3H **,F7.2)
 1025 FORMAT(14H1SPECIAL TESTS//)
 1030 FORMAT(51H THE IDENTITY  ASIN(-X) = -ASIN(X)  WILL BE TESTED.//
     1      8X,1HX,9X,12HF(X) + F(-X)/)
 1031 FORMAT(52H THE IDENTITY ASIN(X) = X , X SMALL, WILL BE TESTED.//
```

```
     1        8X,1HX,9X,8HX - F(X)/)
1035 FORMAT(43H TEST OF UNDERFLOW FOR VERY SMALL ARGUMENT. /)
1050 FORMAT(22H1TEST OF ERROR RETURNS//)
1052 FORMAT(38H ASIN WILL BE CALLED WITH THE ARGUMENT,E15.4/
     1        37H THIS SHOULD TRIGGER AN ERROR MESSAGE//)
1055 FORMAT(24H ASIN RETURNED THE VALUE,E15.4///)
1060 FORMAT(2E15.7/)
1061 FORMAT(6X,6H ASIN(,E13.6,3H) =,E13.6/)
1100 FORMAT(25H THIS CONCLUDES THE TESTS )
C        ---------- LAST CARD OF ASIN/ACOS TEST PROGRAM ----------
     END
```

11.   ATAN/ATAN2

a.   General Discussion

The computation of the arctangent requires three steps: the
reduction of the argument X to a related argument f such that
$|f| \leq 2\text{-sqrt}(3)$, the evaluation of arctan(f), and the reconstruction of
arctan(X) from the results of the first two steps.   Argument reduction
itself is accomplished in several stages.   First the identity

arctan(X) = -arctan(-X)

is used if the argument X is negative to transform the computation to
one for non-negative X.   Next the identity

arctan(X) = pi/2 - arctan(1/X)

is used, if the now non-negative X exceeds 1, to reduce the computation
to the case $X \leq 1$.   Finally, the identity

arctan(X) = pi/6 + arctan(f),

where

f = (X*sqrt(3)-1)/(sqrt(3)+X),

is used,   if needed, to reduce the computation to that of arctan(f),
where $|f| \leq 2\text{-sqrt}(3)$.   Having found f, we evaluate arctan(f) using a
rational approximation generated especially for this work.   Finally, the
above identities are reapplied to reconstruct arctan(X).

The function value is relatively insensitive to small errors in the argument reduction process.   To see this, let $y = \arctan(X)$, and assume that a relative error δf in f leads to a corresponding relative error δy in y according to the equation

$$\delta y = M(X) \cdot \delta f .$$

Approximate expressions for $M(X)$ can be derived for each of the intervals (0,2-sqrt(3)), (2-sqrt(3),1), (1,2+sqrt(3)), and (2+sqrt(3),--) using elementary calculus and the relation $\delta w \doteq dw/w$. The exact form of these expressions is not important. Suffice it to say that $|M(X)|$ is bounded above by 1.0 in the first interval, by .96 in the second, by .32 in the third, and by .20 in the last and vanishes asymptotically.   Thus the error in f is never magnified and is frequently made smaller.   Nevertheless, care should be taken in determining the reduced argument f and in reconstructing $\arctan(X)$.

The function $\arctan(v/u)$, to be implemented as ATAN2(V,U), maps the u-v plane, less the origin, onto the interval (-pi,pi).   Basically, $\arctan(v/u)$ measures the angle between the positive u-axis and the directed line segment from the origin to the point (u,v).   Thus the function is undefined for the origin itself.   The computation of $\arctan(v/u)$ is carried out as follows.   First the identity

$$\arctan(v/u) = -\arctan(-v/u)$$

is used if v is negative to transform the computation to one for non-negative v.   Arctan($v/0$) is then defined to be pi/2, and the relation

$$\arctan(v/u) = pi - \arctan[v/(-u)], \quad u < 0$$

is used if u is negative to transform the computation to one for positive u.   Finally, $\arctan(v/u)$ is calculated directly according to the algorithm outlined above when u is positive.

b. Flow Chart for ATAN(X)/ATAN2(V,U)

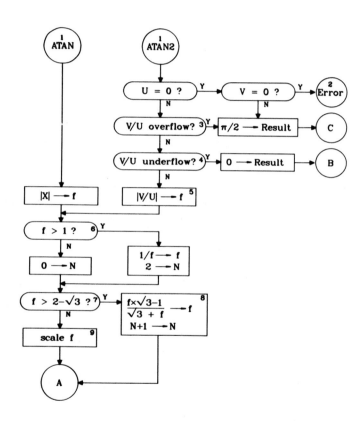

Note: Small integers indicate an implementation note.

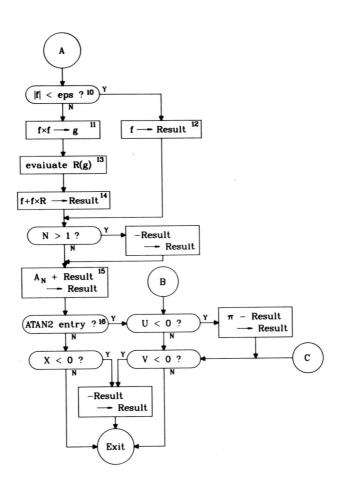

Note: Small integers indicate an implementation note.

c. Implementation Notes, Non-Decimal Fixed-Point Machines

1) These may be alternate entry points to one subroutine, in which case ATAN2 should set a flag and ATAN should clear that flag (see Note 16).

   When multiple entries are not supported, ATAN and ATAN2 must be separate subroutines. In that case ATAN can be a self-contained subroutine which is called by ATAN2 (see Note 5), or there can be a separate computational subroutine starting with the test for $f > 1$ (see Note 6) which is called by both ATAN and ATAN2.

2) If execution is to continue rather than terminate, then a default function value should be provided in addition to the error message. There is no consensus on this default value, with zero and the largest positive floating-point number both being popular choices.

3) It is important in this step and the next that overflow and underflow warnings not be issued to the user. If it is possible to detect overflow in forming V/U while suppressing the diagnostic message, then that approach should be taken in this step. Otherwise, the following approach should be used.

   Assume that both V and U are normalized floating-point numbers (see Glossary) and that $MAXEXP$ is the largest exponent that does not cause overflow in such numbers. ($MAXEXP$ is one of the parameters determined by the subroutine MACHAR given in Appendix B.) Then compare the difference in the exponents of V and U to $MAXEXP-3$, where the 3 is a safety factor. (This difference will also be needed in the next step. See Note 4.) Overflow cannot occur if $MAXEXP-3$ is the larger quantity.

   In terms of our operations (see Chapter 2), the difference in exponents is given by

   INTXP(V) - INTXP(U).

   But it may be quicker to form the difference by considering the absolute values of V and U (or that part of these quantities containing the exponent field) to be integers, subtracting $|U|$ from

$|V|$ using integer operations, and shifting the result, if necessary, so that only the bits corresponding to the exponent field of the floating-point number are retained. Biased exponents are correctly handled by this approach, and the test threshold $MAXEXP$-3 protects against problems associated with small gaps in the sequence of allowable floating-point exponents.

4) If underflow is automatically replaced by zero without issuing a diagnostic, then evaluate V/U and branch on a zero result. Otherwise, the appropriate action here is to compare the difference in exponents (see Note 3) with $MINEXP$+3, where $MINEXP$ is the smallest exponent that does not cause underflow in a normalized floating-point number. ($MINEXP$ is also determined by the subroutine MACHAR in Appendix B.) Underflow cannot occur if $MINEXP$+3 is the smaller quantity.

5) If ATAN2 is a separate subroutine calling ATAN, then replace this step with the call to ATAN using the argument $|V/U|$.

6) On machines that do not support multiple entry points, this is a natural point at which to begin a new subroutine.

7) The strategy from here on is to evaluate a rational function $f + f * R(f^2)$ in scaled fixed point except for the final multiplication by and addition of f, which will be done in floating point. This minimizes the number of floating-point operations while retaining maximum significance for small f. [The fixed-point representation must contain at least two more bits than the floating-point significand (see Glossary) if full precision is to be retained in the final result.] Let f denote the floating-point value of f and y denote a fixed-point quantity. Save f for future use. Then

        FIX(f/2) --> y

(the scaling is necessary because f may be 1).

If magnitude comparisons do not require arithmetic operations, use f in this test. Otherwise compare y to (2-sqrt(3))/2 in fixed point. The necessary constants are

        2-sqrt(3) = 0.26794 91924 31122 70647 (decimal)
                  = 0.21114 12136 47546 52614 (octal)

$$(2-sqrt(3))/2 = 0.13397\ 45962\ 15561\ 35324\ (decimal)$$
$$= 0.10446\ 05057\ 23663\ 25306\ (octal).$$

8) This computation becomes

$$(A \cdot y - 0.25)\ /\ (0.5 \cdot y + B)\ \text{-->}\ y$$

$$REFLOAT(y)\ \text{-->}\ f,$$

where

$A = sqrt(3)/2$
$= 0.86602\ 54037\ 84438\ 64676\ (decimal)$
$= 0.67331\ 72720\ 54114\ 52472\ (octal)$

and

$B = sqrt(3)/4$
$= 0.43301\ 27018\ 92219\ 32338\ (decimal)$
$= 0.33554\ 75350\ 26046\ 25235\ (octal).$

At this point y is the fixed-point representation of f and is no longer scaled.

9) Replace y with $y + y$. A shift operation may be more efficient than the addition.

10) Fixed-point underflow will not hurt in what follows, but we want to be as efficient as possible. We suggest comparing $|y|$ against $eps = 2 \cdot \cdot (-b/2)$ in fixed point, where b is the number of bits in the floating-point significand (see Glossary).

11) This becomes $y \cdot y$ --> g.

12) These are floating-point quantities.

13) We use a fixed-point rational approximation $R(g)$ derived especially for this work. Let b be the number of bits in the significand of a floating-point number. Then

for $b \leq 24$

$p0 = -0.47083\ 25141$
$p1 = -0.05090\ 95825$
$q0 = 0.70625\ 03702$
$q1 = 0.5$

for $25 \leq b \leq 32$

p0 = -0.36002 08621 86
p1 = -0.18000 67122 25
q0 = 0.54003 12986 49
q1 = 0.59402 82307 49
q2 = 0.125

for $33 \leq b \leq 50$

p0 = -0.26714 54200 16400 69
p1 = -0.26715 31158 54956 46
p2 = -0.04964 94559 63021 02
q0 = 0.40071 81300 24749 50
q1 = 0.64116 05517 63182 67
q2 = 0.28743 41765 10949 94
q3 = 0.03125

Evaluate $R(g)$ in fixed point. First form $g \cdot P(g)$ and $Q(g)$ in fixed point using nested multiplication. For example, for $25 \leq b \leq 32$,

$$g \cdot P(g) = (p1 \cdot g + p0) \cdot g$$
and
$$Q(g) = (q2 \cdot g + q1) \cdot g + q0.$$

Finally, form

$$R(g) = .5 \cdot [g \cdot P(g)/Q(g)]$$

in fixed point (use a shift to halve), and convert the result to floating point with $R = \text{REFLOAT}[R(g)]$ (see Chapter 2).

14) Form $f + f \cdot R$ in floating point. The algebraically equivalent form $f \cdot (1+R)$ may be less accurate and should be avoided.

15) The necessary constants are

a(0) = 0.0
a(1) = pi/6 = 0.52359 87755 98298 87308
a(2) = pi/2 = 1.57079 63267 94896 61923
a(3) = pi/3 = 1.04719 75511 96597 74615.

16) Ignore this step if ATAN2 is a separate subroutine. Otherwise, test
    the flag set upon entry.

d. Implementation Notes, All Floating-Point Machines

1) These may be alternate entry points to one subroutine, in which case ATAN2 should set a flag and ATAN should clear that flag (see Note 16).

   When multiple entries are not supported, ATAN and ATAN2 must be separate subroutines. In that case ATAN can be a self-contained subroutine which is called by ATAN2 (see Note 5), or there can be a separate computational subroutine starting with the test for $f > 1$ (see Note 6) which is called by both ATAN and ATAN2.

2) If execution is to continue rather than terminate, then a default function value should be provided in addition to the error message. There is no consensus on this default value, with zero and the largest positive floating-point number both being popular choices.

3) It is important in this step and the next that overflow and underflow warnings not be issued to the user. If it is possible to detect overflow in forming V/U while suppressing the diagnostic message, then that approach should be taken in this step. Otherwise, the following approach should be used.

   Assume that both V and U are normalized floating-point numbers (see Glossary) and that $MAXEXP$ is the largest exponent that does not cause overflow in such numbers. ($MAXEXP$ is one of the parameters determined by the subroutine MACHAR given in Appendix B.) Then compare the difference in the exponents of V and U to $MAXEXP$-3, where the 3 is a safety factor. (This difference will also be needed in the next step. See Note 4.) Overflow cannot occur if $MAXEXP$-3 is the larger quantity.

   In terms of our operations (see Chapter 2), the difference in exponents is given by

   INTXP(V) - INTXP(U).

   But it may be quicker to form the difference by considering the absolute values of V and U (or that part of these quantities containing the exponent field) to be integers, subtracting $|U|$ from

-203-

$|V|$ using integer operations, and shifting the result, if necessary, so that only the bits corresponding to the exponent field of the floating-point number are retained. Biased exponents are correctly handled by this approach, and the test threshold *MAXEXP*-3 protects against problems associated with small gaps in the sequence of allowable floating-point exponents.

4) If underflow is automatically replaced by zero without issuing a diagnostic, then evaluate *V/U* and branch on a zero result. Otherwise, the appropriate action here is to compare the difference in exponents (see Note 3) with *MINEXP*+3, where *MINEXP* is the smallest exponent that does not cause underflow in a normalized floating-point number. (*MINEXP* is also determined by the subroutine MACHAR in Appendix B.) Underflow cannot occur if *MINEXP*+3 is the smaller quantity.

5) If ATAN2 is a separate subroutine calling ATAN, then replace this step with the call to ATAN using the argument $|V/U|$.

6) On machines that do not support multiple entry points, this is a natural point at which to begin a new subroutine.

7) Use the following constant to machine precision:

$$2-\mathrm{sqrt}(3) = 0.26794\ 91924\ 31122\ 70647\ \text{(decimal)}$$
$$= 0.21114\ 12136\ 47546\ 52614\ \text{(octal)}.$$

8) To avoid loss of significance, especially on non-binary machines, rewrite this computation as

$$(((A*f-0.5)-0.5)+f)\ /\ (\mathrm{sqrt}(3)+f),$$

where

$$A = \mathrm{sqrt}(3)-1$$

and

$$\mathrm{sqrt}(3) = 1.73205\ 08075\ 68877\ 29353\ \text{(decimal)}$$
$$= 1.56663\ 65641\ 30231\ 25163\ 55\ \text{(octal)}.$$

9) Ignore this step.

10) We suggest $eps = B**(-t/2)$, where B is the radix of the floating-point number system and t is the number of base-B digits in the floating-point significand (see Glossary).

11) No special comment for floating-point.

12) No special comment for floating-point.

13) We use a rational approximation $R(g)$ derived especially for this work. Let b be the number of bits in the significand of a floating-point number on a non-decimal machine and d the number of digits in the significand on a decimal machine. Then

for b ≤ 24, or d ≤ 8

$p0 = -0.47083\ 25141\ \text{E}+0$
$p1 = -0.50909\ 58253\ \text{E}-1$
$q0 = \ \ 0.14125\ 00740\ \text{E}+1$
$q1 = \ \ 0.10000\ 00000\ \text{E}+1$

For 25 ≤ b ≤ 32, or
9 ≤ d ≤ 10

$p0 = -0.14400\ 83448\ 74\ \text{E}+1$
$p1 = -0.72002\ 68488\ 98\ \text{E}+0$
$q0 = \ \ 0.43202\ 50389\ 19\ \text{E}+1$
$q1 = \ \ 0.47522\ 25845\ 99\ \text{E}+1$
$q2 = \ \ 0.10000\ 00000\ 00\ \text{E}+1$

for 33 ≤ b ≤ 50, or
11 ≤ d ≤ 15

$p0 = -0.42743\ 26720\ 26241\ 096\ \text{E}+1$
$p1 = -0.42744\ 49853\ 67930\ 329\ \text{E}+1$
$p2 = -0.79439\ 12954\ 08336\ 251\ \text{E}+0$
$q0 = \ \ 0.12822\ 98016\ 07919\ 841\ \text{E}+2$
$q1 = \ \ 0.20517\ 13765\ 64218\ 456\ \text{E}+2$
$q2 = \ \ 0.91978\ 93648\ 35039\ 806\ \text{E}+1$
$q3 = \ \ 0.10000\ 00000\ 00000\ 000\ \text{E}+1$

for $51 \leq b \leq 60$, or
$16 \leq d \leq 18$

p0 = -0.13688 76889 41919 26929 E+2
p1 = -0.20505 85519 58616 51981 E+2
p2 = -0.84946 24035 13206 83534 E+1
p3 = -0.83758 29936 81500 59274 E+0
q0 = 0.41066 30668 25757 81263 E+2
q1 = 0.86157 34959 71302 42515 E+2
q2 = 0.59578 43614 25973 44465 E+2
q3 = 0.15024 00116 00285 76121 E+2
q4 = 0.10000 00000 00000 00000 E+1

Form $R = g{\cdot}P(g)/Q(g)$ using nested multiplication.   For example, for $25 \leq b \leq 32$,

$g{\cdot}P(g) = (p1 \cdot g + p0) \cdot g$

and

$Q(g) = (g + q1) \cdot g{+}\ q0.$

Note that because $q2 = 1.0$, $q2{\cdot}g$ can be represented as g, saving one multiplication.

14) Form $f{+}f{\cdot}R$.   The algebraically equivalent form $f{\cdot}(1{+}R)$ may be less accurate and should be avoided.

15) The necessary constants are

a(0) = 0.0
a(1) = pi/6 = 0.52359 87755 98298 87308
a(2) = pi/2 = 1.57079 63267 94896 61923
a(3) = pi/3 = 1.04719 75511 96597 74615

16) Ignore this step if ATAN2 is a separate subroutine.

e. Testing

The tests are divided into four major parts. First is a pair of random argument tests of atan(x) for x in the primary range. Next is a pair of tests for arguments outside the primary range over intervals where progressively more complicated argument reduction is required. Third is a series of cursory checks of the identities

$$\arctan(-x) = -\arctan(x)$$
and
$$\arctan(x) = x$$

to machine precision for $|x| \ll 1$, and a cursory check of the relation between ATAN2 and ATAN. Finally, there is a series of tests of ATAN and ATAN2 with selected arguments at the extremes of the argument ranges to check the resiliency of the subroutines and the error returns.

Because arctan(x) is a bounded monotonic function, the evaluation of the function is generally a stable numerical process. As we saw in the general discussion above, small errors in arguments, especially larger arguments, have little effect on the computed function value. While this means that purification of test arguments is not always necessary, it also means that only tests with arguments in the primary range are likely to uncover numerical deficiencies, barring gross blunders in the argument reduction scheme.

The main accuracy test compares arctan(x) to the truncated Taylor series

$$TS(x) = x \sum_{m=0}^{8} (-1)^m x^{2m}/(2m+1)$$

for $|x| \leq 1/16$. Because the truncation error for this series is bounded in magnitude by $x^{-19}/19$, the relative difference between arctan(x) and TS(x) is bounded in magnitude by $16^{-18}/19$ in the test interval. This is less than the rounding error on all machines with fewer than 19 decimal digits of significance. Additional error due to the numerical evaluation of TS(x) should be limited to one rounding. While it is possible that this test procedure will involve undetected systematic error if the subroutine being tested uses the same Taylor series, there is no problem for implementations of our algorithm.

TABLE 11.1

Typical Results for ATAN/ATAN2 Tests

Test	Machine	B	Library or Program	Reported Loss of Base-B Digits in	
				MRE	**RMS**
1	CDC 6400	2	Ours	0.84	0.00
	IBM/370	16	Ours	1.00	0.38
	CDC 7600	2	FTN 4.8	0.84	0.00
	IBM/370	16	FTX 2.2	1.00	0.37
2	CDC 6400	2	Ours	1.00	0.00
	IBM/370	16	Ours	1.00	0.69
	CDC 7600	2	FTN 4.8	1.00	0.00
	IBM/370	16	FTX 2.2	1.04	0.73
3	CDC 6400	2	Ours	2.50	0.75
	IBM/370	16	Ours	0.76	0.33
	CDC 7600	2	FTN 4.8	1.86	0.39
	IBM/370	16	FTX 2.2	0.76	0.30
4	CDC 6400	2	Ours	2.34	0.05
	IBM/370	16	Ours	1.00	0.67
	CDC 7600	2	FTN 4.8	1.95	0.02
	IBM/370	16	FTX 2.2	1.01	0.68

This test should report a loss of one base-B digit or less for the MRE (see Chapter 3), and a loss of a small fraction of a digit for the RMS, for a good ATAN program. Table 11.1 contains typical test results for various implementations of our algorithm and selected existing library programs.

The second test complements the first by providing an alternate accuracy check for arguments in the primary range. This test is based upon the identity

$$\arctan(u) = \arctan(v) + \arctan[(u-v)/(1+u \cdot v)].$$

In particular, the test measures

$$E = \{\arctan(x) - [\arctan(1/16) + \arctan(y)]\}/\arctan(x),$$

where
$$y = (x-1/16)/(1+x/16),$$

for $1/16 \leq x \leq 2\text{-sqrt}(3)$.   Note that both x and y lie in the primary range of arguments in this case.

It is not practical to purify the argument x to guarantee that the argument y is an exact machine number, but partial purification is useful. The Fortran statement

$$X = ((1.0E0+X*0.625E0)-1.0E0)*16.0E0$$

perturbs x in such a way that both the numerator and denominator terms for y are machine numbers for the interval under consideration. The computation of E is further stabilized by adding the constant $\arctan(1/16)$ in pseudo multiple precision by breaking it into a sum of two constants which are added to $\arctan(y)$ in appropriate order.

Assume in the above test that relative errors of D and d are made in the evaluation of $\arctan(x)$ and $\arctan(y)$, respectively, and that a relative error of e is made in the evaluation of y. Then

$$E = \frac{\arctan(x)(1+D)-\arctan(1/16)-\arctan(y)(1+d+a*e)}{\arctan(x)(1+D)},$$

where
$$a = y/[(1+y^2)\arctan(y)].$$

Simplifying and keeping only terms linear in D, d and e,

$$E = D - bd - ce,$$
where
$$b = \arctan(y)/\arctan(x)$$
and
$$c = a * b.$$

For the interval under consideration, b and c are approximately the same size. Each vanishes for $x = 1/16$, and each is bounded above by 0.77. Thus E measures primarily the relative error in $\arctan(x)$ contaminated by small multiples of the errors in y and $\arctan(y)$. The MRE and RMS errors reported for this test may be slightly greater than those for the first test, but the MRE should still report a loss of one base-B digit or less (see Table 11.1).

Accuracy tests for arguments outside the primary range use the above identity with $u = -v$. In particular, the tests measure

$$E = [2 \arctan(x) - \arctan(y)] / [2 \arctan(x)],$$

where

$$y = 2x/(1-x^2).$$

In the first of two tests x is drawn from the interval $(2-\text{sqrt}(3),\text{sqrt}(2)-1)$, so that y lies in the interval $(\text{sqrt}(3)/3,1)$. This test therefore checks the last stage of argument reduction where arguments are smaller than 1.0 in magnitude. In the second test x is drawn from $(\text{sqrt}(2)-1,1)$, so that y is always greater than 1.0. This test then checks the multistage path for argument reduction.

Argument purification is not practical for these tests, and partial purification does not improve test results. With D, a, d and e defined as above, the error analysis for these tests shows that

$$E = D - d - ae$$

where a monotonically decreases from .83 to .64 for the first interval, and from .64 to 0. for the second. The measured MRE and RMS errors for these tests should be comparable to previous results except that the MRE may report a loss of slightly more than two bits on binary machines. Again, the results reported in Table 11.1 are typical.

```
C      PROGRAM TO TEST ATAN, ATAN2
C
C      DATA REQUIRED
C
C         NONE
C
C      SUBPROGRAMS REQUIRED FROM THIS PACKAGE
C
C         MACHAR - AN ENVIRONMENTAL INQUIRY PROGRAM PROVIDING
C                  INFORMATION ON THE FLOATING-POINT ARITHMETIC
C                  SYSTEM.  NOTE THAT THE CALL TO MACHAR CAN
C                  BE DELETED PROVIDED THE FOLLOWING SIX
C                  PARAMETERS ARE ASSIGNED THE VALUES INDICATED
C
C                     IBETA  - THE RADIX OF THE FLOATING-POINT SYSTEM
C                     IT     - THE NUMBER OF BASE-IBETA DIGITS IN THE
C                              SIGNIFICAND OF A FLOATING-POINT NUMBER
C                     IRND   - 0 IF FLOATING-POINT ADDITION CHOPS,
C                              1 IF FLOATING-POINT ADDITION ROUNDS
C                     MINEXP - THE LARGEST IN MAGNITUDE NEGATIVE
C                              INTEGER SUCH THAT FLOAT(IBETA)**MINEXP
C                              IS A POSITIVE FLOATING-POINT NUMBER
C                     XMIN   - THE SMALLEST NON-VANISHING FLOATING-POINT
C                              POWER OF THE RADIX
C                     XMAX   - THE LARGEST FINITE FLOATING-POINT NO.
C
C         RAN(K) - A FUNCTION SUBPROGRAM RETURNING RANDOM REAL
C                  NUMBERS UNIFORMLY DISTRIBUTED OVER (0,1)
C
C      STANDARD FORTRAN SUBPROGRAMS REQUIRED
C
C         ABS, ALOG, AMAX1, ATAN, ATAN2, FLOAT, SQRT
C
C
C      LATEST REVISION - DECEMBER 6, 1979
C
C      AUTHOR - W. J. CODY
C               ARGONNE NATIONAL LABORATORY
C
C
       INTEGER I,IBETA,IEXP,IOUT,IRND,II,IT,I1,J,K1,K2,K3,MACHEP,
      1         MAXEXP,MINEXP,N,NEGEP,NGRD
       REAL A,AIT,ALBETA,B,BETA,BETAP,DEL,EM,EPS,EPSNEG,EXPON,HALF,OB32,
```

```
     1     ONE,RAN,R6,R7,SUM,TWO,W,X,XL,XMAX,XMIN,XN,XSQ,X1,Y,Z,ZERO,ZZ
C
      IOUT = 6
      CALL MACHAR(IBETA,IT,IRND,NGRD,MACHEP,NEGEP,IEXP,MINEXP,
     1               MAXEXP,EPS,EPSNEG,XMIN,XMAX)
      BETA = FLOAT(IBETA)
      ALBETA = ALOG(BETA)
      AIT = FLOAT(IT)
      ONE = 1.0E0
      HALF = 0.5E0
      TWO = 2.0E0
      ZERO = 0.0E0
      A = -0.0625E0
      B = -A
      OB32 = B * HALF
      N = 2000
      XN = FLOAT(N)
      I1 = 0
C-------------------------------------------------------------------
C     RANDOM ARGUMENT ACCURACY TESTS
C-------------------------------------------------------------------
      DO 300 J = 1, 4
         K1 = 0
         K3 = 0
         X1 = ZERO
         R6 = ZERO
         R7 = ZERO
         DEL = (B - A) / XN
         XL = A
C
         DO 200 I = 1, N
            X = DEL * RAN(I1) + XL
            IF (J .EQ. 2) X = ((1.0E0+X*A)-ONE)*16.0E0
            Z = ATAN(X)
            IF (J .NE. 1) GO TO 100
            XSQ = X * X
            EM = 17.0E0
            SUM = XSQ / EM
C
            DO 80 II = 1, 7
               EM = EM - TWO
               SUM = (ONE/EM - SUM) * XSQ
   80       CONTINUE
```

```
C
            SUM = -X * SUM
            ZZ = X + SUM
            SUM = (X - ZZ) + SUM
            IF (IRND .EQ. 0) ZZ = ZZ + (SUM + SUM)
            GO TO 110
 100        IF (J .NE. 2) GO TO 105
            Y = X - .0625E0
            Y = Y / (ONE + X*A)
            ZZ = (ATAN(Y) - 8.1190004042651526021E-5) + OB32
            ZZ = ZZ + OB32
            GO TO 110
 105        Z = Z + Z
            Y = X / ((HALF + X * HALF)*((HALF - X) + HALF))
            ZZ = ATAN(Y)
 110        W = ONE
            IF (Z .NE. ZERO) W = (Z - ZZ) / Z
            IF (W .GT. ZERO) K1 = K1 + 1
            IF (W .LT. ZERO) K3 = K3 + 1
            W = ABS(W)
            IF (W .LE. R6) GO TO 120
            R6 = W
            X1 = X
 120        R7 = R7 + W * W
            XL = XL + DEL
 200    CONTINUE
C
        K2 = N - K3 - K1
        R7 = SQRT(R7/XN)
        IF (J .EQ. 1) WRITE (IOUT,1000)
        IF (J .EQ. 2) WRITE (IOUT,1001)
        IF (J .GT. 2) WRITE (IOUT,1002)
        WRITE (IOUT,1010) N,A,B
        WRITE (IOUT,1011) K1,K2,K3
        WRITE (IOUT,1020) IT,IBETA
        W = -999.0E0
        IF (R6 .NE. ZERO) W = ALOG(ABS(R6))/ALBETA
        WRITE (IOUT,1021) R6,IBETA,W,X1
        W = AMAX1(AIT+W,ZERO)
        WRITE (IOUT,1022) IBETA,W
        W = -999.0E0
        IF (R7 .NE. ZERO) W = ALOG(ABS(R7))/ALBETA
        WRITE (IOUT,1023) R7,IBETA,W
```

```
            W = AMAX1(AIT+W,ZERO)
            WRITE (IOUT,1022) IBETA,W
            A = B
            IF (J .EQ. 1) B = TWO - SQRT(3.0E0)
            IF (J .EQ. 2) B = SQRT(TWO) - ONE
            IF (J .EQ. 3) B = ONE
     300 CONTINUE
C-------------------------------------------------------------------
C     SPECIAL TESTS
C-------------------------------------------------------------------
        WRITE (IOUT,1025)
        WRITE (IOUT,1030)
        A = 5.0E0
C
        DO 320 I = 1, 5
            X = RAN(I1) * A
            Z = ATAN(X) + ATAN(-X)
            WRITE (IOUT,1060) X, Z
     320 CONTINUE
C
        WRITE (IOUT,1031)
        BETAP = BETA ** IT
        X = RAN(I1) / BETAP
C
        DO 330 I = 1, 5
            Z = X - ATAN(X)
            WRITE (IOUT,1060) X, Z
            X = X / BETA
     330 CONTINUE
C
        WRITE (IOUT,1032)
        A = -TWO
        B = 4.0E0
C
        DO 340 I = 1, 5
            X = RAN(I1) * B + A
            Y = RAN(I1)
            W = -Y
            Z = ATAN(X/Y) - ATAN2(X,Y)
            ZZ = ATAN(X/W) - ATAN2(X,W)
            WRITE (IOUT,1059) X, Y, Z, ZZ
     340 CONTINUE
C
```

```
      WRITE (IOUT,1035)
      EXPON = FLOAT(MINEXP) * 0.75E0
      X = BETA ** EXPON
      Y = ATAN(X)
      WRITE (IOUT,1061) X, Y
C------------------------------------------------------------------------
C     TEST OF ERROR RETURNS
C------------------------------------------------------------------------
      WRITE (IOUT,1050)
      WRITE (IOUT,1051) XMAX
      Z = ATAN(XMAX)
      WRITE (IOUT,1061) XMAX, Z
      X = ONE
      Y = ZERO
      WRITE (IOUT,1053) X, Y
      Z = ATAN2(X,Y)
      WRITE (IOUT,1062) X, Y, Z
      WRITE (IOUT,1053) XMIN, XMAX
      Z = ATAN2(XMIN,XMAX)
      WRITE (IOUT,1062) XMIN, XMAX, Z
      WRITE (IOUT,1053) XMAX, XMIN
      Z = ATAN2(XMAX,XMIN)
      WRITE (IOUT,1062) XMAX, XMIN, Z
      X = ZERO
      WRITE (IOUT,1054) X, Y
      Z = ATAN2(X,Y)
      WRITE (IOUT,1062) X, Y, Z
      WRITE (IOUT,1100)
      STOP
1000 FORMAT(43H1TEST OF ATAN(X) VS TRUNCATED TAYLOR SERIES   //)
1001 FORMAT(20H1TEST OF ATAN(X) VS ,
    1 40HATAN(1/16) + ATAN((X-1/16)/(1+X/16))     //)
1002 FORMAT(40H1TEST OF 2*ATAN(X) VS ATAN(2X/(1-X*X))      //)
1010 FORMAT(I7,47H RANDOM ARGUMENTS WERE TESTED FROM THE INTERVAL /
    1 6X,1H(,E15.4,1H,,E15.4,1H))//)
1011 FORMAT(19H ATAN(X) WAS LARGER,I6,7H TIMES,/
    1    12X,7H AGREED,I6,11H TIMES, AND /
    1    8X,11HWAS SMALLER,I6,7H TIMES.//)
1020 FORMAT(10H THERE ARE,I4,5H BASE,I4,
    1    46H SIGNIFICANT DIGITS IN A FLOATING-POINT NUMBER   //)
1021 FORMAT(30H THE MAXIMUM RELATIVE ERROR OF,E15.4,3H = ,I4,3H **,
    1 F7.2/4X,16HOCCURRED FOR X =,E17.6)
1022 FORMAT(27H THE ESTIMATED LOSS OF BASE,I4,
```

```
      1   22H SIGNIFICANT DIGITS IS,F7.2//)
 1023 FORMAT(40H THE ROOT MEAN SQUARE RELATIVE ERROR WAS,E15.4,
      1      3H = ,I4,3H **,F7.2)
 1025 FORMAT(14H1SPECIAL TESTS//)
 1030 FORMAT(53H THE IDENTITY   ATAN(-X) = -ATAN(X)   WILL BE TESTED.//
      1      8X,1HX,9X,12HF(X) + F(-X)/)
 1031 FORMAT(52H THE IDENTITY ATAN(X) = X , X SMALL, WILL BE TESTED.//
      1        8X,1HX,9X,8HX - F(X)/)
 1032 FORMAT(51H THE IDENTITY ATAN(X/Y) = ATAN2(X,Y) WILL BE TESTED /
      1 57H THE FIRST COLUMN OF RESULTS SHOULD BE 0, THE SECOND +-PI//
      2 8X,1HX,13X,1HY,5X,15HF1(X/Y)-F2(X,Y),18HF1(X/Y)-F2(X/(-Y)) /)
 1035 FORMAT(43H TEST OF UNDERFLOW FOR VERY SMALL ARGUMENT. /)
 1050 FORMAT(22H1TEST OF ERROR RETURNS //)
 1051 FORMAT(38H ATAN WILL BE CALLED WITH THE ARGUMENT,E15.7/
      1        41H THIS SHOULD NOT TRIGGER AN ERROR MESSAGE/)
 1053 FORMAT(40H ATAN2 WILL BE CALLED WITH THE ARGUMENTS/2E15.7/
      1        41H THIS SHOULD NOT TRIGGER AN ERROR MESSAGE/)
 1054 FORMAT(40H ATAN2 WILL BE CALLED WITH THE ARGUMENTS/2E15.7/
      1        37H THIS SHOULD TRIGGER AN ERROR MESSAGE//)
 1059 FORMAT(4E15.7/)
 1060 FORMAT(2E15.7/)
 1061 FORMAT(6X,6H ATAN(,E13.6,3H) =,E13.6/)
 1062 FORMAT(6X,7H ATAN2(,2E13.6,3H) =,E13.6/)
 1100 FORMAT(25H THIS CONCLUDES THE TESTS )
C     ---------- LAST CARD OF ATAN/ATAN2 TEST PROGRAM ----------
      END
```

12. SINH/COSH

a. General Discussion

We consider first the computation of sinh(X) whose mathematical definition is

$$sinh(X) = [exp(X)-exp(-X)]/2,$$

from which it follows that

$$sinh(-X) = -sinh(X).$$

This definition could be used to compute the function over much of the argument range, but there are some problems. The definition is not useful for small $|X|$ because the subtraction of nearly equal quantities causes severe loss of precision, nor is it useful for $|X|$ near the point at which sinh(X) is too large in magnitude to be represented in the machine.

The problem in the first case is obvious and is solved by using a rational minimax approximation to sinh(X) for $|X| \leq 1$. But the problem in the second case is subtle and requires some care to solve. Because the overflow threshold for sinh(X) is beyond the overflow threshold for exp(X), it appears natural to reformulate the computation as

$$sinh(X) = exp(X-ln(2))$$

when $|X|$ is sufficiently large that the negative exponential term in the definition can safely be ignored. But, if

$$y = exp(X),$$

then it easily follows that

    dy/y = dX,

i.e., that the transmitted error in the exponential function is roughly
equal to the absolute error in the argument (see Glossary). Because
ln(2) is not an exact machine number, the finite word length of the
machine implies that the absolute error in X-ln(2), hence the
transmitted error in sinh(X), is proportional to the magnitude of X even
when X is error-free. To avoid this problem, revise the computation to

    sinh(X) = (v/2)·exp(X-ln(v)),   X >> 1,

where ln(v) is an exact machine number slightly larger than ln(2) with
the last few digits of its significand zero. Now the argument for the
exponential function is error-free whenever X is, and the transmitted
error depends only upon the error in X.

     This latter formulation also avoids some of the numerical problems
inherent in the computation of sinh(X) from its definition on machines
with wobbling precision (see Glossary). On a hexadecimal machine, for
example, there exist X for which exp(X) = $(1+e)\cdot16**n$, $e > 0$. The
floating-point significand for this quantity has three leading zero
bits. For many of the same X, sinh(X) = $(1-d)\cdot16**n$, $d > 0$. The
floating-point significand for this quantity has no leading zero bits.
But then the last three bits of the significand of sinh(X) are probably
incorrect if the computation involves explicit evaluation of exp(X). In
the alternate formulation, however, $v/2 > 1$, and exp(X-ln(v)) < sinh(X)
for X moderately large. For these X the significand for the exponential
contains no leading zero bits unless the significand for sinh does, and
the computation is stable despite wobbling precision. For smaller X
there are still regions of instability, but these regions are smaller
than before.

     We could extend this more stable computation to all $|X| > 1$ by
setting

    sinh(X) = (v/2)·[exp(X-ln(v))-v⁻²/exp(X-ln(v))].

On the one hand this obviates a logical test to determine when the
revised formulation should be used instead of the definition, and adds
numerical stability on non-binary machines. On the other hand the

revised formulation is more complicated and does not contribute extra
stability on binary machines.   We will therefore restrict use of this
extended revision to floating-point non-binary machines.

Consider now the computation of cosh(X) which is defined as

$$\cosh(X) = [\exp(X)+\exp(-X)]/2,$$

whence

$$\cosh(-X) = \cosh(X).$$

This function is well behaved for small $|X|$ but has the same problems as
sinh(X) for large $|X|$.   Thus the method just discussed for sinh(X)
should also be used here when $|X| > 1$. However, the original definition
in terms of exp(X) should be used for $|X| < 1$ because it is numerically
more stable.

b. Flow Chart for SINH(X)/COSH(X)

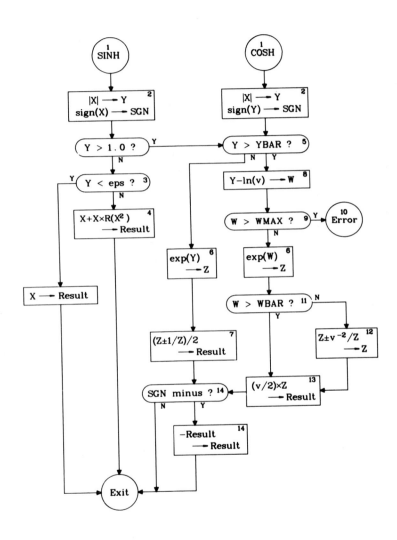

Note: Small integers indicate an implementation note.

c. Implementation Notes, Non-Decimal Fixed-Point Machines

1) These may be alternate entries to one subroutine, in which case a flag must be set to indicate which entry is active (see Notes 7 and 12). When multiple entries are not supported, we suggest that SINH and COSH be independent of each other and not access a common computational subroutine. The portions of the flow chart applicable to each program should be obvious in that case.

2) The algebraic sign of X will be needed later for the computation of SINH. *SGN* may be designated by either a flag or a floating-point number, depending upon the most efficient method of implementing the uses of *SGN* described in Notes 10 and 14. Thus ±1 or X might be appropriate values of *SGN* for the SINH entry, with +1 or Y the corresponding values for the COSH entry. Note, however, that if SINH and COSH are independent programs, then *SGN* is not needed in the COSH program and should be deleted from it.

3) *Eps* should be chosen so that $\sinh(X) = X$ to machine precision for $|X| < eps$, and so that X^3 will not underflow in floating point. We suggest $eps = B**(-t/2)$, where B is the radix of the floating-point representation and there are t base-B digits in the significand (see Glossary).

4) We evaluate a polynomial approximation $X+X*[X^2*P(X^2)]$, derived especially for this work, using fixed-point arithmetic for all except the final operations with X. This minimizes the number of floating-point operations while maximizing the accuracy for small $|X|$. Let b be the number of bits in the significand of a floating-point number. Then

for b ≤ 24

p0 = 0.16666 7338 E+0
p1 = 0.83299 1192 E-2
p2 = 0.20393 9897 E-3

for $25 \leq b \leq 32$

p0 = 0.16666 66643 02 E+0
p1 = 0.83333 52592 90 E-2
p2 = 0.19835 81244 79 E-3
p3 = 0.28185 23941 73 E-5

for $33 \leq b \leq 40$

p0 = 0.16666 66666 7209 E+0
p1 = 0.83333 33269 0119 E-2
p2 = 0.19841 29762 2826 E-3
p3 = 0.27551 91453 3845 E-5
p4 = 0.25535 00764 7784 E-7

for $41 \leq b \leq 50$

p0 = 0.16666 66666 66657 93 E+0
p1 = 0.83333 33333 47538 58 E-2
p2 = 0.19841 26975 50150 70 E-3
p3 = 0.27557 34409 51771 46 E-5
p4 = 0.25048 43562 94822 61 E-7
p5 = 0.16327 26568 62665 98 E-9

Let

f = FIX(X)

Using fixed-point arithmetic, form $g = f^2$. Then use nested multiplication to evaluate $g \cdot P(g)$, a polynomial in g with coefficients $p0, p1, \ldots, pN$. For example, for $25 \leq b \leq 32$,

g·P(g) = (((p3·g + p2)·g + p1)·g + p0)·g

Finally, set $R = \text{REFLOAT}[g \cdot P(g)]$ (see Chapter 2), and evaluate $X + X \cdot R$ using floating-point arithmetic. Avoid the form $X \cdot [1.0 + R]$, which is less accurate.

5) For binary machines, let *YBAR* be the largest floating-point number which is acceptable to the EXP program and for which $1.0/\text{EXP}(YBAR)$ does not underflow. For non-binary machines link the test for $Y > 1.0$ in the path for SINH to Step 8 instead of this step, and set *YBAR* = 1.0 here.

6) Invoke the standard EXP program.

7) Use the "-" sign for SINH and the "+" sign for COSH on binary machines. If SINH and COSH are alternate entries to the same program, this decision on sign requires that the active entry be flagged (see Note 1). This path is followed only for the COSH entry on non-binary machines. In that case replace the computation with $Z \cdot 0.5 + 0.5/Z$ for increased accuracy.

8) Values of $\ln(v)$, v^{-2} and $v/2-1$ will be needed at this step and below (see Notes 12 and 13). An octal value is given for $\ln(v)$ because it is important that this constant be represented exactly in the machine. The decimal value is also given for use in Note 9.

$$\ln(v) = 0.542714 \ \ (octal)$$
$$= 0.69316 \ 10107 \ 42187 \ 50000 \ E+0 \ (decimal)$$
$$v^{-2} = 0.24999 \ 30850 \ 04514 \ 99336 \ E+0$$
$$v/2-1 = 0.13830 \ 27787 \ 96019 \ 02638 \ E-4$$

9) To protect against overflow, WMAX should be the smaller of a) the largest argument acceptable to the EXP program and b) $\ln(XMAX)-\ln(v)+0.69$, where XMAX is the largest positive floating-point number.

10) If execution is to continue rather than terminate, then a default function value of $\pm XMAX$ should be returned, where XMAX is the largest positive floating-point number and the algebraic sign agrees with SGN (see Note 2). If $SGN = \pm 1.0$, we do not recommend the explicit construction of $SGN \cdot XMAX$ here because floating-point multiplication by ± 1.0 may not be accurate and/or may trigger an overflow.

11) Omit this box on binary machines. On non-binary machines WBAR should be chosen large enough that $EXP(W)-EXP(-W) = EXP(W)$ for all $W > WBAR$. We suggest $WBAR = 0.35 \cdot (b+1)$, where b is defined in Note 4.

12) Omit this box on binary machines. On non-binary machines the value of v^{-2} is given in Note 8. Use the "-" sign for SINH and the "+" sign for COSH. If SINH and COSH are alternate entries to the same program, this decision on sign requires that the active entry be flagged (see Note 1).

13) Rewrite this computation as

$$Z + (v/2-1.0) \cdot Z,$$

where $(v/2-1)$ is given in Note 8.

14) There are two obvious ways to implement the decision on *SGN*: One is to treat *SGN* as a floating-point number and branch on the algebraic sign of that number, and the other is to treat *SGN* as a flag. (Because floating-point multiplication by 1.0 introduces error on some machines, we do not advise collapsing these two boxes in the flow chart into a simple replacement of *Result* with *SGN·Result* when *SGN* = ±1.0.)   The particular implementation chosen depends upon the available repertoire of branching instructions.   Note that if SINH and COSH are independent programs, then these steps should be omitted in the COSH program only.

d. Implementation Notes, All Floating-Point Machines

1) These may be alternate entries to one subroutine, in which case a flag must be set to indicate which entry is active (see Notes 7 and 12). When multiple entries are not supported, we suggest that SINH and COSH be independent of each other and not access a common computational subroutine. The portions of the flow chart applicable to each program should be obvious in that case.

2) The algebraic sign of X will be needed later for the computation of SINH. SGN may be designated by either a flag or a floating-point number, depending upon the most efficient method of implementing the uses of SGN described in Notes 10 and 14. Thus ± 1 or X might be appropriate values of SGN for the SINH entry, with $+1$ or Y the corresponding values for the COSH entry. Note, however, that if SINH and COSH are independent programs, then SGN is not needed in the *COSH* program and should be deleted from it.

3) *Eps* should be chosen so that $\sinh(X) = X$ to machine precision for $|X| < eps$, and so that X^3 will not underflow. We suggest $eps = B**(-t/2)$, where B is the radix of the floating-point representation and there are t base-B digits in the significand (see Glossary).

4) We use a rational approximation $R(x^2)$ derived especially for this work. Let b be the number of bits in the significand on a non-decimal machine, and d be the number of digits in the significand on a decimal machine. Then

for $b \leq 24$, or $d \leq 7$

p0 = -0.71379 3159 E+1
p1 = -0.19033 3399 E+0
q0 = -0.42827 7109 E+2
q1 = 0.10000 0000 E+1

for $25 \leq b \leq 40$, or
8 $\leq d \leq 12$

```
p0 =  0.10622 28883 7151 E+4
p1 =  0.31359 75645 6058 E+2
p2 =  0.34364 14035 8506 E+0
q0 =  0.63733 73302 1822 E+4
q1 = -0.13051 01250 9199 E+3
q2 =  0.10000 00000 0000 E+1
```

for $41 \leq b \leq 50$, or
13 $\leq d \leq 15$

```
p0 =  0.23941 43592 30500 69 E+4
p1 =  0.85943 28483 85490 10 E+2
p2 =  0.13286 42866 92242 29 E+1
p3 =  0.77239 39820 29419 23 E-2
q0 =  0.14364 86155 38302 92 E+5
q1 = -0.20258 33686 64278 69 E+3
q2 =  0.10000 00000 00000 00 E+1
```

for $51 \leq b \leq 60$, or
16 $\leq d \leq 18$

```
p0 = -0.35181 28343 01771 17881 E+6
p1 = -0.11563 52119 68517 68270 E+5
p2 = -0.16375 79820 26307 51372 E+3
p3 = -0.78966 12741 73570 99479 E+0
q0 = -0.21108 77005 81062 71242 E+7
q1 =  0.36162 72310 94218 36460 E+5
q2 = -0.27773 52311 96507 01667 E+3
q3 =  0.10000 00000 00000 00000 E+1
```

Let $f = x^2$ and evaluate $P(f)$ and $Q(f)$, polynomials in f with coefficients $p0$, $p1$, ..., pN and $q0$, $q1$, ..., qM, respectively. Use nested multiplication. For example, for $25 \leq b \leq 40$,

    Q(f) = (f + q1)•f + q0.

Note that explicit multiplication by $q2 = 1.0$ is avoided. Finally, let $R(f) = f•[P(f)/Q(f)]$, and form $X + X•R$. Avoid the form $X•[1.0 + R]$, which is less accurate.

5) For binary machines, let *YBAR* be the largest floating-point number which is acceptable to the EXP program, and for which $1.0/EXP(YBAR)$ does not underflow. For non-binary machines link the test for $Y > 1.0$ in the path from SINH to Step 8 instead of this step, and set *YBAR* = 1.0 here.

6) Invoke the standard EXP program.

7) Use the "-" sign for SINH and the "+" sign for COSH on binary machines. If SINH and COSH are alternate entries to the same program, this decision on sign requires that the active entry be flagged (see Note 1). This path is followed only for the COSH entry on non-binary machines. In that case replace the computation with $Z \cdot 0.5 + 0.5/Z$ for increased numerical stability.

8) Values of $\ln(v)$, v^{-2} and $v/2-1$ will be needed at this step and below (see Notes 12 and 13). The following list of constants for non-decimal machines includes an octal value for $\ln(v)$ because it is important that this constant be represented exactly in the machine. The decimal value is also given for use in Note 9.

$$\ln(v) = 0.542714 \text{ (octal)}$$
$$= 0.69316\ 10107\ 42187\ 50000\ E+0 \text{ (decimal)}$$
$$v^{-2} = 0.24999\ 30850\ 04514\ 99336\ E+0$$
$$v/2-1 = 0.13830\ 27787\ 96019\ 02638\ E-4$$

For decimal machines, use the following constants:

$$\ln(v) = 0.6932\ E+0$$
$$v^{-2} = 0.24997\ 35916\ 74870\ 15965\ E+0$$
$$v/2-1 = 0.52820\ 83502\ 58748\ 52469\ E-4$$

9) To protect against overflow *WMAX* should be the smaller of a) the largest argument acceptable to the EXP program, and b) $\ln(XMAX)-\ln(v)+0.69$, where *XMAX* is the largest positive floating-point number.

10) If execution is to continue rather than terminate, then a default function value of $\pm XMAX$ should be returned, where *XMAX* is the largest positive floating-point number and the algebraic sign agrees with *SGN* (see Note 2). If *SGN* = ±1.0, we do not recommend the explicit construction of $SGN \cdot XMAX$ here because floating-point

multiplication by ±1.0 may not be accurate and/or may trigger an overflow.

11) Omit this box on binary machines. On non-binary machines $WBAR$ should be chosen large enough that $EXP(W)-EXP(-W) = EXP(W)$ for all $W > WBAR$. We suggest $WBAR = 0.35 \cdot (b+1)$ for non-decimal machines, and $WBAR = 1.16 \cdot (d+1)$ for decimal machines, where b and d are defined in Note 4.

12) Omit this box on binary machines. On non-binary machines the value of v^{-2} is given in Note 8. Use the "-" sign for SINH and the "+" sign for COSH. If SINH and COSH are alternate entries to the same program, this decision on sign requires that the active entry be flagged (see Note 1).

13) Rewrite this computation as

$$Z + (v/2-1.0) \cdot Z,$$

where $(v/2-1)$ is given in Note 8.

14) There are two obvious ways to implement the decision on SGN: One is to treat SGN as a floating-point number and branch on the algebraic sign of that number, and the other is to treat SGN as a flag. (Because floating-point multiplication by 1.0 introduces error on some machines, we do not advise collapsing these two boxes in the flow chart into a simple replacement of $Result$ with $SGN \cdot Result$ when $SGN = ±1.0$.) The particular implementation chosen depends upon the available repertoire of branching instructions. Note that if SINH and COSH are independent programs, then these steps should be omitted in the COSH program only.

e. Testing

The tests are divided into four major parts. First is a pair of random argument accuracy tests of the computation of sinh(x) and cosh(x) for arguments in the interval (0,0.5) where the obvious algorithm for sinh(x) leads to subtraction error. Second is a pair of tests for arguments greater than 2.0 based on mathematical identities. Third is a cursory check of the properties

$$sinh(-x) = -sinh(x),$$

$$cosh(-x) = cosh(x),$$

and

$$sinh(x) = x$$

to machine precision for $|x| \ll 1$, and a check for underflow for small $|x|$. Finally there is a test with two large arguments, one lying beyond the point at which EXP(X) will overflow but within the theoretical domain of SINH(X), thus checking whether the domain of SINH is greater than that of EXP, and the other lying outside the domain of SINH, thus testing the error return.

The random argument tests for x in the interval (0,0.5) compare sinh(x) and cosh(x) against the usual Taylor series expansions truncated so as to provide accuracy over the test interval to at least the working precision of the machine. The final evaluation of the series is usually correct to within rounding error and is frequently correctly rounded even on computers with truncating arithmetic. These tests should therefore be almost as discriminating as direct comparisons against higher precision computations except possibly in cases where the program being tested implements the same Taylor series. In that case systematic error might go undetected. This is normally not the case for programs for cosh(x), which usually implement the definition in terms of exp(x) for all x, and is certainly not the case for implementations of the algorithms recommended here.

Satisfactory programs for sinh(x) should result in a loss of about one base-B digit in the measured MRE (see Chapter 3) and a half digit or less in the measured RMS error. Satisfactory programs for cosh(x) may report a loss of one digit for the MRE, and almost one digit for the RMS error. Both RMS errors may be much smaller on binary machines with

TABLE 12.1

Typical Results for SINH/COSH Tests

Test	Machine	B	Library or Program	Reported Loss of Base-B Digits in	
				MRE	RMS
1	CDC 6400	2	Ours	1.00	0.00
	IBM/370	16	Ours	1.00	0.48
	CDC 6400	2	FTN 4.6	1.48	0.08
	IBM/370	16	FTX 2.2	1.00	0.45
2	CDC 6400	2	Ours	1.00	0.00
	IBM/370	16	Ours	1.00	0.85
	CDC 6400	2	FTN 4.6	1.00	0.41
	IBM/370	16	FTX 2.2	1.00	0.76
3	CDC 6400	2	Ours	2.36	0.98
	IBM/370	16	Ours	1.26	0.77
	CDC 6400	2	FTN 4.6	2.50	1.00
	IBM/370	16	FTX 2.2	1.25	0.76
4	CDC 6400	2	Ours	2.04	0.98
	IBM/370	16	Ours	1.25	0.77
	CDC 6400	2	FTN 4.6	2.19	0.99
	IBM/370	16	FTX 2.2	1.24	0.75

rounding arithmetic, but the MRE errors will probably still involve a loss of about one digit. Table 12.1 reports test results for several implementations of our algorithm and for selected existing library programs.

The random argument accuracy test for $\sinh(x)$, $x > 2.0$, is based on the identity

$$2 \sinh(x) \cosh(1) = \sinh(x+1) + \sinh(x-1).$$

Thus we measure

$$E = \{\sinh(x) - C[\sinh(x+1)+\sinh(x-1)]\} / \sinh(x),$$

where

$$C = 1/[2 \cosh(1)] = 0.324027...$$

Because x is to be a random argument generated in the computer, we can safely assume it is error-free. But $x+1$ and $x-1$ must also be error-free. Therefore we generate the random argument $x+1$ and determine x and $x-1$ from it by subtraction. This process is always error-free for $x > 2$ provided the constant 1.0 is error-free.

Under these assumptions the only error involved in the evaluation of E is that associated with the several evaluations of sinh and the roundoff in the arithmetic manipulation of these values. Assume that relative errors of D, d and e are made in the evaluations of $\sinh(x)$, $\sinh(x+1)$ and $\sinh(x-1)$, respectively. Then $\sinh(x)$ is replaced by $\sinh(x) \cdot (1+D)$ in the expression for E, and similar replacements are made for $\sinh(x+1)$ and $\sinh(x-1)$. Retaining only terms linear in D, d and e, the resulting expression can be simplified to give

$$E = D - [cd + (1-c)e]$$

$$c = C \sinh(x+1)/\sinh(x);$$

c varies between 0.895 and 0.881 as x varies between 2 and infinity. The measured quantity E is therefore roughly the difference between D and d, scrambled a little by the roundoff error in evaluating E. Assuming D and d are of the same order of magnitude, E can be about twice D or can almost vanish, even though D is significant. In practice the MRE and RMS errors determined from E range between 1/2 and 3/2 those for D.

The corresponding test for $\cosh(x)$ uses the identity

$$2 \cosh(x) \cosh(1) = \cosh(x+1) + \cosh(x-1).$$

An analysis similar to that just given shows that

$$E = D - [cd + (1-c)e]$$

in this case as well, where E, D, d and e are defined analogously to the sinh case,

$$c = C \cosh(x+1)/\cosh(x),$$

and c varies between 0.867 and 0.881 as x varies between 2 and infinity. The MRE and RMS errors for E bear the same relation to those for D as before.

These identity tests are not as sensitive as the previous tests based upon truncated Taylor series, but they do detect gross errors. In general, the errors detected here should compare with errors associated with the exponential function for large arguments. Satisfactory programs for $\sinh(x)$ and $\cosh(x)$ should lose no more than one and a small fraction base-B digits in the reported MRE (perhaps 2 bits on a binary machine), and perhaps half of that loss in the reported RMS error. See Table 12.1 for typical test results.

```
C       PROGRAM TO TEST SINH/COSH
C
C       DATA REQUIRED
C
C          NONE
C
C       SUBPROGRAMS REQUIRED FROM THIS PACKAGE
C
C          MACHAR - AN ENVIRONMENTAL INQUIRY PROGRAM PROVIDING
C                   INFORMATION ON THE FLOATING-POINT ARITHMETIC
C                   SYSTEM.  NOTE THAT THE CALL TO MACHAR CAN
C                   BE DELETED PROVIDED THE FOLLOWING SIX
C                   PARAMETERS ARE ASSIGNED THE VALUES INDICATED
C
C                      IBETA  - THE RADIX OF THE FLOATING-POINT SYSTEM
C                      IT     - THE NUMBER OF BASE-IBETA DIGITS IN THE
C                               SIGNIFICAND OF A FLOATING-POINT NUMBER
C                      IRND   - 0 IF FLOATING-POINT ADDITION CHOPS,
C                               1 IF FLOATING-POINT ADDITION ROUNDS
C                      MINEXP - THE LARGEST IN MAGNITUDE NEGATIVE
C                               INTEGER SUCH THAT FLOAT(IBETA)**MINEXP
C                               IS A POSITIVE FLOATING-POINT NUMBER
C                      EPS    - THE SMALLEST POSITIVE FLOATING-POINT
C                               NUMBER SUCH THAT 1.0+EPS .NE. 1.0
C                      XMAX   - THE LARGEST FINITE FLOATING-POINT NO.
C
C          RAN(K) - A FUNCTION SUBPROGRAM RETURNING RANDOM REAL
C                   NUMBERS UNIFORMLY DISTRIBUTED OVER (0,1)
C
C
C       STANDARD FORTRAN SUBPROGRAMS REQUIRED
C
C          ABS, ALOG, AMAX1, COSH, FLOAT, INT, SINH, SQRT
C
C
C       LATEST REVISION - DECEMBER 6, 1979
C
C       AUTHOR - W. J. CODY
C                ARGONNE NATIONAL LABORATORY
C
C
        INTEGER I,IBETA,IEXP,II,IOUT,IRND,IT,I1,I2,J,K1,K2,K3,
     1          MACHEP,MAXEXP,MINEXP,N,NEGEP,NGRD,NIT
```

```
      REAL  A,AIND,AIT,ALBETA,ALXMAX,B,BETA,BETAP,C,C0,DEL,DEN,EPS,
     1       EPSNEG,FIVE,ONE,RAN,R6,R7,THREE,W,X,XL,XMAX,XMIN,XN,X1,
     2       XSQ,Y,Z,ZERO,ZZ
C
      IOUT = 6
      CALL MACHAR(IBETA,IT,IRND,NGRD,MACHEP,NEGEP,IEXP,MINEXP,
     1            MAXEXP,EPS,EPSNEG,XMIN,XMAX)
      BETA = FLOAT(IBETA)
      ALBETA = ALOG(BETA)
      ALXMAX = ALOG(XMAX)
      AIT = FLOAT(IT)
      ZERO = 0.0E0
      ONE = 1.0E0
      THREE = 3.0E0
      FIVE = 5.0E0
      C0 = FIVE/16.0E0 + 1.152713683194269979E-2
      A = ZERO
      B = 0.5E0
      C = (AIT + ONE) * 0.35E0
      IF (IBETA .EQ. 10) C = C * THREE
      N = 2000
      XN = FLOAT(N)
      I1 = 0
      I2 = 2
      NIT = 2 - (INT(ALOG(EPS)*THREE))/20
      AIND = FLOAT(NIT+NIT+1)
C-----------------------------------------------------------------
C     RANDOM ARGUMENT ACCURACY TESTS
C-----------------------------------------------------------------
      DO 300 J = 1, 4
         IF (J .NE. 2) GO TO 30
         AIND = AIND - ONE
         I2 = 1
   30    K1 = 0
         K3 = 0
         X1 = ZERO
         R6 = ZERO
         R7 = ZERO
         DEL = (B - A) / XN
         XL = A
C
         DO 200 I = 1, N
            X = DEL * RAN(I1) + XL
```

```
            IF (J .GT. 2) GO TO 80
            XSQ = X * X
            ZZ = ONE
            DEN = AIND
C
            DO 40 II = I2, NIT
               W = ZZ * XSQ/(DEN*(DEN-ONE))
               ZZ = W + ONE
               DEN = DEN - 2.0E0
   40       CONTINUE
C
            IF (J .EQ. 2) GO TO 50
            W = X*XSQ*ZZ/6.0E0
            ZZ = X + W
            Z = SINH(X)
            IF (IRND .NE. 0) GO TO 110
            W = (X - ZZ) + W
            ZZ = ZZ + (W + W)
            GO TO 110
   50       Z = COSH(X)
            IF (IRND .NE. 0) GO TO 110
            W = (ONE - ZZ) + W
            ZZ = ZZ + (W + W)
            GO TO 110
   80       Y = X
            X = Y - ONE
            W = X - ONE
            IF (J .EQ. 4) GO TO 100
            Z = SINH(X)
            ZZ = (SINH(Y) + SINH(W)) * C0
            GO TO 110
  100       Z = COSH(X)
            ZZ = (COSH(Y) + COSH(W)) * C0
  110       W = ONE
            IF (Z .NE. ZERO) W = (Z - ZZ)/Z
            IF (W .GT. ZERO) K1 = K1 + 1
            IF (W .LT. ZERO) K3 = K3 + 1
            W = ABS(W)
            IF (W .LE. R6) GO TO 120
            R6 = W
            X1 = X
  120       R7 = R7 + W * W
            XL = XL + DEL
```

```
      200      CONTINUE
C
               K2 = N - K3 - K1
               R7 = SQRT(R7/XN)
               I = (J/2) * 2
               IF (J .EQ. 1) WRITE (IOUT,1000)
               IF (J .EQ. 2) WRITE (IOUT,1005)
               IF (J .EQ. 3) WRITE (IOUT,1001)
               IF (J .EQ. 4) WRITE (IOUT,1006)
               WRITE (IOUT,1010) N,A,B
               IF (I .NE. J) WRITE (IOUT,1011) K1,K2,K3
               IF (I .EQ. J) WRITE (IOUT,1012) K1,K2,K3
               WRITE (IOUT,1020) IT,IBETA
               W = -999.0E0
               IF (R6 .NE. ZERO) W = ALOG(ABS(R6))/ALBETA
               WRITE (IOUT,1021) R6,IBETA,W,X1
               W = AMAX1(AIT+W,ZERO)
               WRITE (IOUT,1022) IBETA,W
               W = -999.0E0
               IF (R7 .NE. ZERO) W = ALOG(ABS(R7))/ALBETA
               WRITE (IOUT,1023) R7,IBETA,W
               W = AMAX1(AIT+W,ZERO)
               WRITE (IOUT,1022) IBETA,W
               IF (J .NE. 2) GO TO 300
               B = ALXMAX
               A = THREE
      300 CONTINUE
C--------------------------------------------------------------------
C     SPECIAL TESTS
C--------------------------------------------------------------------
      WRITE (IOUT,1025)
      WRITE (IOUT,1030)
C
      DO 320 I = 1, 5
         X = RAN(I1) * A
         Z = SINH(X) + SINH(-X)
         WRITE (IOUT,1060) X, Z
      320 CONTINUE
C
      WRITE (IOUT,1031)
      BETAP = BETA ** IT
      X = RAN(I1) / BETAP
C
```

```
      DO 330 I = 1, 5
         Z = X - SINH(X)
         WRITE (IOUT,1060) X, Z
         X = X / BETA
  330 CONTINUE
C
      WRITE (IOUT,1032)
C
      DO 340 I = 1, 5
         X = RAN(I1) * A
         Z = COSH(X) - COSH(-X)
         WRITE (IOUT,1060) X, Z
  340 CONTINUE
C
      WRITE (IOUT,1035)
      X = BETA ** (FLOAT(MINEXP)*0.75E0)
      Y = SINH(X)
      WRITE (IOUT,1061) X, Y
C-------------------------------------------------------------------
C     TEST OF ERROR RETURNS
C-------------------------------------------------------------------
      WRITE (IOUT,1050)
      X = ALXMAX + 0.125E0
      WRITE (IOUT,1051) X
      Y = SINH(X)
      WRITE (IOUT,1055) Y
      X = BETAP
      WRITE (IOUT,1052) X
      Y = SINH(X)
      WRITE (IOUT,1055) Y
      WRITE (IOUT,1100)
      STOP
 1000 FORMAT(45H1TEST OF SINH(X) VS T.S. EXPANSION OF SINH(X) //)
 1001 FORMAT(43H1TEST OF SINH(X) VS C*(SINH(X+1)+SINH(X-1))   //)
 1005 FORMAT(45H1TEST OF COSH(X) VS T.S. EXPANSION OF COSH(X) //)
 1006 FORMAT(43H1TEST OF COSH(X) VS C*(COSH(X+1)+COSH(X-1))   //)
 1010 FORMAT(I7,47H RANDOM ARGUMENTS WERE TESTED FROM THE INTERVAL /
     1 6X,1H(,E15.4,1H,,E15.4,1H)//)
 1011 FORMAT(19H SINH(X) WAS LARGER,I6,7H TIMES, /
     1      12X,7H AGREED,I6,11H TIMES, AND /
     1      8X,11HWAS SMALLER,I6,7H TIMES.//)
 1012 FORMAT(19H COSH(X) WAS LARGER,I6,7H TIMES, /
     1      12X,7H AGREED,I6,11H TIMES, AND /
```

```
      1    8X,11HWAS SMALLER,I6,7H TIMES.//)
 1020 FORMAT(10H THERE ARE,I4,5H BASE,I4,
      1    46H SIGNIFICANT DIGITS IN A FLOATING-POINT NUMBER  //)
 1021 FORMAT(30H THE MAXIMUM RELATIVE ERROR OF,E15.4,3H = ,I4,3H **,
      1 F7.2/4X,16HOCCURRED FOR X =,E17.6)
 1022 FORMAT(27H THE ESTIMATED LOSS OF BASE,I4,
      1 22H SIGNIFICANT DIGITS IS,F7.2//)
 1023 FORMAT(40H THE ROOT MEAN SQUARE RELATIVE ERROR WAS,E15.4,
      1    3H = ,I4,3H **,F7.2)
 1025 FORMAT(14H1SPECIAL TESTS//)
 1030 FORMAT(51H THE IDENTITY  SINH(-X) = -SINH(X)  WILL BE TESTED.//
      1    8X,1HX,9X,12HF(X) + F(-X)/)
 1031 FORMAT(52H THE IDENTITY SINH(X) = X , X SMALL, WILL BE TESTED.//
      1    8X,1HX,9X,8HX - F(X)/)
 1032 FORMAT(50H THE IDENTITY  COSH(-X) = COSH(X)  WILL BE TESTED.//
      1    8X,1HX,9X,12HF(X) - F(-X)/)
 1035 FORMAT(43H TEST OF UNDERFLOW FOR VERY SMALL ARGUMENT. /)
 1050 FORMAT(22H1TEST OF ERROR RETURNS//)
 1051 FORMAT(38H SINH WILL BE CALLED WITH THE ARGUMENT,E15.4/
      1    41H THIS SHOULD NOT TRIGGER AN ERROR MESSAGE//)
 1052 FORMAT(38H0SINH WILL BE CALLED WITH THE ARGUMENT,E15.4/
      1    37H THIS SHOULD TRIGGER AN ERROR MESSAGE//)
 1055 FORMAT(24H SINH RETURNED THE VALUE,E15.4///)
 1060 FORMAT(2E15.7/)
 1061 FORMAT(6X,6H SINH(,E13.6,3H) =,E13.6/)
 1100 FORMAT(25H THIS CONCLUDES THE TESTS )
C     ---------- LAST CARD OF SINH/COSH TEST PROGRAM ----------
      END
```

13. TANH

a. General Discussion

The hyperbolic tangent is defined and computable for all floating-point arguments. The computation is reduced to one for positive arguments by the identity

$$\tanh(-x) = -\tanh(x).$$

The computation for positive arguments in turn relies upon the exponential function through the equation

$$\tanh(x) = 1 - 2/(\exp(2x)+1),$$

provided the argument is large enough to avoid loss of significance in the subtraction but not so large that the subtracted term is negligible with respect to 1. The possibility of subtraction error exists whenever $|\tanh(x)| < .5$, i.e., whenever $|x| < \ln(3)/2$. Therefore a rational approximation generated especially for this work is used to evaluate $\tanh(x)$ for small x. The point at which $\tanh(x) = 1$ to machine precision varies with the machine. Let B be the radix of the floating-point number system, and let there be t base-B digits in the significand of a floating-point number (see Glossary). Then the second term in the above equation is negligible whenever

$$[\exp(2x)+1] \cdot B^{**}(-t-1) > 2,$$

and the equation reduces to $\tanh(x) = 1$ for $x > [\ln(2)+(t+1)\ln(B)]/2$.

Numerical stability of the above computation for small arguments depends upon the form of the rational approximation. The forms to be used here are stable.   For intermediate-size arguments the major source of error   is the evaluation   of exp($2x$),   but again the   computation is stable.   To show this, let $y = \tanh(x)$, and $z = \exp(2x)$.   Then

    $dy/y = \text{csch}(2x)\ dz/z$,

where dy/y is the relative   error in $\tanh(x)$ directly traceable   to a relative   error dz/z in exp($2x$).   The   magnification factor   csch($2x$) achieves   its   maximum   value   of   0.75 for x = $\ln(3)/2$ and   rapidly diminishes for larger x,   assuming a value of about 0.04 for x = 2,   for example.   Thus small   errors   in   exp($2x$)   have little   effect on   the computed value of $\tanh(x)$.

b. Flow Chart for TANH(X)

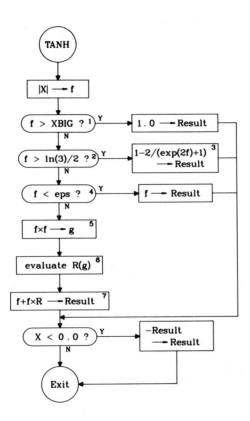

Note: Small integers indicate an implementation note.

c. Implementation Notes, Non-Decimal Fixed-Point Machines

1) In this case the radix B of the floating-point number system is $2**k$. Let b be the number of bits in the significand of a floating-point number (see Glossary). Then

$$XBIG = (b+k+1)\ln(2)/2.$$

2) Use the following value to machine precision:

$$\ln(3)/2 = 0.54930\ 61443\ 34054\ 84570.$$

3) There are no easy ways to avoid calling the exponential subroutine or performing the floating-point divide. For numerical accuracy, especially on non-binary machines, we suggest that the computation be reformulated as

$$0.5 - 1.0/(EXP(f+f)+1.0) \ \text{--> Result}$$

$$\text{Result} + \text{Result} \ \text{--> Result.}$$

4) Fixed-point underflow will not hurt here, but we want to be efficient. *Eps* should be chosen small enough that $\tanh(f) = f$ to machine precision for $f < eps$, but large enough that the shorter computational path will be followed whenever $R(g)$ would underflow (see Note 6). We suggest $eps = 2**(-b/2)$.

5) The strategy from here on is to evaluate a rational function $f + f * R(f*f)$ in scaled fixed point except for the final multiplication by and addition of f, which will be done in floating point. This minimizes the number of floating-point operations while retaining maximum significance for small f. (The fixed-point representation must contain at least $b+2$ bits if full precision is to be retained in the final result.) Let f denote the floating-point value of f and y denote a fixed-point quantity. Save f for future use. Then (see Chapter 2)

$$FIX(f) \ \text{--> } y$$

$$y*y \ \text{--> } g.$$

The value of y need not be retained further.

6) We use a fixed-point rational approximation $R(g)$ derived especially for this work.   Let b be the number of bits in the significand of a floating-point number.   Then

for b ≤ 24

```
p0 = -0.20594 32032
p1 = -0.00095 77527
q0 =  0.61782 99136
q1 =  0.25
```

for 25 ≤ b ≤ 36

```
p0 = -0.16456 21718 76916
p1 = -0.00729 40215 35344
q0 =  0.49368 65157 46738
q1 =  0.21935 66677 38052
q2 =  0.00781 25
```

for 37 ≤ b ≤ 48

```
p0 = -0.14890 25189 60799 158
p1 = -0.00721 23976 13392 670
p2 = -0.00000 28314 39213 644
q0 =  0.44670 75568 82545 442
q1 =  0.20032 02155 87335 741
q2 =  0.00781 25
```

We evaluate $R(g)$ in fixed point.   First form $P(g)$ and $Q(g)$ in fixed point using nested multiplication.   For example, for $25 \le b \le 36$,

$$P(g) = p1 \cdot g + p0$$
and
$$Q(g) = (q2 \cdot g + q1) \cdot g + q0.$$

Finally, form

$$R(g) = g \cdot [P(g)/Q(g)]$$

in fixed point, and convert back to floating point with R = REFLOAT$[R(g)]$ (see Chapter 2).

7) Form $f+f \cdot R$ in floating point. The algebraically equivalent form $f \cdot (1+R)$ may be less accurate and should be avoided.

d. Implementation Notes, All Floating-Point Machines

1) Let B be the radix of the floating-point number system and t the number of base-B digits in the significand of a floating-point number (see Glossary). Then

   XBIG = [ln(2)+(t+1)ln(B)]/2.

2) Use the following value to machine precision:

   ln(3)/2 = 0.54930 61443 34054 84570.

3) For numerical accuracy, especially on non-binary machines, we suggest that the computation be reformulated as

   0.5 - 1.0/(EXP(f+f)+1.0) --> Result

   Result + Result --> Result

4) *Eps* should be chosen so that $\tanh(f) = f$ to machine precision for $f < eps$, and so that $R(g)$ will not underflow for $f > eps$ (see Note 6). We suggest *eps* $= B**(-t/2)$, where B and t are as defined in Note 1.

5) No special comment for floating point.

6) We use a rational approximation $R(g)$ derived especially for this work. Let b be the number of bits in the significand of a floating-point number on a non-decimal machine and d the number of digits in the significand on a decimal machine. Then

   for b ≤ 24, or d ≤ 8

   p0 = -0.82377 28127 E+0
   p1 = -0.38310 10665 E-2
   q0 = 0.24713 19654 E+1
   q1 = 0.10000 00000 E+1

for $25 \leq b \leq 36$, or
$$9 \leq d \leq 11$$

p0 = -0.21063 95800 0245 E+2
p1 = -0.93363 47565 2401 E+0
q0 = 0.63191 87401 5582 E+2
q1 = 0.28077 65347 0471 E+2
q2 = 0.10000 00000 0000 E+1

for $37 \leq b \leq 48$, or
$$12 \leq d \leq 14$$

p0 = -0.19059 52242 69822 92 E+2
p1 = -0.92318 68945 14261 77 E+0
p2 = -0.36242 42193 46421 73 E-3
q0 = 0.57178 56728 09658 17 E+2
q1 = 0.25640 98759 51789 75 E+2
q2 = 0.10000 00000 00000 00 E+1

for $49 \leq b \leq 60$, or
$$15 \leq d \leq 18$$

p0 = -0.16134 11902 39962 28053 E+4
p1 = -0.99225 92967 22360 83313 E+2
p2 = -0.96437 49277 72254 69787 E+0
q0 = 0.48402 35707 19886 88686 E+4
q1 = 0.22337 72071 89623 12926 E+4
q2 = 0.11274 47438 05349 49335 E+3
q3 = 0.10000 00000 00000 00000 E+1

Evaluate $g \cdot P(g)$ and $Q(g)$ using nested multiplication.   For example,
for $25 \leq b \leq 36$,

$$g \cdot P(g) = (p1 \cdot g + p0) \cdot g$$
and
$$Q(g) = (g + q1) \cdot g + q0.$$

Note that because $q2 = 1.0$, $q2 \cdot g$ can be represented as g, saving one
multiplication. Finally, form

$$R(g) = g \cdot [P(g)/Q(g)].$$

7) The algebraically equivalent form $f*(1+R)$ may be less accurate and should be avoided.

e. Testing

The tests are divided into three major parts. First is a random argument test for the interval (0,ln(3)/2), where direct computation of tanh(x) is performed. Second is a similar test for the interval where the exponential function is used to compute tanh(x), i.e., for (ln(3)/2,*XBIG*), where *XBIG* is the point beyond which tanh(x) = 1 to machine precision. Finally there is a series of cursory checks of the properties

$$\tanh(-x) = -\tanh(x),$$

$$\tanh(x) = x, \quad |x| \ll 1,$$

and

$$\tanh(x) = 1, \quad x \gg 1,$$

where the last two relations need only hold to machine precision. There are also a number of tests with special arguments to be sure the computation is free of underflow and overflow.

The random argument accuracy tests are based upon the identity

$$\tanh(u+v) = [\tanh(u)+\tanh(v)]/[1+\tanh(u)\tanh(v)].$$

In particular, the tests measure

$$E = \{\tanh(x)-[\tanh(y)+A]/[1+\tanh(y)A]\} / \tanh(x),$$

where

$$y = x - 1/8,$$

and

$$A = \tanh(1/8).$$

The first test measures E when both x and y are in the interval (0,ln(3)/2), while for the second both are in the interval (ln(3)/2,*XBIG*).

Assume that relative errors of D and d are made in the evaluation of tanh(x) and tanh(y), respectively, but that no error is made in evaluating y given x. By restricting x to be greater than 1/8 this

TABLE 13.1

Typical Results for TANH Tests

Test	Machine	B	Library or Program	Reported Loss of Base-B Digits in	
				MRE	RMS
1	CDC 6400	2	Ours	1.75	0.03
	IBM/370	16	Ours	1.05	0.72
	CDC 6400	2	FTN 4.6	3.90	1.81
	IBM/370	16	FTX 2.2	1.05	0.72
2	CDC 6400	2	Ours	1.73	0.00
	IBM/370	16	Ours	1.00	0.61
	CDC 6400	2	FTN 4.6	2.25	0.00
	IBM/370	16	FTX 2.2	1.00	0.60

latter condition is guaranteed to hold without argument purification. Then

$$E = \frac{\tanh(x)(1+D)-[\tanh(y)(1+d)+A]/[1+\tanh(y)A(1+d)]}{\tanh(x)(1+D)}.$$

Simplifying and keeping only terms linear in D and d, we get

$$E = D - ad,$$

where

$$a = [\tanh(x)-A]/[\tanh(y)+A].$$

The term a vanishes for $x = 1/8$ but rises rapidly to assume a value of about 0.74 for $x = \ln(3)/2$ and an asymptotic value of 7/9 for large x.

These tests may report a loss of about one base-B digit in the MRE (see Chapter 3), and a loss of a fraction of a digit in the RMS error for good implementations of $\tanh(x)$ on non-binary machines. On binary machines the MRE may report a loss of almost two bits, but the RMS error should report almost no loss. Table 13.1 lists test results for various implementations of our algorithm and for several existing library programs. The only unusually large errors listed are those for the FTN 4.6 library program on the CDC 6400. These may indicate problems that should be corrected, especially for arguments in the first test interval.

```
C     PROGRAM TO TEST TANH
C
C     DATA REQUIRED
C
C        NONE
C
C     SUBPROGRAMS REQUIRED FROM THIS PACKAGE
C
C        MACHAR - AN ENVIRONMENTAL INQUIRY PROGRAM PROVIDING
C                 INFORMATION ON THE FLOATING-POINT ARITHMETIC
C                 SYSTEM.  NOTE THAT THE CALL TO MACHAR CAN
C                 BE DELETED PROVIDED THE FOLLOWING FIVE
C                 PARAMETERS ARE ASSIGNED THE VALUES INDICATED
C
C                 IBETA  - THE RADIX OF THE FLOATING-POINT SYSTEM
C                 IT     - THE NUMBER OF BASE-IBETA DIGITS IN THE
C                          SIGNIFICAND OF A FLOATING-POINT NUMBER
C                 MINEXP - THE LARGEST IN MAGNITUDE NEGATIVE
C                          INTEGER SUCH THAT FLOAT(IBETA)**MINEXP
C                          IS A POSITIVE FLOATING-POINT NUMBER
C                 XMIN   - THE SMALLEST NON-VANISHING FLOATING-POINT
C                          POWER OF THE RADIX
C                 XMAX   - THE LARGEST FINITE FLOATING-POINT NO.
C
C        RAN(K) - A FUNCTION SUBPROGRAM RETURNING RANDOM REAL
C                 NUMBERS UNIFORMLY DISTRIBUTED OVER (0,1)
C
C
C     STANDARD FORTRAN SUBPROGRAMS REQUIRED
C
C        ABS, ALOG, AMAX1, FLOAT, SQRT, TANH
C
C
C     LATEST REVISION - DECEMBER 6, 1979
C
C     AUTHOR - W. J. CODY
C              ARGONNE NATIONAL LABORATORY
C
C
      INTEGER I,IBETA,IEXP,IOUT,IRND,IT,I1,J,K1,K2,K3,MACHEP,
     1        MAXEXP,MINEXP,N,NEGEP,NGRD
      REAL A,AIT,ALBETA,B,BETA,BETAP,C,D,DEL,EPS,EPSNEG,EXPON,HALF,
     1     ONE,RAN,R6,R7,W,X,XL,XMAX,XMIN,XN,X1,Y,Z,ZERO,ZZ
```

```
      C
            IOUT = 6
            CALL MACHAR(IBETA,IT,IRND,NGRD,MACHEP,NEGEP,IEXP,MINEXP,
           1              MAXEXP,EPS,EPSNEG,XMIN,XMAX)
            BETA = FLOAT(IBETA)
            ALBETA = ALOG(BETA)
            AIT = FLOAT(IT)
            ZERO = 0.0E0
            ONE = 1.0E0
            HALF = 0.5E0
            A = 0.125E0
            B = ALOG(3.0E0) * HALF
            C = 1.2435300177159620805E-1
            D = ALOG(2.0E0) + (AIT+ONE) * ALOG(BETA) * HALF
            N = 2000
            XN = FLOAT(N)
            I1 = 0
      C----------------------------------------------------------------
      C     RANDOM ARGUMENT ACCURACY TESTS
      C----------------------------------------------------------------
            DO 300 J = 1, 2
               K1 = 0
               K3 = 0
               X1 = ZERO
               R6 = ZERO
               R7 = ZERO
               DEL = (B - A) / XN
               XL = A
      C
               DO 200 I = 1, N
                  X = DEL * RAN(I1) + XL
                  Z = TANH(X)
                  Y = X - 0.125E0
                  ZZ = TANH(Y)
                  ZZ = (ZZ + C) / (ONE + C*ZZ)
                  W = ONE
                  IF (Z .NE. ZERO) W = (Z - ZZ) / Z
                  IF (W .GT. ZERO) K1 = K1 + 1
                  IF (W .LT. ZERO) K3 = K3 + 1
                  W = ABS(W)
                  IF (W .LE. R6) GO TO 120
                  R6 = W
                  X1 = X
```

```
 120         R7 = R7 + W * W
             XL = XL + DEL
 200     CONTINUE
C
         K2 = N - K3 - K1
         R7 = SQRT(R7/XN)
         WRITE (IOUT,1000)
         WRITE (IOUT,1010) N,A,B
         WRITE (IOUT,1011) K1,K2,K3
         WRITE (IOUT,1020) IT,IBETA
         W = -999.0E0
         IF (R6 .NE. ZERO) W = ALOG(ABS(R6))/ALBETA
         WRITE (IOUT,1021) R6,IBETA,W,X1
         W = AMAX1(AIT+W,ZERO)
         WRITE (IOUT,1022) IBETA,W
         W = -999.0E0
         IF (R7 .NE. ZERO) W = ALOG(ABS(R7))/ALBETA
         WRITE (IOUT,1023) R7,IBETA,W
         W = AMAX1(AIT+W,ZERO)
         WRITE (IOUT,1022) IBETA,W
         A = B + A
         B = D
 300 CONTINUE
C------------------------------------------------------------------
C    SPECIAL TESTS
C------------------------------------------------------------------
     WRITE (IOUT,1025)
     WRITE (IOUT,1030)
C
     DO 320 I = 1, 5
         X = RAN(I1)
         Z = TANH(X) + TANH(-X)
         WRITE (IOUT,1060) X, Z
 320 CONTINUE
C
     WRITE (IOUT,1031)
     BETAP = BETA ** IT
     X = RAN(I1) / BETAP
C
     DO 330 I = 1, 5
         Z = X - TANH(X)
         WRITE (IOUT,1060) X, Z
         X = X / BETA
```

```
  330 CONTINUE
C
      WRITE (IOUT,1032)
      X = D
      B = 4.0E0
C
      DO 340 I = 1, 5
         Z = (TANH(X) - HALF) - HALF
         WRITE (IOUT,1060) X, Z
         X = X + B
  340 CONTINUE
C
      WRITE (IOUT,1035)
      EXPON = FLOAT(MINEXP) * 0.75E0
      X = BETA ** EXPON
      Z = TANH(X)
      WRITE (IOUT,1061) X, Z
      WRITE (IOUT,1040) XMAX
      Z = TANH(XMAX)
      WRITE (IOUT,1061) XMAX, Z
      WRITE (IOUT,1040) XMIN
      Z = TANH(XMIN)
      WRITE (IOUT,1061) XMIN, Z
      X = ZERO
      WRITE (IOUT,1040) X
      Z = TANH(X)
      WRITE (IOUT,1061) X, Z
      WRITE (IOUT,1100)
      STOP
 1000 FORMAT(20H1TEST OF TANH(X) VS ,
     1  50H(TANH(X-1/8)+TANH(1/8))/(1+TANH(X-1/8)TANH(1/8))   //)
 1010 FORMAT(I7,47H RANDOM ARGUMENTS WERE TESTED FROM THE INTERVAL /
     1  6X,1H(,E15.4,1H,,E15.4,1H)//)
 1011 FORMAT(19H TANH(X) WAS LARGER,I6,7H TIMES, /
     1    12X,7H AGREED,I6,11H TIMES, AND /
     2   8X,11HWAS SMALLER,I6,7H TIMES.//)
 1020 FORMAT(10H THERE ARE,I4,5H BASE,I4,
     1    46H SIGNIFICANT DIGITS IN A FLOATING-POINT NUMBER  //)
 1021 FORMAT(30H THE MAXIMUM RELATIVE ERROR OF,E15.4,3H = ,I4,3H **,
     1  F7.2/4X,16HOCCURRED FOR X =,E17.6)
 1022 FORMAT(27H THE ESTIMATED LOSS OF BASE,I4,
     1  22H SIGNIFICANT DIGITS IS,F7.2//)
 1023 FORMAT(40H THE ROOT MEAN SQUARE RELATIVE ERROR WAS,E15.4,
```

```
      1    3H = ,I4,3H **,F7.2)
 1025 FORMAT(14H1SPECIAL TESTS//)
 1030 FORMAT(53H THE IDENTITY    TANH(-X) = -TANH(X)    WILL BE TESTED.//
      1        8X,1HX,9X,12HF(X) + F(-X)/)
 1031 FORMAT(52H THE IDENTITY TANH(X) = X , X SMALL, WILL BE TESTED.//
      1        8X,1HX,9X,8HX - F(X)/)
 1032 FORMAT(52H THE IDENTITY TANH(X) = 1 , X LARGE, WILL BE TESTED.//
      1        8X,1HX,9X,8H1 - F(X)/)
 1035 FORMAT(43H TEST OF UNDERFLOW FOR VERY SMALL ARGUMENT. /)
 1040 FORMAT(51H THE FUNCTION TANH WILL BE CALLED WITH THE ARGUMENT,
      1    E15.7)
 1060 FORMAT(2E15.7/)
 1061 FORMAT(6X,6H TANH(,E13.6,3H) =,E13.6/)
 1100 FORMAT(25H THIS CONCLUDES THE TESTS )
C     ---------- LAST CARD OF TANH TEST PROGRAM ----------
      END
```

APPENDIX A.   RANDOM NUMBER GENERATORS

```
      REAL FUNCTION RAN(K)
C
C     RANDOM NUMBER GENERATOR - BASED ON ALGORITHM 266 BY PIKE AND
C       HILL (MODIFIED BY HANSSON), COMMUNICATIONS OF THE ACM,
C       VOL. 8, NO. 10, OCTOBER 1965.
C
C     THIS SUBPROGRAM IS INTENDED FOR USE ON COMPUTERS WITH
C       FIXED POINT WORDLENGTH OF AT LEAST 29 BITS.  IT IS
C       BEST IF THE FLOATING POINT SIGNIFICAND HAS AT MOST
C       29 BITS.
C
      INTEGER IY,J,K
      DATA IY/100001/
C
      J = K
      IY = IY * 125
      IY = IY - (IY/2796203) * 2796203
      RAN = FLOAT(IY) / 2796203.0E0
      RETURN
C     ---------- LAST CARD OF RAN ----------
      END



      REAL FUNCTION RANDL(X)
C
C     RETURNS PSEUDO RANDOM NUMBERS LOGARITHMICALLY DISTRIBUTED
C       OVER (1,EXP(X)).  THUS A*RANDL(ALOG(B/A)) IS
C       LOGARITHMICALLY DISTRIBUTED IN (A,B).
C
C     OTHER SUBROUTINES REQUIRED
C
C        EXP(X) - THE EXPONENTIAL ROUTINE
```

```
C
C          RAN(K) - A FUNCTION PROGRAM RETURNING RANDOM REAL
C                     NUMBERS UNIFORMLY DISTRIBUTED OVER (0,1).
C                     THE ARGUMENT K IS A DUMMY.
C
C
      REAL RAN,X
      INTEGER K
      DATA K/1/
C
      RANDL = EXP(X*RAN(K))
      RETURN
C     ---------- LAST CARD OF RANDL ----------
      END
```

APPENDIX B.   ENVIRONMENTAL INQUIRY SUBPROGRAM

The subroutine MACHAR is intended to dynamically determine thirteen parameters relating to the floating-point arithmetic system.   The first three--the radix B, the number of base-B digits in the significand, and the question of whether floating-point addition rounds or truncates--are determined with an algorithm developed by M. Malcolm [1972].   Several of the remaining parameters are determined with "folk algorithms," but most of them   are determined   using algorithms   we believe   to be   new.   The methods are sometimes *ad hoc,*   and the program is not guaranteed to work on all machines.   Not all of the conditions under which MACHAR will fail are known,   but it   is known to   fail on   Honeywell machines   where the active arithmetic   registers are   wider than   storage registers.   This particular   failure   can   be   corrected   by   forcing   the   storage   of intermediate   results at   critical points   (see   Gentleman   and   Marovich [1974]).   We   have deliberately not   followed that procedure   in MACHAR because   the   program   is   already very   complicated   and   difficult   to understand.

Aside from the   Honeywell machines the program has   run properly on all other machines we have tried.   These include, in alphabetical order, BESM-6 (Russian),   Burroughs 6700,   CDC   6000/7000 series,   CRAY-1,   IBM 360/370 series, IBM 3033, PDP-10, PDP-11, Univac 1108,   Varian V76,   and Z-80 (with Microsoft   Fortran).   MACHAR has been   translated into Basic and run on the Datapoint 2200,   IBM   5100 and PDP-10.   It has even been translated   and run   on the   HP-67 and   TI-59 programmable   calculators. Despite these successes we strongly   urge that parameter values returned by this program be   examined critically the first time it   is run on any machine.

```
      SUBROUTINE MACHAR(IBETA,IT,IRND,NGRD,MACHEP,NEGEP,IEXP,MINEXP,
     1                 MAXEXP,EPS,EPSNEG,XMIN,XMAX)
C
      INTEGER I,IBETA,IEXP,IRND,IT,IZ,J,K,MACHEP,MAXEXP,MINEXP,
     1        MX,NEGEP,NGRD
      REAL A,B,BETA,BETAIN,BETAM1,EPS,EPSNEG,ONE,XMAX,XMIN,Y,Z,ZERO
CD    DOUBLE PRECISION A,B,BETA,BETAIN,BETAM1,EPS,EPSNEG,ONE,XMAX,
CD   1                 XMIN,Y,Z,ZERO
C
C     THIS SUBROUTINE IS INTENDED TO DETERMINE THE CHARACTERISTICS
C     OF THE FLOATING-POINT ARITHMETIC SYSTEM THAT ARE SPECIFIED
C     BELOW.  THE FIRST THREE ARE DETERMINED ACCORDING TO AN
C     ALGORITHM DUE TO M. MALCOLM, CACM 15 (1972), PP. 949-951,
C     INCORPORATING SOME, BUT NOT ALL, OF THE IMPROVEMENTS
C     SUGGESTED BY M. GENTLEMAN AND S. MAROVICH, CACM 17 (1974),
C     PP. 276-277.  THE VERSION GIVEN HERE IS FOR SINGLE PRECISION.
C     CARDS CONTAINING  CD  IN COLUMNS 1 AND 2 CAN BE USED TO
C     CONVERT THE SUBROUTINE TO DOUBLE PRECISION BY REPLACING
C     EXISTING CARDS IN THE OBVIOUS MANNER.
C
C
C        IBETA   - THE RADIX OF THE FLOATING-POINT REPRESENTATION
C        IT      - THE NUMBER OF BASE IBETA DIGITS IN THE FLOATING-POINT
C                  SIGNIFICAND
C        IRND    - 0 IF FLOATING-POINT ADDITION CHOPS,
C                  1 IF FLOATING-POINT ADDITION ROUNDS
C        NGRD    - THE NUMBER OF GUARD DIGITS FOR MULTIPLICATION.  IT IS
C                  0 IF  IRND=1, OR IF  IRND=0 AND ONLY  IT  BASE  IBETA
C                  DIGITS PARTICIPATE IN THE POST NORMALIZATION SHIFT
C                  OF THE FLOATING-POINT SIGNIFICAND IN MULTIPLICATION
C                  1 IF  IRND=0  AND MORE THAN  IT  BASE  IBETA  DIGITS
C                  PARTICIPATE IN THE POST NORMALIZATION SHIFT OF THE
C                  FLOATING-POINT SIGNIFICAND IN MULTIPLICATION
C        MACHEP  - THE LARGEST NEGATIVE INTEGER SUCH THAT
C                  1.0+FLOAT(IBETA)**MACHEP .NE. 1.0, EXCEPT THAT
C                  MACHEP IS BOUNDED BELOW BY  -(IT+3)
C        NEGEPS  - THE LARGEST NEGATIVE INTEGER SUCH THAT
C                  1.0-FLOAT(IBETA)**NEGEPS .NE. 1.0, EXCEPT THAT
C                  NEGEPS IS BOUNDED BELOW BY  -(IT+3)
C        IEXP    - THE NUMBER OF BITS (DECIMAL PLACES IF IBETA = 10)
C                  RESERVED FOR THE REPRESENTATION OF THE EXPONENT
C                  (INCLUDING THE BIAS OR SIGN) OF A FLOATING-POINT
C                  NUMBER
```

```
C          MINEXP  - THE LARGEST IN MAGNITUDE NEGATIVE INTEGER SUCH THAT
C                    FLOAT(IBETA)**MINEXP IS A POSITIVE FLOATING-POINT
C                    NUMBER
C          MAXEXP  - THE LARGEST POSITIVE INTEGER EXPONENT FOR A FINITE
C                    FLOATING-POINT NUMBER
C          EPS     - THE SMALLEST POSITIVE FLOATING-POINT NUMBER SUCH
C                    THAT  1.0+EPS .NE. 1.0. IN PARTICULAR, IF EITHER
C                    IBETA = 2   OR   IRND = 0, EPS = FLOAT(IBETA)**MACHEP.
C                    OTHERWISE,  EPS = (FLOAT(IBETA)**MACHEP)/2
C          EPSNEG  - A SMALL POSITIVE FLOATING-POINT NUMBER SUCH THAT
C                    1.0-EPSNEG .NE. 1.0. IN PARTICULAR, IF IBETA = 2
C                    OR   IRND = 0, EPSNEG = FLOAT(IBETA)**NEGEPS.
C                    OTHERWISE,  EPSNEG = (IBETA**NEGEPS)/2.  BECAUSE
C                    NEGEPS IS BOUNDED BELOW BY -(IT+3), EPSNEG MAY NOT
C                    BE THE SMALLEST NUMBER WHICH CAN ALTER 1.0 BY
C                    SUBTRACTION.
C          XMIN    - THE SMALLEST NON-VANISHING FLOATING-POINT POWER OF THE
C                    RADIX.  IN PARTICULAR,  XMIN = FLOAT(IBETA)**MINEXP
C          XMAX    - THE LARGEST FINITE FLOATING-POINT NUMBER.  IN
C                    PARTICULAR   XMAX = (1.0-EPSNEG)*FLOAT(IBETA)**MAXEXP
C                    NOTE - ON SOME MACHINES  XMAX WILL BE ONLY THE
C                    SECOND, OR PERHAPS THIRD, LARGEST NUMBER, BEING
C                    TOO SMALL BY 1 OR 2 UNITS IN THE LAST DIGIT OF
C                    THE SIGNIFICAND.
C
C       LATEST REVISION - OCTOBER 22, 1979
C
C       AUTHOR - W. J. CODY
C                ARGONNE NATIONAL LABORATORY
C
C-----------------------------------------------------------------
      ONE = FLOAT(1)
CD    ONE = DBLE(FLOAT(1))
      ZERO = 0.0E0
CD    ZERO = 0.0D0
C-----------------------------------------------------------------
C       DETERMINE IBETA,BETA ALA MALCOLM
C-----------------------------------------------------------------
      A = ONE
   10 A = A + A
      IF (((A+ONE)-A)-ONE .EQ. ZERO) GO TO 10
      B = ONE
   20 B = B + B
```

```
          IF ((A+B)-A .EQ. ZERO) GO TO 20
       IBETA = INT((A+B)-A)
CD     IBETA = INT(SNGL((A + B) - A))
       BETA = FLOAT(IBETA)
CD     BETA = DBLE(FLOAT(IBETA))
C-----------------------------------------------------------------
C     DETERMINE IT, IRND
C-----------------------------------------------------------------
       IT = 0
       B = ONE
   100 IT = IT + 1
          B = B * BETA
           IF (((B+ONE)-B)-ONE .EQ. ZERO) GO TO 100
       IRND = 0
       BETAM1 = BETA - ONE
       IF ((A+BETAM1)-A .NE. ZERO) IRND = 1
C-----------------------------------------------------------------
C     DETERMINE NEGEP, EPSNEG
C-----------------------------------------------------------------
       NEGEP = IT + 3
       BETAIN = ONE / BETA
       A = ONE
C
       DO 200 I = 1, NEGEP
          A = A * BETAIN
   200 CONTINUE
C
       B = A
   210 IF ((ONE-A)-ONE .NE. ZERO) GO TO 220
          A = A * BETA
          NEGEP = NEGEP - 1
       GO TO 210
   220 NEGEP = -NEGEP
       EPSNEG = A
       IF ((IBETA .EQ. 2) .OR. (IRND .EQ. 0)) GO TO 300
       A = (A*(ONE+A)) / (ONE+ONE)
       IF ((ONE-A)-ONE .NE. ZERO) EPSNEG = A
C-----------------------------------------------------------------
C     DETERMINE MACHEP, EPS
C-----------------------------------------------------------------
   300 MACHEP = -IT - 3
       A = B
   310 IF((ONE+A)-ONE .NE. ZERO) GO TO 320
```

```
          A = A * BETA
          MACHEP = MACHEP + 1
      GO TO 310
  320 EPS = A
      IF ((IBETA .EQ. 2) .OR. (IRND .EQ. 0)) GO TO 350
      A = (A*(ONE+A)) / (ONE+ONE)
      IF ((ONE+A)-ONE .NE. ZERO) EPS = A
C-------------------------------------------------------------------
C     DETERMINE NGRD
C-------------------------------------------------------------------
  350 NGRD = 0
      IF ((IRND .EQ. 0) .AND. ((ONE+EPS)*ONE-ONE) .NE. ZERO) NGRD = 1
C-------------------------------------------------------------------
C     DETERMINE IEXP, MINEXP, XMIN
C
C     LOOP TO DETERMINE LARGEST I AND K = 2**I SUCH THAT
C          (1/BETA) ** (2**(I))
C     DOES NOT UNDERFLOW
C     EXIT FROM LOOP IS SIGNALED BY AN UNDERFLOW.
C-------------------------------------------------------------------
      I = 0
      K = 1
      Z = BETAIN
  400 Y = Z
          Z = Y * Y
C-------------------------------------------------------------------
C         CHECK FOR UNDERFLOW HERE
C-------------------------------------------------------------------
          A = Z * ONE
          IF ((A+A .EQ. ZERO) .OR. (ABS(Z) .GE. Y)) GO TO 410
CD        IF ((A+A .EQ. ZERO) .OR. (DABS(Z) .GE. Y)) GO TO 410
          I = I + 1
          K = K + K
      GO TO 400
  410 IF (IBETA .EQ. 10) GO TO 420
      IEXP = I + 1
      MX = K + K
      GO TO 450
C-------------------------------------------------------------------
C     FOR DECIMAL MACHINES ONLY
C-------------------------------------------------------------------
  420 IEXP = 2
      IZ = IBETA
```

```
  430 IF (K .LT. IZ) GO TO 440
         IZ = IZ * IBETA
         IEXP = IEXP + 1
      GO TO 430
  440 MX = IZ + IZ - 1
C--------------------------------------------------------------------
C    LOOP TO DETERMINE MINEXP, XMIN
C    EXIT FROM LOOP IS SIGNALED BY AN UNDERFLOW.
C--------------------------------------------------------------------
  450 XMIN = Y
         Y = Y * BETAIN
C--------------------------------------------------------------------
C        CHECK FOR UNDERFLOW HERE
C--------------------------------------------------------------------
         A = Y * ONE
         IF (((A+A) .EQ. ZERO) .OR. (ABS(Y) .GE. XMIN)) GO TO 460
CD       IF (((A+A) .EQ. ZERO) .OR. (DABS(Y) .GE. XMIN)) GO TO 460
         K = K + 1
      GO TO 450
  460 MINEXP = -K
C--------------------------------------------------------------------
C    DETERMINE MAXEXP, XMAX
C--------------------------------------------------------------------
      IF ((MX .GT. K+K-3) .OR. (IBETA .EQ. 10)) GO TO 500
      MX = MX + MX
      IEXP = IEXP + 1
  500 MAXEXP = MX + MINEXP
C--------------------------------------------------------------------
C    ADJUST FOR MACHINES WITH IMPLICIT LEADING
C    BIT IN BINARY SIGNIFICAND AND MACHINES WITH
C    RADIX POINT AT EXTREME RIGHT OF SIGNIFICAND
C--------------------------------------------------------------------
      I = MAXEXP + MINEXP
      IF ((IBETA .EQ. 2) .AND. (I .EQ. 0)) MAXEXP = MAXEXP - 1
      IF (I .GT. 20) MAXEXP = MAXEXP - 1
      IF (A .NE. Y) MAXEXP = MAXEXP - 2
      XMAX = ONE - EPSNEG
      IF (XMAX*ONE .NE. XMAX) XMAX = ONE - BETA * EPSNEG
      XMAX = XMAX / (BETA * BETA * BETA * XMIN)
      I = MAXEXP + MINEXP + 3
      IF (I .LE. 0) GO TO 520
C
      DO 510 J = 1, I
```

```
          IF ( IBETA .EQ. 2) XMAX = XMAX + XMAX
          IF ( IBETA .NE. 2) XMAX = XMAX * BETA
  510 CONTINUE
C
  520 RETURN
C      ---------- LAST CARD OF MACHAR ----------
      END
```

REFERENCES

Abramowitz, M., and I. A. Stegun, eds. [1964]. *Handbook of Mathematical Functions with Formulas, Graphs, and Mathematical Tables.* Nat. Bur. Standards Appl. Math. Series, 55, U. S. Government Printing Office, Washington, D. C.

American National Standards Institute [1966]. *American National Standard Programming Language FORTRAN, ANSI X3.9-1966.* American National Standards Institute, Inc., New York.

American National Standards Institute [1978]. *American National Standard Programming Language FORTRAN, ANSI X3.9-1978.* American National Standards Institute, Inc., New York.

Clark, N. A., and W. J. Cody [1969]. "Self-contained exponentiation." *AFIPS Conf. Proc. 35.* AFIPS Press, Montvale, N.J., pp. 701-706.

Clark, N. A., W. J. Cody, and H. Kuki [1971]. "Self-contained power routines." *Mathematical Software.* Ed. J. Rice. Academic Press, New York, pp. 399-415.

Clenshaw, C. W. [1962]. *Mathematical Tables.* Vol. 5, *Chebyshev Series for Mathematical Functions.* Her Majesty's Stationery Office, London.

Cody, W. J. [1969]. "Performance testing of function subroutines." *AFIPS Conf. Proc. SJCC.* AFIPS Press, Montvale, N. J., pp. 759-763.

---------- [1977]. "Machine parameters for numerical analysis." *Portability of Numerical Software.* Ed. W. Cowell. Springer-Verlag, New York, pp. 49-67.

Forsythe, G. E., M. A. Malcolm and C. B. Moler [1977]. *Computer Methods for Mathematical Computations.* Prentice-Hall, Englewood Cliffs, N. J.

Fike, C. T. [1968]. *Computer Evaluation of Mathematical Functions.* Prentice-Hall, Englewood Cliffs, N. J.

Gentleman, W. M., and S. B. Marovich [1974]. "More on algorithms that reveal properties of floating point arithmetic units." *CACM* 17:276-277.

Haddon, B. K., and W. M. Waite [1978]. *The Universal Intermediate Language Janus (Draft Definition).* Tech. Report SEG-78-3. Department of Electrical Engineering, University of Colorado, Boulder.

Hart, J. F., E. W. Cheney, C. L. Lawson, H. J. Maehly, C. K. Mesztenyi, J. R. Rice, H. C. Thacher, Jr., and C. Witzgall [1968]. *Computer Approximations.* Wiley, New York.

Knuth, D. E. [1969]. *The Art of Computer Programming.* Vol. 2. Addison Wesley, Reading, Mass.

Lyusternik, L. A., O. A. Chervonenkis, and A. R. Yanpol'skii [1965]. *Handbook for Computing Elementary Functions.* Pergamon, Oxford.

Malcolm, M. A. [1972]. "Algorithms to reveal properties of floating-point arithmetic." *CACM* 15:949-951.

Ralston, A. [1976]. "Arithmetic, Computer." *Encyclopedia of Computer Science.* Ed. A. Ralston and C. L. Meek. Petrocelli/Charter, New York.

Schrage, L. [1979]. "A more portable Fortran random number generator." *TOMS* 5:132-138.

Sterbenz, P. H. [1974]. *Floating-point Computation.* Prentice-Hall, Englewood Cliffs, N. J.

Waite, W. M. [1973]. *Implementing Software for Non-Numeric Applications.* Prentice-Hall, Englewood Cliffs, N. J.

Glossary

ADX(A,N):   an operation that augments the integer exponent in the floating-point representation of A by N. See Chapter 2.

AINT(X):   the standard Fortran intrinsic function which returns the floating-point representation, with correct sign, of the integer part of the floating-point number X. See Chapter 2.

AINTRND(X):   an operation that rounds a floating-point number X to the nearest floating-point integer. See Chapter 2.

Binary machine: a computer in which the floating-point radix is 2.

Exponent: see "Floating-point number representation."

FIX(X):   an operation that converts the floating-point number X to the equivalent fixed-point fraction. See Chapter 2.

Fixed-point arithmetic: binary arithmetic in which the operands are binary fractions of magnitude less than one.

Fixed-point machine: a computer in which the floating-point operations are extremely slow in comparison to the fixed-point operations. Typically, the floating-point operations are software implementations on these machines. We assume that the number of bits in a fixed-point number is at least as great as the number of bits in the floating-point significand, and is actually greater for certain functions, such as SQRT.

FLOAT(N):   the standard Fortran intrinsic function which converts the integer N to floating point. See Chapter 2.

Floating-point machine: a computer in which the floating-point arithmetic operations are reasonably fast. Typically, the operations are in the hardware or are micro-coded on these machines.

Floating-point number representation: the bit or digit pattern representing a floating-point number. Although the details of the representation may vary from machine to machine, every non-zero floating-point number can be thought of as being represented in the form

$$X = \pm f * B^{**}e, \quad 1/B \leq f < 1,$$

where B is called the base or radix of the representation, f is the significand, and e is the exponent. See Chapter 2.

Generated error: that part of the relative error in the function value that is not attributable to the inherited error. See "Inherited error" below.

Guard digits: extra digits generated at an intermediate stage of a floating-point arithmetic operation. They specifically protect the accuracy of low-order digit positions during shifting of the result significand to eliminate leading zero digits. Digits in the guard position at the end of the operation are lost and do not participate in subsequent operations.

Inherited error: the relative error in the function argument(s).

INT(X): the standard Fortran intrinsic function which truncates a floating-point number to an integer and converts it to integer format. See Chapter 2.

INTRND(X): an operation that rounds the floating-point number X to the nearest integer and converts it to integer format. See Chapter 2.

INTXP(A): an operation that returns as a signed integer the exponent e in the floating-point representation of A. See Chapter 2.

Non-binary machine: a computer in which the radix for the floating-point number representation is not 2. Radices of 4, 8, 10 and 16 are most common for non-binary machines.

Radix: see "Floating-point number representation."

REFLOAT(f): an operation that converts the fixed-point fraction f to the equivalent floating-point number X. See Chapter 2.

Relative error (RE): if X is an approximation to Y, then the relative error in X is $(X-Y)/Y$, provided $Y \neq 0$.

SETXP(A,N): an operation that returns the floating-point number with the same significand as A and with exponent N. See Chapter 2.

Significand: see "Floating-point number representation."

Transmitted error: that part of the relative error in the function value which is directly attributable to the inherited error. See "Inherited error."

Wobbling precision: the variation in the number of significant bits in the significands of different floating-point numbers on a non-decimal machine with a radix other than 2. See "Floating-point number representation." For example, if b bits are available for the representation of f in a base-16 system, there are 3 leading zero bits and hence only $b-3$ significant bits in f whenever $1/16 \leq f < 1/8$. In contrast, all b bits are significant whenever $1/2 \leq f < 1$.